PLAY RE[SUMED]
WITH CARDUS

Neville Cardus

Macdonald
Queen Anne Press

A QUEEN ANNE PRESS BOOK

First published in Great Britain in 1979 by Souvenir Press Ltd

First published in paperback in Great Britain in 1990 by
Queen Anne Press, a division of
Macdonald & Co (Publishers)
Orbit House
1 New Fetter Lane
London EC4A 1AR

A member of Maxwell Macmillan Pergamon Publishing
Corporation

Cover illustration and design: Deborah Holmes

British Library Cataloguing in Publication Data
Cardus, Neville, *1888–1975*
   Play resumed with Cardus.
   1. Cricket
   I. Title
   796.35′8

   ISBN 0–356–19049–8

ACKNOWLEDGMENTS

The publishers are grateful to the editor of *The Guardian*, to
Richards Press, to William Collins for their co-operation in the
assembly of articles in *Play Resumed With Cardus*. The publishers are particularly grateful to Margaret Hughes for her generous
assistance in planning and compiling the book.

Reproduced, printed and bound in Great Britain
by Richard Clay Ltd, Bungay, Suffolk

CONTENTS

FROM SECOND INNINGS

INTRODUCTION

SUMMER after summer up and down England, with my eyes on green grass for hours and my face receiving the brown of sun and air; autumns and Salzburg or Worcester or Gloucester or Hereford for music. Then winter and the Hallé Concerts and Queen's Hall. Thursday in Manchester, back next day in a first-class restaurant car to St. Pancras, arriving in London just in time for cocktails before dinner. Here and there and everywhere—London and Sydney; and as the important musical and cricket events were arranged to take place much at the same dates each season, I could say, 'Why, at this very time last twelve months ago I was in this very same place, and next year I shall be here again.'

The years flashed by like a kaleidoscope, with one's experiences exquisitely related, each a separate 'shot', so to say, in the continuous film of full imaginative living. But–I am asked this question by nearly everybody who meets me for the first time—cricket and music? 'How could you mix them?'—with the implication that cricket is, to echo Smee, a bit of a 'come-down' for a musical pirate. It is a silly question. As well might a man be asked how can he mix breathing with walking, or wine with song, or George Meredith with gardening, or mountaineering with Wagner. If we are not clods of earth, or worse still, 'experts' and 'specialists', we will expand our way of life according to where our antennæ of sensibility lead us. I would be an intellectual snob if I were to maintain that I have not loved days at Lord's as intensely as nights at Covent Garden and in both places found in equal abundance material for my writings and—more important—for my memory's granary of good things fully experienced—rich wine of temperament for the day's diet of sights and sounds. Only an æsthete would pretend that an innings by Woolley could not approach as closely to an expression of personal art, plus skill and character, all presented in a significant scene, as the performance of the next fashionable tenor, or somebody's slick, quick exploitation of technique in a Rachmaninoff concerto.

Whether any happening in art or in life is of consequence depends not on the form in which the happening is presented; it depends on our capacity for *experiencing*, or whether our 'receiving sets' are sensitively attuned. The silent room we sit in is full of sounds and sweet airs that will give delight and,

11

possibly, hurt not—if the apparatus is there. But most people's lives are like deaf rooms, silent for want of a responsive 'pick-up':

> *... Such harmony is in immortal souls;*
> *But, whilst this muddy vesture of decay*
> *Doth grossly close it in, we cannot hear it.*

Did grace fall the more blissfully upon me when I heard the 'Echo' nocturne on a summer night at Salzburg while the candles on the music-stands burned steadily, and the stars above were like the pulsation of the notes of Mozart's music? Or when I watched Spooner rippling the sunlit grass with strokes that were without solidity or earthly momentum, and he leaned gracefully forward and flicked his wrists and the whole of the June day and the setting of sky and white tents and the trees of Canterbury were as though the created element of this lovely player's every motion and breath of being? Or when I walked in daylight to Covent Garden, white tie and tails, for all the workaday world to see, on my way from my club for the beginning of the *Ring* at Covent Garden, a leisurely walk along Henrietta Street and through the market, savouring the hour as the sun cast its evening glow on London? Or when I listened to Friedman, then walked soon after under the starry sky of Vaucluse? Or when I heard Toscanini transform an orchestra into shot silk and gold of tone while conducting 'Daphnis et Chloe' of Ravel; or when I heard Seth Lomas conducting at a rehearsal the choir in a Lancashire town where the cobbled streets resound at the crack of dawn from the impact of hurrying clogs? It was Christmas time and they were at a 'Messiah' practice, and Seth sounded his tuning-fork and the basses made humming noises like wasps; then Seth spoke and said, 'And all you open thi mouths. Foller mi beat. And never mind what tha was listenin' to at t' 'Allé Concert last week. It's me that's conducting thi now—not 'Amilton 'Arty.'

Only the material, the rare stuff for imagination's manufacture, is given to us, whether by Bach or by the Matterhorn or by César Franck or by the stillness of snow at Christmas or by Dickens or by Harry Dean or Seth Lomas. We must ourselves fashion it into spirit and sensibility and weave it into the texture of our being. Whether the shape or symbol be sonnet or sunset, curve of fiddle-bow or curve of cricket bat, only with our own vision may we see the light and be free to say,

> *I was for that time lifted above earth,*
> *And possest joys not promised in my birth.*

12

FROM MANCHESTER GUARDIAN

IDLE THOUGHTS

WHEN I was very young I hated cricket because every respectable and gentlemanly boy was supposed to play it. To play soccer was to be outside the pale, amongst the urchins of the pavement. Cricket in my youth was class-conscious. As a result, I played soccer; and regarded cricket as the pastime of milksops.

It was when I first went to a county match at Old Trafford that I realized the truth about cricket: the first batsman I ever saw was G. L. Jessop. On this occasion he was hitting the Lancashire bowling all over the field—cutting good length balls, and driving perfect off-breaks for six into the frenzied crowd. This didn't seem to my young mind a little bit respectable or nicely bred—Jessop stirred something primitive and untamable. He was a great force of nature, incalculable, free, violent, grand! Then I saw Tom Richardson bowling, a sight that made my nerves tingle. He ran over the ground with long strides, and leaped into the air magnificently as his arm swung over. Then I saw Johnny Briggs—a little indiarubber man, who bounced about as though unable to control his own comic energy. And I saw A. C. MacLaren batting with the lordly air of a man who is not making runs, but squandering them all over the field as though he had thousands to spare. When he first went out to bat with little Harry Makepeace, I saw a vision of Don Quixote and Sancho Panza—MacLaren ready to tilt at windmills romantically; Makepeace content to wait cannily for his little island of runs at the day's end.

PERSONAL ELEMENT IN THE CRICKET FIELD

These great players taught me that cricket was far better than anybody had ever told me it was; here I found not only a game, but a splendid picture of English life. And now today after some thirty-five summers spent on cricket fields, I find myself thinking of the great characters of the game much as I think of characters in Charles Dickens, or, if you like, in Shakespeare; they all mingle together,

Grace and Falstaff, Patsy Hendren and Sam Weller, Walter Brearley and Mr Boythorne; Parkin and the Artful Dodger. When you come to think of all the jolly days you have spent at cricket, you do not dwell particularly on the mere results, the points won or lost, the averages and the percentages. These things are soon forgotten; what remains in your memory is the tingle of delight which ran up your spine when you made a drive through the covers, the ecstasy experienced when you knocked somebody's stumps flying, or the quiet enjoyment of watching the afternoon draw near to sunset. More than any other game, cricket is a thing of personal art and skill; it depends not mainly on results, but on the amount of genius and character which is put into it minute by minute by the players. The spaciousness of cricket, the very form and procedure of it, helps the personal contribution. We hear a lot of cant about team-work at cricket, the truth is that the game is great only when the players have minds and styles of their own. Cricket allows a man to express his own personal arts; it puts him on the pedestal in splendid isolation. When he bowls he is alone in the world with a thousand eyes on him; he is alone in the world when he defends his wicket against Larwood's thunderbolts; and he is alone in the world when a catch comes to him in the deep field—and when he drops it. The style is the man himself at cricket; what's bred in the bone comes out in an innings.

The game gives up its secret charm only to those who see the fun and varied life of it. Never worry about the results—it might rain; don't trouble over the averages; only the newspapers really want them. Play the game as the impulses of imagination move you. Play it in your own way, and after you have learned the first principles, put your own heart in every action. I am not asking everybody to play like Jessop; there is room in cricket for the stonewaller. But if you are a stonewaller by nature, stonewall with passion. There is as much force of character, as much energy of imagination, in the stonewalling of Woodfull as there is in the brilliant offensive play of Hammond. The great commandment of cricket is 'Thou shalt not be negative!'

A GAME FOR IMAGINATION AND ENTERPRISE

Every boy comes to cricket instinctively along the right lines. He doesn't think of the game as a sort of arithmetic or accountancy; it is only after he has read the newspapers that he begins to waste his delight on records. His first fresh response is one of joy in the game's activity, the opportunity it gives for free play of limb and muscle, and for personal adventure. You cannot lift up a bat without feeling a thrill of pleasure throughout the body. Once I used to coach young cricketers at a school in Shropshire, a famous school in a beautiful place. I found that nearly every boy approached cricket imaginatively; he loved to take a risk or to imitate some delightful deed he had seen performed in the holidays at Lord's or Old Trafford. This instinct to imitate the great artists of the cricket field is sound; the cricket coach should not discourage it; he should only see that imitation is in agreement with natural style. A boy who is essentially cautious by temperament is not likely to improve his play if, in a momentary fit of hero-worship, he imitates a fierce hitter. When I was a boy, I would go to Old Trafford one day and decide that fast bowling was my purpose in life; that was after I had looked long and dotingly on Walter Brearley. But the next day I would see the delicious action of Blythe, and decide that henceforth I would be not a demon bowler, but a slow and cunning fellow, a dealer in spinning balls of great evil. Thus did the game lose a great cricketer, for I could not make up my mind about the best way of directing my undoubted abilities.

I urge you all to watch and play cricket as though taking part in a romance of adventure, with every ball a challenge to your enterprise. That is the way all the great cricketers have played. Avoid the dull, easy way of doing things. Give me the cricketer who is always ready to answer a challenge. Many years ago the Australians brought to England a new bowler. When the team arrived at Lord's, W. G. Grace went into the Australian dressing-room, and saw W. L. Murdoch, the captain. 'I hear you've got a new bowler,' said W. G. 'Yes,' was the answer, 'he's a terror.' 'What does he bowl,' asked W. G., 'fast or slow, leg or off-breaks?' 'Ah!' was the sinister reply, 'he mixes 'em; he mixes 'em.' 'Very well,' replied the Old Man in his high-pitched voice, 'I'll look at him this afternoon; I'll look at him.' And that afternoon W. G. went on to bat with an M.C.C. Professional, whom we'll call Harry. And when W. G. faced the new bowler, he played him for a while as though evil spirits lurked in every ball. He bent over his broad bat, the picture of suspicion. Then he hit the new 'demon' bowler for four, four, and a three. And as he rushed across the wicket for the third run, he cried out to his partner, 'Run up, Harry; run up; we'll mix 'em for him; we'll mix 'em.'

'CRICKET MUST NEVER BE SHORT OF WIT AND LIFE'

There can be no dreary play with quick humorous minds on the job. Cricket must never be short of wit and life, dullness at cricket comes out of a dull mind. It doesn't matter whether runs are made or not made if the antagonism is keen, if the fight is being fought with all your energy, humorous as well as other. Remember the gorgeous comedy once played by David Denton and George Hirst in a game between Yorkshire and Derbyshire. Derbyshire were giving a trial to an unknown bowler. When Hirst reached the wicket Denton was fifty not out. He met Hirst, and said behind his hand, 'This lad's a reight bowler, George; keep him on, he's just our sort.' And so Hirst and Denton played a rich bluff for half-an-hour, tapping the new bowler for discreet singles, defending with a great show of respect, and now and then hitting a four, so as not to give the game away. Then suddenly Hirst hit the new bowler for four fours in one over—bang! bang! bang! At the end of the over, Denton came down the wicket and said, 'Why, George, what were't thinkin' of? That's busted t'contract. They'll take him off after that—tha's spoiled t'fun . . .' 'It's all right, David,' said George, 'Ah heard his captain tell him it were his last over afore he bowled it.'

That is a fair example of Yorkshire humour, and one of the extraordinary facts about this national game of cricket is the way it will accommodate itself to the expression, not only of every man in his humour, but of the spirit of the various counties who play the game. There was no mistaking the Yorkshire quality of Emmott Robinson's play, just as there was no mistaking the quality of the aristocratic cricket which was exhibited at Lord's day by day by the Hon. C. M. Bruce. And not only can a cricketer express his own nature through bat and ball; if he has genius enough he can express his race. In the 'nineties there was a wonderful example of how through the game of cricket a batsman displayed a genius that was not even English. At that period cricket was about as English a game as it has ever been. It was the time when batsmen trusted to the straight bat with the left leg forward, and bowlers believed in the good-length ball. Everything was stately, and not only English, but Victorian, and it was at this time that something came into cricket that had never been seen there before.

ORIENTAL GENIUS IN A WESTERN SPORT

A batsman began to play as no Englishman had ever played or could play. A dark oriental colour came into cricket, sinuous and

16

subtle. No straight bat or stately left leg forward, but mysterious flashes and conjurings at the wicket, so that bowlers crossed themselves as though in the presence of witchcraft. This was no English cricket; this was cricket from the East, from the land of snake-charmers and rope-dancers, from the land of fakirs and magic carpets. For the man who was batting now was none other than Ranjitsinhji. He put the genius of his own race into an English game that was born in the meadows of Hambledon, and this, as I say, was the most emphatic proof of how cricket can express individual genius. I once asked a famous Yorkshire player what he thought of Ranjitsinhji, and he said: 'Ranjitsinhji never made a Christian stroke in his life!'—which was first-class criticism, for why should Ranjitsinhji make a Christian stroke, seeing that he was not a Christian?

WHEN AN 'OBSTINATE RABBIT' SAVED A MATCH

You should never go on to a cricket-field without realizing that you are playing the most uncertain game in the world, a game in which anything might happen any minute. One ball might make you into a hero or into a nobly inglorious duffer. There was once a cricket match in Australia not long ago when the last man came in to bat a few minutes before close of play, and his side hundreds of runs behind. Much to the annoyance of the other side, he batted out time, which made it necessary for the match to be continued the next morning. Imagine the disgust of the other side when they had to turn up again, change into flannels, merely in order, as they thought, to bowl a few balls to get rid of this obstinate rabbit who so unreasonably refused to get out the night before, when everybody, the scorers included, wanted to go home with the match well and truly finished. Well, they all went on the field again, and still this last man in declined to get out. At the other end of the wicket was one of the great batsmen of the world—his name, Kippax—a member of the present Australian Eleven who will play in England this summer. And the obstinate rabbit proceeded to stay in the whole of the day, and when stumps were drawn at six o'clock, he was as invincible as he had been twenty-four hours before. That last wicket scored over 300 runs. And the rabbit's name was Hooker. And what he did that day with unsuspected ability, but with a good deal of pluck, any one of you may very well do tomorrow if you play cricket not just with your hands, eyes and feet, but with your imagination.

A SMALL WIRY YOUTH

LARWOOD

NOT until the closing hour of today's play did we get the challenging air, the sense of fearless antagonism that we have a right to expect in a representative cricket match. The Rest's innings of 211 on an easy wicket lasted as long as four and a half hours, and it seemed much longer than that. Excepting Duleepsinhji, the Rest's batsmen were palpably taking the event much too seriously. I wish some of our cricketers would cultivate a broad view of their places within the cosmic process, link up a game of cricket with the dog-star, and see themselves in the light of humorous proportion.

The match first commanded attention when young Larwood bowled at England's batsmen. This happened as the sun was going down and throwing its softness aslant over the grass. It is somehow always a magical time of day on a cricket field—this closing scene. Larwood, a small youth but wiry, flung himself into his attack with a bitterness which was at one and the same time admirable and comical. Here we had a sturdy boy with his career still to forge—and a responsible occasion did not check in the slightest youth's own confidence—'cheek' if you like. Larwood bowled fast through the air and faster from the pitch. He quickly upset Holmes's wicket. Then he dropped a catch in the slips from Hobbs of all men. Did this unhappy lapse daunt the lad? It did not; on the contrary, it obviously outraged him, his temper became very stern. A terrier that has snapped at a bone offered to him and missed it by an inch could not have shown us a more aggressive spirit than Larwood's, the moment he bowled again after letting Hobbs escape from his fingers. He ran to the wicket with an increase of tenacity, he got Woolley caught in the slips, and next ball he had the effrontery to bowl Carr (captain of his own county as well as of England) off the pads.

LARWOOD'S 'NIP'

None of the England bowlers was able to find in the turf as much 'nip' as Larwood. Larwood's ability to give the ball great pace from the ground is rather astonishing, for a lad of his size cannot of course hurl down his attack with a high action. Cricketers have always agreed that 'nip' in bowling comes from some sting in young blood

18

and some beautiful unison of healthy, untired nerve and muscle. 'Ah can bowl a length as well as ever Ah could,' said an old England player to me once, 'And Ah can spin 'em yet. But, bless ye, Ah've got no "nip" now; that goes when tha's gettin' on in years.' Granted careful nursing, Larwood might prove a deadlier bowler on a firm wicket than Macaulay (who yet again has fallen below his best away from the Yorkshire XI). Larwood makes the new ball swing from the bat, also he has the ability to break the ball back—not by deliberate spin but because of the natural sweep of his arm across the line of the ball at the 'moment of release'. Now and again he drops a short length, a sign maybe of effort beyond his strength, yet today he was canny enough to send Carr for his first ball a length tossed far enough up to the bat to compel a stroke. Larwood is already a better bowler than Allen—the best is yet to come.

When the Rest's innings began the turf was so lifeless that even Tate's attack had little energy after pitching. Hallows and Sandham scored 33 for the first wicket in an hour. At lunch, after 90 minutes' apparent activity, 50 runs had been hoarded. A 'silly point' was used while Kilner bowled. Many years ago batsmen considered they were 'on their honour' to remove a silly point from their view imme-diately—remove him either to some other and more respectful position in the field or to the nearest hospital. 'Silly point,' with the opportunities it gives for intimate conversation, is a popular fielding place nowadays. Emmott Robinson is an artist in this position, both as fieldsman and conversationalist. Hearne had the bad luck to get caught in the slips from the only ball that 'kicked' in the afternoon. Sandham batted two hours and a quarter for 34 and Ernest Tyldesley an hour for 17. Neither cricketer would trust the scoring strokes nature has given to him. Tyldesley frequently pushed short balls fruitlessly to the fieldsmen. What has become of his powerful and dramatic hook? The pace of the wicket was surely convenient for a resolute use of the hook-stroke, especially when Macaulay bowled a short length with an inward turn towards the bat. Hallows was bowled trying to drive. As at Birmingham he got out just as he looked to be shaping for free and cultivated cricket.

The longest stand in the Rest's innings, achieved by Duleepsinhji and Jupp, added 52 for the sixth wicket in forty minutes. Duleep-sinhji's innings had its defeats. None the less it did remind us in good time that we were watching a big game at Lord's. His play has style—that indescribable touch or current of personal spirit and energy which seems to run out of a fine cricketer's very being and pass down and through his bat into the ball. Duleepsinhji's back-play is pretty, he blends it (and few batsmen of today do) with a live circling stroke which sometimes seems to begin and end around the wrists. We need not compare him with 'Ranji', for Duleepsinhji will remain fairly orthodox even when he has come to maturity. But his wrist-work will put bloom on the orthodox. When Duleepsinhji allowed a leg ball to hit his pads and go for byes, I thought, 'There we may see the difference between Duleepsinhji and Ranjitsinhji.' Let us be content with this young Indian's own gifts, and, echoing Whistler, let us say, 'Why drag in "Ranji"?' Duleepsinhji has not grown out of the mistake of letting his left foot lag some distance away from the off-side ball. It is high time he did. He batted an hour and three-quarters. His charming late-cut might be safer if he got his body more over the ball and did not make it almost wholly 'with his arms', as cricketers say. Jupp drove powerfully once or twice, the occasion, at any rate, did not bother him. His cricket was in excellent contrast to that of Duleepsinhji—one thought of silk and good cloth. I dislike Duleepsinhji's crouch at the wicket while he is waiting for the ball, but his stance as he plays a stroke is pure enough.

THE ENGLAND BOWLING

The England bowling was treated with more respect than it deserved. Tate, despite his good results, had a laboured action, and little of his true vitality went into the ball. Kilner was the only genuine finger-spin bowler on his side. Macaulay gets his occasional breakback by 'cutting under' the ball, not by finger-spin. It was very occasional indeed today. Allen's length could not be trusted, and Woolley's analysis is frankly a misrepresentation of the true facts. The England eleven will be the better for another spin bowler, though it is hard to see how (if he exists) he can be put into the team with Root almost a 'certainty' now. The XI, though, is likely to have too many bowlers whose best work depends on the new ball and the high but perishable seam. Root did not play today because (so it was announced) he has a cold. The England fielding was only moderate. Woolley 'in the deep' presented an unfamiliar and monumental sight. Hendren did a lot of work on twinkling feet, still I do wish that the Lord's crowd would not cheer wildly every time Hendren runs to a quite stationary ball, picks it up, and throws it in. Smith kept the safe undemonstrative wicket of the 'old-hand' at the game.

THE REST

First Innings

Hallows, b Kilner	17	W. W. C. Jupp, b Tate	23
Sandham, c Allen, b Tate	34	P. G. H. Fender, b Allen	4
Hearne, c Carr, b Tate	11	Larwood, b Tate	16
Tyldesley (E.), c Smith, b Tate	17	Durston, b Woolley	0
K. S. Duleepsinhji, c and b Woolley	51	Strudwick, not out	9
Shepherd, c Smith, b Kilner	8	B 10, lb 8, nb 3	21
		Total	211

ENGLAND—First Innings

Hobbs, not out	13	Hendren, not out	1
Holmes, b Larwood	3	W. W. Carr, b Larwood	0
Woolley, c Fender, b Larwood	21		
		Total (for 3)	38

A. P. F. Chapman, G. O. Allen, Tate, Macaulay, Kilner (R.), and Smith (E. J.) to bat.

BOWLING ANALYSIS

THE REST—First Innings

	O.	M.	R.	W.		O.	M.	R.	W.
Allen	26	5	51	1	Kilner	31	13	50	2
Tate	28·3	10	44	5	Woolley	7	3	15	2
Macaulay	16	6	30	0					

Allen bowled three no-balls

LANCASHIRE WIN THE 1926 TITLE

SATURDAY'S play in this crucial game at Old Trafford was even. Lancashire did well to get Notts. all out on a beautiful turf for 292, but Hallows's wicket is gone already. The Lancashire attack is so worn out that it is hard for us to hope for victory outright over the Notts. batsmen. There is the question, too, whether Larwood will not run through a Lancashire innings like a whirlwind. But this is to put wicked ideas into his young head.

Saturday found us all back in June again. Who in this lovely sunshine could believe that we were at the season's end, that in a day or two Old Trafford's happy companionship in the open-air will be over and far away, that Old Trafford will soon stand deserted, a place of forlorn silences—even the ladies' pavilion will be quiet and still! Only the true cricketer knows of the ache that comes to the heart at this time of the year. In the soft falling light of Old Trafford's last Saturday evening for many long months to come, a barbarous voice was heard selling a football edition. (Actually the voice pronounced it 'Fuhbadishane.') I am sorry to say that many people were to be seen looking for Manchester City's score, even while Makepeace and Sibbles played out an anxious ten minutes before the close. Sometimes I wish football went on throughout the summer; then cricket would always get a crowd pure and undefiled.

GUNN'S INNINGS

Green was unable, because of a wrist damaged in the Hampshire match, to win the toss for Lancashire. Thus George Gunn and Whysall had first use of a pitch so excellent that in the absence of devastating bowlers there seemed no reason why a good batsman should ever get out on it, unless he sighed for the shady pavilion or was moved to compassion by a weary attack. Gunn and Whysall made 120 for the first wicket in just over two hours. Then Gunn carelessly flicked his bat at an offside ball and pulled it into his stumps—an appropriate finish to as nonchalant a piece of cricket as even Gunn has ever given us. He is one of the world's two most fascinating batsmen; Macartney is the other. Those spectators on Saturday who complained that Gunn's scoring was slow rather misunderstand Gunn's relationship to cricket. An innings by Gunn cannot be referred to the scoreboard or even to the state of the game. His batsmanship is, like every other precious thing on the earth, free from any obligation to be other than itself; Gunn is an artist, and therefore answerable to none but his own temperamental promptings. You may grumble, if you wish, at Gunn because he frequently gets runs slowly—just as you may grumble at Kreisler whenever he plays bad music. But the art for art's sake of Gunn's cricket will captivate you as entirely as the art for art's sake of Kreisler's fiddling.

On Saturday Gunn was at his best, genius in all that he did, every stroke significant with the style that is the man. Perhaps his injured finger prevented him from hitting as many balls to the boundary as he easily could have done. But Gunn does not require the excuse of a damaged hand to justify an inactive moment: on Saturday he was at times insolently inactive; I suspect that he toyed with tired bowlers because it was his pleasure so to do. Several times he walked leisurely to the pitch of a half-volley and then stopped it dead with a bat solemn and straight. Or perhaps, instead, he leaned on the ball carelessly, pushed it away, beginning a lazy run for a single at the same time. Yet the challenge of Macdonald's fastest and best length would see Gunn's bat suddenly turned into a strong broadsword; his left leg would go quickly over the wicket, and then we had the most classic off drive in cricket. That is the way with Gunn; he will bat seriously and flippantly in, so to speak, one and the same breath. He flicked Macdonald to third man with a bat as haphazard as a man's cane flicking at a hedge. Once he brushed a good ball away contemptuously, and almost before the stroke was finished he was looking at his bat critically, as though in search of some vital flaw. With all his apparent leisureliness, he gets into position for the bowling perhaps quicker than any other English batsman; fast as Macdonald sent them down on Saturday morning Gunn was ready—one might even say his bat was waiting for them with a half-concealed yawn.

Gunn hit only three boundaries in his innings of two hours: that was because he did not choose to hit thirteen. A bat in Gunn's hands is endowed with sensibility. He gives it delicate, fastidious life; he gives it a witty, sardonic tongue: at times he gives it dignity and beauty. Had Gunn been a cricketer of earnest mind he might easily have attained to the fame of a Hobbs. But a consistently responsible George Gunn will not bear thinking of for a moment. Who of us would have him different from the incalculable spirit he is? Cricket is not all match-winning and match-saving; the mind and fancy of man will be served, even while he is at his games. Gunn's cricket is a whimsical compound of skill and wit, impudence and dignity, brilliance and idleness, insolence and charm. It is his very own art, and with him it will pass from the game for ever. Let us enjoy our George Gunn while we may.

CARR'S GREAT RECEPTION

After Gunn played on, Duckworth caught A. Staples magnificently, falling to the earth and holding an 'impossible' chance. Then Carr came in cheered all the way to the wicket. He could not have expected a more tumultuous reception even if he had (according to his deserts) been captain of England in the Oval Test match. Carr was much moved by Old Trafford's tribute, and he wishes he could somehow express his appreciation of it. His innings on Saturday, I thought, was appreciation quite eloquent enough. It must have given as much pleasure to the crowd as the crowd's applause gave to Carr. He was in his proper form, once again he let us admire his old devil-may-care power. But this time there was always real cricket-sense in his play; Carr is a better batsman today than ever he has been before. His defence is sounder, and there are now in his range of hits many of those excellent short-armed strokes which are required against the fast-medium ball that drops at slightly less than the good length. Carr reached fifty in little over the hour, and all the time he looked the great cricketer. It is not the many but the few that have deposed him from the English captaincy. Carr fell to a capital running catch by Iddon—a good end to an innings essentially rhetorical. He and Whysall added 98 in seventy minutes by cricket of the highest class. Whysall had the misfortune to play on to a ball that kept low; he missed a hundred by three runs, after three hours and a half's good craftsmanship. His offdrive is so beautiful that he ought to trust it much more implicitly. At tea, Notts. were 234 for four; afterwards six wickets fell for 58. Macdonald worked hard in the heavy heat; in the flesh he was obviously at an end even before lunch. But he persisted by some sheer act of grace; at twenty minutes to six he returned to the attack and tried again to bowl fast, though an hour of unceasing work after lunch must have left him, as the man in Dickens says, 'considerably used-up'. None of Lancashire's other bowlers seemed likely to get a wicket on Saturday.

When Lancashire batted in the afternoon's last quarter of an hour, Hallows was caught near square leg, close to the wicket, from a ball that jumped up towards his body. Hallows had a sketchy sort of day; he turned into the field late in the morning, left it before the Notts. innings was finished, and then got a duck as quickly as it is humanly possible for one to be obtained.

MONDAY

Given fine weather today, and—but this is to anticipate. Let the historian be dispassionate and relate the facts as they happened in a great day of cricket at Old Trafford. Lancashire went out for the laurels in the temper of champions. The situation at the morning's outset favoured Notts.; only cricket resolute and imaginative could serve Lancashire's ambition. Mere mechanical skill was not wanted; the game's position had to be taken by storm. And of all men in the Lancashire side, it was Makepeace who was our Danton, saying with a militant bat: 'What we need for victory is audacity, audacity, and always audacity.' Makepeace played always the innings of his career; he was the first to set the conqueror's pace for his county and did so by an astonishing change from his customary methods. The old warhorse forgot his years and scars; he was mettlesome, crying 'Ha! Ha!' amongst the trumpets. He scored 180 out of 358 in four hours and a half; in two hours after lunch he galloped from 56 to 180, and hit the ball into most parts of the field. At half-past two, he had made 68; thirty-five minutes afterwards he reached 101.

In the first hour following the lunch interval Makepeace and Ernest Tyldesley scored 100—Makepeace 67 of them and Tyldesley 33. Old Trafford looked upon this wonderful *tour de force* of Makepeace—it was nothing less—with eyes almost incredulous. It was an innings which moved one by its devotion to Lancashire county. For Makepeace is weary after a long, hard, and responsible summer; his brilliance yesterday probably strained him in limb as much as in temperament. Probably his better instincts were slightly outraged by his riotous bat. 'This,' perhaps his heart said, 'is vain show—sounding brass. But it is for Lancashire.' As a fact, Makepeace's quick scoring did not do any hurt at all to his usual technical conscientiousness. His strokes were always discreet and thoroughly respectable. It was the authentic Makepeace, seen as it were in 'quick motion'. He polished his periods in the familiar way, only this time he was in a tremendous hurry about it all.

A QUIET BEGINNING

At the morning's beginning the cricket was circumspect enough. The Notts. attack hereabout possessed some edge. Larwood's pace, though not at its deadliest, needed watching, and Staples caused the new ball to swing cleverly. Later Barratt came on and pitched a length just too short for strong forward play. Makepeace countered him fruitfully by means of his own late forearm strokes. Sibbles batted manfully at this searching moment, and when at 73 he was well caught in the slips 69 runs had come in some 75 minutes. Sibbles's innings was most valuable, and he got out at the right time, for the Notts. bowling was wavering and we wanted to see Ernest Tyldesley attack it. Makepeace was nearly run out with his score 34; he fell hopelessly to the earth, yards outside of his crease; but a bad return saved him. From twenty-five minutes to one till lunch Makepeace and Tyldesley played the wearing-down game politically; when the interval came 126 runs had been scored in two hours and a quarter. So far the news from Old Trafford that reached

Emmott Robinson and his friends at Swansea could not have been too bitter to bear.

Almost from the first over bowled in the afternoon Makepeace flung his bat about him as though it were a stimulating banner. His footwork was swift and his judgment of the ball's flight unfailing. Many times he cut Barratt's short length late, leaning over the ball, his right leg thrown towards the slips—a J. T. Brown stroke. His share of 65 in 35 minutes was 45; Ernest Tyldesley proceeded elegantly enough, but, unlike Makepeace, occasionally remembered he was playing in a first-class engagement. It was now that Makepeace scored at twice the speed of Tyldesley. Makepeace completed his 100 out of 195 in three hours and five minutes. At 118 he let us see his first doubtful hit, a 'fluke' over the slips' heads from Larwood, who with the new ball began to bowl like the Larwood the Australians have learned to respect.

TYLDESLEY'S TENTH 100

Tyldesley kept pace with Makepeace while the total flashed from 200 to 250 in 33 minutes; he arrived at his hundred, out of 201, in two hours and twenty minutes, his tenth of the summer. Then his cricket burst into gaudy fire, and for the while the Notts. attack was utterly consumed. In less than half an hour Tyldesley hit 40 in sixteen blows, thus—4 4 4 4 1 1 1 4 4 4 1 1 4 1 1 1. Between five minutes to four and a quarter past four the Lancashire total went like a dizzy wheel from 300 to 350. Then Tyldesley was caught on the off side from a mis-hit; one of the finest partnerships in the records of the county was finished. Makepeace and Tyldesley made 279 in two hours and three-quarters; despite the headlong action of both batsmen after lunch only three strokes were of the kind that offends good taste. In 1904 Lancashire won the championship by playing the handsome cavalier game; if the championship should come to Lancashire today, after long years of waiting, it will be good to know that it has been won at the pinch by cricket true to the MacLaren, Spooner, and J. T. Tyldesley tradition.

Ernest Tyldesley's innings had bloom on its every stroke; this play of Makepeace and Tyldesley, indeed, ought to have happened weeks ago; I am left with no words that have not been worn out. Makepeace's innings was ended by a stroke good enough for at least four runs; it was a strong and pretty glance, and Staples caught it one-handed at short leg. Makepeace hit 16 boundaries and Tyldesley 19.

The Lancashire innings now became frankly dissolute. It was good policy to send in the hitters, immediately Tyldesley was out. At half-past five the Notts. bowlers were able to rest: in five and a quarter hours yesterday Lancashire looted them to the tune of 450. For three hours and a quarter after lunch the rate of scoring was 108 an hour. Up to a point the Notts. attack stuck to a gruelling job, and the ball with which Larwood put an end to the Lancashire foray was not that of a sick and tired bowler. It shot the middle stump yards out of the earth—always a satisfying sight to see. Carr nurses Larwood wisely; the future of English Test cricket may depend largely on this young man.

Every Notts fieldsman had much hot running about to do; consequently it was bad luck that any of them should have had to tackle Macdonald at the day's end in a fading light. George Gunn, for the second time in the match, pulled a ball into his wicket—the stroke of a tired man. A. Staples was caught in the slips at 16; seven runs afterwards Whysall fell to a ball from Macdonald which looked to break back. Richard Tyldesley was put on in the closing moments, obviously to get Richmond out; his first ball made pace from the turf, and Carr was lbw, after accomplishing one sledge-hammer cut. A good day went to its fall with Richmond holding his bat with exasperating straightness to many balls which, in common decency, he ought to have let bowl him. We were all greedy for the Notts. fifth wicket.

TUESDAY

Yesterday, at twenty-five minutes past one, Makepeace hit a ball from George Gunn (the same George that is a great batsman) and won Lancashire the county cricket championship for the first time since 1904. It was right and proper for Makepeace to make this stroke, for it was Makepeace who on Monday first showed Lancashire the only way to the heights. There was, of course, a scene of tumult and applause at the end of the match; the crowd forgot the unwritten law of Old Trafford (which ordains that the best turf in England is not to be trod by any but cricketers) and gathered in front of the pavilion. The game's heroes were commanded to show themselves, and the whole team, man and boy, was given a grand 'All hail'. Then there were speeches, more cheers, and then—a last look at Old Trafford, and a longing in the heart for all the summer days to come back again.

EARLY TORMENT

Victory did not reach us until we had passed through an amount of torment. In the early hours of yesterday morning some of us were wakened by the sound of rain; granted that it did not last too long we did not protest (fair play and a wicket as good for Notts. as it had been for Lancashire were now matters absurdly academic; who would not be an unashamed partisan at such a moment and throw morality to the winds?) But the rain passed by without even hurting the pitch overmuch. With joy we heard, as the Lancashire XI took the field, that play at Swansea was held up.

Flint was out almost at once, leg-before-wicket to Richard Tyldesley. I thought the ball hit Flint too high on the leg; Flint, too, obviously was of that opinion. Still, he had to go, and I cheered his passing, with everybody else. (In this game I have lived in Lancashire county, not on aloof Olympus.) Richmond persisted in his delusion (so aggravating on Monday evening) that he was about to make a century in county cricket. And some of his strokes were preposterously stylish and strong. Macdonald could not bowl him till his score was 30. And now Lilley and Payton put Old Trafford on the rack with a vengeance. For 55 minutes they batted with an ease maddening to see. And all the time the sky threatened rain. Payton often chanced his bat at the overtossed length and lofted the ball. Ernest Tyldesley missed him from a hit in front of the Stretford sight screen, and was silently though affectionately cursed for his blunder. Lilley drove through the covers like William Gunn; against our proper Lancastrian instincts we applauded these strokes. 'He'll play for England yet, will Lilley,' said somebody, and somebody else answered rather illogically, 'Then he ought to get out at once.'

ANNOYING NOTTS. PERSISTENCE

The Notts. innings seemed to be settling down for the day. Payton was at his best and, of course, he ought to have been No. 4 in the England batting order for these many years. The innings defeat was saved by Notts. at half-past twelve; Eckersley consulted Makepeace freely, and the bowling was changed with depressing frequency. Hereabouts we hated the very thought of Emmott Robinson. Young Woolley was called up from the boundary to bowl when Notts. were two in front and four wickets in hand—a state of affairs which in our now quite morbid minds meant certain defeat for Lancashire. Woolley's first ball got Lilley caught in the slips and Old Trafford blessed him, for it was a good ball—the kind that makes a batsman play forward with a speculative bat.

Nine runs after Payton had reached his 50, Duckworth caught him off Macdonald, thus making it possible for us to enjoy the Notts. innings from here onwards to its end.

Lancashire opened with Makepeace and Tyldesley to get the runs. Outside the ground a little crowd mainly of ardent but not wealthy supporters of Lancashire cricket, had been trying all morning to get a glimpse of the scoreboard. They were admitted free of charge to the pavilion side in time to see the finish.

LANCASHIRE'S HEART'S DESIRE

Carr opened the Notts. bowling and set a field which made the most of his forces. His style of attack was, in intention, true to the Attewell tradition, for he aimed at the off stump. Before he began his first ball, a photographer took a picture of the state of the game from a position near mid-on, close to the wicket. The players placed themselves in attitudes confidently assumed to be indicative of defence and offence. Then Carr ran ambitiously to the wicket and let his arm swing. His bowling apparently proceeded upon some dark laid scheme; at any rate, he altered his field for no reason palpable to the common eye. Carr, I take it, is essentially a new-ball bowler, for after he had kept one end going for three overs he retired, amidst applause, in favour of George Gunn who straightway began to bowl with his head, so much so that only two runs were hit from the only four balls he sent down. He was clearly about to get a subtle length when the winning hit was made and Lancashire came into their heart's desire.

After the shouting finished, a man with a very hoarse and tired voice asked me whether, now that this match was won, Lancashire were 'absolutely certain' to be champions, no matter what happened to Yorkshire. And when I told him Lancashire were indeed champion county now, he seemed taken aback and he said, making his wan voice audible with an effort, 'Good Lord, I didn't know that till now!' Apparently he went home regretting he had not shouted a little louder than he did.

NOTTINGHAMSHIRE

First Innings		Second Innings	
Gunn, b Macdonald	56	b Sibbles	2
Whysall, b Sibbles	97	b Macdonald	6
Staples (A.), c Duckworth, b Macdonald	0	c Tyldesley (R.), b M'nald	10
A. W. Carr, c Iddon, b Macdonald	67	lbw, b Tyldesley (R.)	10
Payton, lbw, b Macdonald	2	c D'worth, b M'donald	59
Lilley, b Tyldesley (R)	13	c Watson, b Woolley	45
Flint, c Sibbles, b Macdonald	2	lbw, b Tyldesley (R.)	17
Staples (S.), b Tyldesley (R.)	27	not out	9
Larwood, lbw, b Tyldesley (R.)	10	c Woolley, b Macdonald	3
Barratt, not out	6	b Macdonald	4
Richmond, b Woolley	0	b Macdonald	30
B 5, lb 6, nb 1	12	B 4	4
Total	292	Total	199

LANCASHIRE

First Innings		Second Innings	
Makepeace, c Staples (A.), b Staples (S.)	180	not out	15
Hallows, c Carr, b Larwood	0		
Sibbles, c Staples (S.), b Staples (A.)	34		
Tyldesley (E.), c Carr, b Staples (S.)	140	not out	18
Iddon, c and b Staples (S.)	18		
Macdonald, st Lilley, b Staples (S.)	24		
Tyldesley (R.), b Larwood	28		
Watson, b Barratt	15		
P. T. Eckersley, b Larwood	8		
Woolley, run out	0		
Duckworth, not out	0		
B 1, lb 4, w 2	7	B 4, w 1	5
Total	454	Total (for 0)	38

BOWLING ANALYSIS
NOTTINGHAMSHIRE

NOTTINGHAMSHIRE—First Innings

	O.	M.	R.	W.		O.	M.	R.	W.
Macdonald	34	7	93	5	Woolley	17	3	52	1
Sibbles	23	5	46	1	Iddon	4	1	13	0
Tyldesley (R.)	25	7	76	3					

Sibbles bowled one no-ball.

Second Innings

	O.	M.	R.	W.		O.	M.	R.	W.
Macdonald	21·1	8	80	6	Iddon	5	1	21	0
Sibbles	12	2	25	1	Woolley	4	1	18	1
Tyldesley (R.)	11	0	51	2					

LANCASHIRE—First Innings

Barratt	23	5	68	1	Richmond	23	4	112	0
Larwood	18·5	5	42	3	Flint	16	4	50	0
Staples (S.)	25	2	125	4	Staples (A.)	19	2	50	1

Flint and Richmond each bowled one wide

Second Innings

Carr	3	0	7	0	Gunn	0·4	0	2	0
Richmond	3	0	24	0					

Carr bowled one wide

ROOT'S GREAT DAY

THERE were sensations at Edgbaston this sunny June morning. Root bowled the Australians out neck and heels, and not only that—he rendered them as helpless as boys from a preparatory school. It was a clear case of a success of surprise. Australian batsmen get little practice in their own country against the swerving ball. The air is not heavy enough in Australia for a deadly exploitation of the swerve—George Hirst was for that reason a failure in Australia as a bowler. Today the circumstances gave Root a rare opportunity, and he turned it all to advantage. He was privileged to attack cricketers who had never before seen his curious style of bowling, and there were also these other points in his favour—a breeze that blew diagonally down the wicket, and a turf which, having dried after the recent rains, lent to the ball a good amount of pace after pitching.

Root's line of attack, is, of course, familiar enough to English batsmen; he bowls a ball which swings in from the off and passes across the wicket towards the leg side, where a circle of fieldsmen await catches. Sometimes Root's swerve is so wide that at the moment it has to be played its direction is not unlike the direction of a throw-in from mid-off. The batsman is often at liberty to allow Root's swerve to pass by his legs aimlessly a yard away from the danger zone, but on certain days Root's in-swinger comes towards the bat on the off wicket and then hits the leg or middle stump. When Root is exploiting this latter ball the batsman, of course, must make some sort of stroke; if he misses he is bowled, and if he plays the stroke too hard a catch flies to the leg trap. The mistake of the

Australians today was that, though they usually permitted the more pronounced swerves to go by outside their legs harmlessly enough, they did not know how to tackle the swerve which came across and yet remained always on the wicket. There is indeed only one safe way whereby to frustrate this ball and that is the way of Makepeace, for example. The use of the dead bat is necessary. Makepeace, as the good length in-swinger pitches on his wicket, faces the bowler, backs up with his pads, and, if the ball still keeps in the danger zone and simply must be played, holds out his bat straight enough but without positive resistance. Thus the ball works its vitality away and falls well in front of the crouching fieldsmen all around him on the leg side. The Australians did not let this nasty delivery hit a yielding bat and defeat itself; instead they mostly tried to make positive hits, and were clean bowled or sent a catch to the leg trap with ample carrying force. As I have suggested the Australians cut a tragic comical picture. All of their customary strokes, learned on true wickets against straightish bowling, were useless now. The Australians' very lack of acquaintance with the despised two-eyed stance was here a weakness and not a strength. A good forward style of batting is exactly the style which Root thrives on.

HOW THE WICKETS FELL

Mailey's wicket was the first to fall today; he attempted a leg stroke from Larwood, and sheer pace from the turf defeated his intentions. Taylor watched Root circumspectly for a while before he drove an inswinger to mid-on, where Whysall made a running catch. Andrews played for rather more swerve than actually happened, and he was comprehensively bowled. Ryder's innings had an almost farcical ineptitude; he could scarcely have looked a more bothered man if Root's swerve had been describing corkscrews through the air. His wicket fell to another fairly imaginary swerve. Root, indeed, gave a clever variation to his attack; now and then he would insinuate a slightly slower and tolerably straight ball—at any rate one with no more swerve than was caused by the breeze coming slantwise down the wicket. Gregory resorted to desperation tactics: being a left-handed batsman, his problem while facing Root was not, of course, quite so acute as that of his colleagues. He threw his bat violently at everything, and just missed giving a catch on the off side. Then he hit across Root's biggest swing, and sent the ball as high as a tower. Smith let the ball drop into his capacious gloves with a richly decisive noise. Richardson and Ponsford scratched for a while like hens on very barren ground, and the follow-on was saved.

ROOT AND THE TEST MATCHES

In some ninety minutes we witnessed today the downfall of eight Australian wickets for 71. Carr's swift catch, which was a sort of last nail in the coffin, had the old MacLaren dive and swiftness. Macartney, the only Australian, excepting Taylor, not to make a foolish sight when tackling Root, was frequently beaten by Larwood's excellent nip from the ground—the question we need to ask ourselves now is this, 'Has a mistake been made by giving the Australians an opportunity of looking into Root's methods? If he is indeed England's rod, ought he not to have remained in pickle till next Saturday?' My own view is that if Root bowls at Trent Bridge as cleverly as he has bowled in this game, and if also he is lucky enough to get the right wicket and the right wind, I cannot imagine that the Australians will play him with confidence. I do not suppose he will ever again render them quite so helpless as he has done today; but the moral effect of this superb piece of bowling and opportunist strategy will not be lost in a hurry. At Trent Bridge next Saturday the Australians may contrive to hold their wickets against Root by declining to risk a positive stroke. But if this plan is adopted the Australians will be compelled to get runs from Tate—and the risks they will therefore need to take with Tate will possibly make Tate a bowler of even more than his customary deadliness. As a rule batsmen play for safety against Tate and find the runs at the other end. Root thoroughly deserves the glory now descending on him. For years he has worked hard in a weak, unfashionable county. The Australians may master him in time, even as many English batsmen have done after finding him first of all a sore trial. Let us hope he will win us a Test Match before his method is understood by Collins and his men. For, I believe, Root's success is a success of method rather than of technique—though this is not to deny the accuracy with which he deploys his trick.

The North's attack all round was far better than the Australians'. Larwood is a good bowler, with much devil from the pitch and no mean offbreak. He is inexperienced yet, and will gain with greater strength. Smith's wicket-keeping could be relied upon, though it did not suggest Test Match class.

Carr declared the North's second innings closed with an hour and a half left for cricket. Larwood forced Woodfull to play on and uprooted Taylor's leg stump with consecutive balls—a sorry day for the Australians, indeed. Larwood again achieved immense speed after the ball hit the earth—a likely youngster, and no mistake.

NORTH OF ENGLAND

First Innings		Second Innings	
Sutcliffe, retired hurt	35		
Holmes, run out	43	c and b Richardson	15
Hallows, c Gregory, b Macartney	34	not out	7
A. W. Carr, st Oldfield, b Macartney	14		
Whysall, b Macartney	0	not out	47
Watson, b Richardson	20		
V. W. C. Jupp, c Woodfull, b Richardson	23		
Smith, c Oldfield, b Mailey	23		
Geary, not out	39		
Root, b Richardson	1		
Larwood, run out	0		
B 1, lb 2, nb 4	7	B 2, lb 5, nb 1	8
Total	239	Total (for 1)	77
		Innings declared	

AUSTRALIANS

First Innings		Second Innings	
W. Bardsley, c Carr, b Root	11	run out	10
W. M. Woodfull, c Larwood, b Root	8	b Larwood	7
J. M. Taylor, c Whysall, b Root	22	b Larwood	0
A. A. Mailey, lbw, b Larwood	3		
C. G. Macartney, c sub., b Geary	15	not out	20
T. J. Andrews, b Root	5	not out	68
J. S. Ryder, b Root	4		
W. H. Ponsford, c Carr, b Root	14		
J. M. Gregory, c Smith, b Root	6		
A. J. Richardson, not out	13		
W. Oldfield, c Carr, b Geary	0		
B 1, lb 3	4	Lb 5	5
Total	105	Total (for 3)	110

BOWLING ANALYSIS
NORTH OF ENGLAND

First Innings

	O.	M.	R.	W.		W.	M.	R.	W
Gregory	26	9	55	0	Richardson	24·2	12	31	3
Ryder	18	5	40	0	Mailey	9	1	34	1
Macartney	34	13	72	3					

Richardson bowled two no-balls and Ryder and Macartney one each

Second Innings

	O	M	R	W		O	M	R	W
Gregory	7	1	10	0	Richardson	11	5	7	1
Macartney	8	5	8	0	Mailey	8	2	29	0
Ryder	6	4	15	0					

Ryder bowled one no-ball

AUSTRALIANS

First Innings

	O	M	R	W		O	M	R	W
Larwood	14	4	29	1	Geary	14·4	6	25	2
Root	28	11	42	7	Jupp	1	0	5	0

Second Innings

	O	M	R	W		O	M	R	W
Larwood	7	3	18	2	Jupp	7	0	39	0
Geary	7	1	26	0	Watson	7	1	22	0

THE OLD FEUD

FIRST DAY

The year's wheel has gone round again, and here is the old feud with its slow fires ready to break into flames at the first breath of antagonism. On Saturday, at Bradford, the crowd, though big, was not unwieldy; it had the proper Yorkshire pride in the cricketers of its county, but enthusiasm remained tolerant the day long; never was the game's action dramatic enough to stir the multitude to the fine clannish vehemence which makes a Yorkshire crowd the most loyal and the most vociferous in the land.

Today, maybe we shall hear the authentic Yorkshire roar splitting the skies; these dour conflicts usually begin in a calm that hints bodefully of the brewing storm; the first day's play is given mainly to a suspicious searching for position; then the hurly-burly bubbles and passion spins the plot. This morning we shall see Macaulay running his intense run to the wicket, moving bitterly along as though a battleaxe and not a cricket ball were in his grip—Macaulay, the image of lean enmity ('Let me have men about me that are fat.'); Macaulay bowling like a Fury crowned with snakes—Lancashire batsmen must 'circumwent' him (as Sam Weller would say) on this Whit-Monday or the Yorkshire roar will send us mad.

I would rather watch Yorkshire in attack than Yorkshire making runs. Saturday's play sometimes compelled a watcher here and there to emulate the Frenchmen at the Court of Frederick the Great and conjugate the verb *s'ennuyer*. Not that the cricket had quite the Lethe'd dullness of other Lancashire and Yorkshire matches of recent times; some event was usually taking place, and now and again Kilner and Holmes scored runs at a speed almost vulgar for an occasion so heavy and solemn. My complaint against Saturday's cricket is that (like this account of it) it was a long time 'coming to the point'; the style of the play was loose and the action drifted rather aimlessly.

A missed catch in the morning's first quarter of an hour obviously upset for a while the confidence of Lancashire; another Lancashire fielding blunder proved that the stars were shining for Yorkshire, and yet Yorkshire apparently could not decide whether to meet good luck half-way, and take the offensive, or whether to regard as warnings the fortunate escapes of one or two of her best batsmen, and draw in horns and go warily. Thus the day and the policy of the match lacked much of the traditional sense of stern steel crossing stern steel.

SUTCLIFFE'S 'LIVES'

Sutcliffe gave an easy slip catch when his score was two and Yorkshire's total was nine; the mistake happened in Macdonald's third over. A ball swung away rather late and Sutcliffe edged it straight to Watson at second slip; and easier catch it would be hard to imagine. Watson somehow contrived to drop it, whereat everybody that has ever played cricket sent out his heart to the unhappy Watson; the erring fieldsman always suffers for a blunder of this sort sorrows of humiliation far more painful than the bitter frustration felt in the partisan crowd. Yet while Watson's dropped catch was calculated to make one laugh as well as cry. The simplicity of it! Once, long ago, the present writer missed such a catch, and at the over's end the irate bowler declared: 'I suppose you prefer a catch handed to you on a plate with parsley round the ball.'

Macdonald palpably accepted his bad luck on Saturday with the utmost philosophy; he proceeded to bowl a half-dozen fastish overs, some very good and some not good at all, and then, as the saying goes, 'surrendered the ball' to Richard Tyldesley. Sutcliffe gave another chance, when the Yorkshire score was 45 and his own 21; this time he cut a ball from Watson hard and low to Makepeace at backward point; Makepeace gripped the catch after a desperate fling forward of the whole of his being, but dropped it. And as he did so lines of care marked his face.

Lancashire's fielding, keen enough on the ground, could not be trusted in the air. The costliest mishap was Ernest Tyldesley's. Kilner flashed his bat at a short rising ball from Macdonald; the hit was quick and Tyldesley had to jump a little to reach the catch; he stopped the ball but could not hold it. When this happened Kilner was 0—he made 85. Iddon gave him yet another innings at 70, missing a dainty 'caught and bowled' opportunity.

A WAVERING ATTACK

These dropped catches, of course, did Lancashire damage; yet I do not grumble at them now half so much as I grumble at the lack of consistent length in the Lancashire attack. The best fieldsman in the world cannot safeguard himself, try as he may, against missing a catch; a good bowler, by concentration of mind, *can* avoid bowling a long-hop. On Saturday I saw a dozen rank long-hops bowled by one Lancashire bowler in half an hour.

Apart from Holmes, Yorkshire did not too clearly possess more than one batsman in true form; had the Lancashire bowlers 'pegged away' at the good length *all the time*; had they acted on the Rhodes doctrine (which we shall witness in force today)—'Length, length! Mak' 'em fetch 'em. Length, length!'—Yorkshire could scarcely have made 298. The Lancashire attack was good whenever 'things were coming off', as cricketers say, for Lancashire; it wavered in technique and spirit at the first sign of an unfavourable wind. The grim efficiency of Yorkshire bowling may be relied upon never to throw runs away in the face of the most conquering batsman; today Lancashire will have to fight for every run, even if not a single wicket should fall to Yorkshire for hours. A third of Yorkshire's 298, I imagine, was given—a present from Lancashire, Whitsuntide, 1926.

Richard Tyldesley bowled accurately for a while; at the afternoon's fall it seemed he would go through the Yorkshire 'tail' (and there is one nowadays) in quick time; but he was 'taken off', and Macdonald put on instead; I could understand Green's move; he probably thought, like MacLaren of old, that fast bowling in a fading light is the specific at an innings's finish. Taking the day in the lump Watson provided Lancashire's most reliable attack; Parkin was steady at times but the easy pitch deprived his spin of sting.

MACDONALD'S 'BUMPERS'

Macdonald bowled with a perplexing changefulness. In one over his speed and length would be good; the next it would dwindle to medium pace; then, suddenly, the man's energy would shoot out in a violent bumping ball, terribly short, which would fly at a batsman's head like a deadly bolt. As a fact, a great batsman would more often than not have hit this fast 'bumper' out of the field. MacLaren's way with crude violence of this kind was to assume a position, which placed him not full-fronted to the ball, but rather across its flight, so that if he missed his stroke the ball would pass safely by the left side of his head and not hit him. MacLaren's stroke for the bumper was not the blind short-armed sweep frequently attempted on Saturday; it was a calm, deliberate stroke to the on, rather to leg, made by moving over the wicket and hitting the ball, with a turn of the wrist, as it passed by, with little or no chance of doing him physical hurt. How magnificently he would achieve his stroke; he would lift himself up to his proudest height: the sweep of his bat was like a disdainful gesture at the sight of bowling that was merely so much brute strength. MacLaren did not *hit* the bumping ball; he dismissed it from his presence.

Holmes countered Macdonald's shock tactics like the Test-match cricketer he is; he hit the short ball to leg, not across the flight but from the side of it; sometimes he even got behind it! Holmes never seemed likely to lose his wicket; his batting was the best of the day by far. His footwork is as quick as it is scientific and pretty; few other cricketers possess Holmes's elegance and versatility on the leg side. In contrast to Holmes, whose feet are always in nimble motion, Sutcliffe is an almost static (or shall we say statuesque?) batsman. On Saturday Sutcliffe was not in a good vein; his bat had more than its customary edge. But his style was as polished as ever; it was his timing, not his strokes, that was wrong. Fast, hard grounds will find Sutcliffe an England batsman still.

THE HAPPY CAVALIER

Oldroyd's innings of 64 lasted beyond two hours and a half—sturdy work, more body than bouquet, to reverse Mr. Asquith's description of Dr. Jowett's conversation. Kilner's cricket, as I have suggested, possessed a liveliness that was even flippant, considering the day and the occasion. He did not go into the safe shell of circumspection, as most batsmen would have been glad to, after his lucky escape from Tyldesley's fingers. His bat made many a merry impudent fling in the face of Fortune—her humorous ladyship. Some of his cover-hits were dazzling; some were 'off'n the edge', as the old 'pro' used to say of Shrewsbury. Good or bad hits were all the same to Kilner, who is a happy cavalier in a company of Ironsides. I often wonder what Emmot Robinson thinks of Kilner's riskily-flung bat; he must regard it as a vain pagan thing. Kilner hit two sixes and 10 fours, batted one hour and fifty minutes for 85.

Rhodes fell to a lovely diving catch by Macdonald, who also caught Holmes cleverly after getting himself into a position totally unscientific. Yorkshire's fifth wicket did not fall till the score was 273, and the long day closed with the stirring sight of Waddington and Major Lupton holding back the advancing Lancashire bowlers.

SECOND DAY

The air was stirring with the proper Yorkshire temper when the match went on this morning. A great crowd sat in the sun-shine and expectancy stood on tip-toe. Major Lupton astonished and delighted the multitude (and possibly himself by achieving a superb off-drive from Macdonald, also a savage blow to the on—both boundary hits.

Yorkshire scored 326: then at high noon, with summer opening graciously all around us, the game got to grips fiercely; Lancashire's innings began in the teeth of an attack far more determined than any I have yet seen this year. Robinson and Macaulay bowled—the familiar Emmott Robinson, with the same old grizzled face, the same lumbering yet antagonistic run to the wicket, the same old Yorkshire faith in rough honest muscle—and with the same old boots, though today I thought they looked to be suspiciously clean. Makepeace passed through an over of tribulation straightway; Macaulay broke down his defences with balls that swung away very late and at a rare speed from the ground. In Robinson's fourth over Makepeace again was beaten, but he got his pads there in time. Robinson's appeal might easily have stunned the umpire into deaf-ness, and as he heard judgment given against him he stood in the middle of the wicket and seemed to arraign justice eternal. How magnificent is the fighting passion of these ancient Yorkshiremen—the younger cricketers of the county, clever though they be, possess a manner that is mildness itself in contrast to the vehemence of the old clan.

Hallows, though compelled to play a defensive game, was pleasant to watch; his cricket made one think of young Samson in chains:

time after time he accomplished a strong blow for freedom with a defiant bat, only to find his strokes and his runs checked by the tight prison made by Yorkshire's close and watchful field. Forty minutes passed before Hallows drove the first Lancashire boundary—a lovely hit straight by the bowler, which was Emmott, now rather more outraged than ever. 'There ought to be no fours allowed by high heaven against Yorkshire in a match like this,' he was apparently saying.

YORKSHIRE BOWLERS ON TOP

From the outset the Yorkshire bowlers were on top: despite the easeful movement of Hallows's bat Lancashire had the aspect of a struggling team. The field was set with a silly mid-off and a silly mid-on while Makepeace batted to Kilner, whose first five overs were maidens. Oh, the royal agony of these Lancashire and York-shire matches! Some of us are growing grey in the service of them. In fifty minutes this morning Lancashire scored 27: then Hallows was caught at slip off a ball from Macaulay that made spiteful pace from the turf and swung a little at the last second away from the bat. Thus was the promise of Hallows suddenly and sadly ended.

Immediately before getting this wicket Macaulay's attack was wavering, and he seemingly asked his captain to give him a rest. At any rate, he was seen to be taking his sweater back from the umpire. But as he did so Rhodes had a word with Lupton—and Macaulay returned to work and ensnared Hallows without loss of time. Whereat the crowd wagged a sage admiring head and said, 'Good owd Wilfred; he knows a thing or two'—which, of course, he does.

Makepeace fell to a ball like that which baffled Hallows; the stroke was much the same, and Sutcliffe again was the fieldsman. Lancashire's honourable old 'Stonewall' Jackson had batted seventy minutes, suffering devotedly in the cause of his county. Watson did not do justice to his talents—his bat was without sight, and Kilner quickly had him confused and confounded. And now Yorkshire were definitely winning, for the Lancashire score read 49 for three.

BARNES AND TYLDESLEY TO THE RESCUE

The crowd roared out delight as these wickets were taken, and the occasion assumed a fine irony—we saw the aspect of tragedy come over the Lancashire batsmen as each understood that he was ruined, and shouts of savage joy must have been in the ears of the victims as they passed out of our sight. In this trying situation Barnes came into Lancashire cricket for the first time this summer. And no sooner had he got to the intense middle than he saw Ernest Tyldesley missed by Waddington from a hard hit to the leg side. Had this catch been held Lancashire's score would now have been 50 for four. Barnes entered the responsible air like a brave cricketer: true, he was nearly bowled immediately by a capital break from Kilner. This, though, was Barnes's only mistake in a stern innings: his ability to stop the advancing Yorkshiremen for a long period is proof, if proof were needed, that a sound method will serve well even a cricketer who is out of practice.

Ernest Tyldesley was disconcerted by his indiscreet stroke to Waddington; he quickly settled down to cool, manly cricket, subdued maybe, but deliberate. Tyldesley and Barnes slowly, very slowly, heaved the match round a little in Lancashire's way. The cautious play hereabouts was no longer that of batsmen overwhelmed by circumstances and severe bowling. We were watching at this point the stubbornness of batsmen who themselves chose to be stubborn: defensive measures were not any longer being forced on Lancashire—Lancashire was of purpose cultivating obstinacy. The crowd in a while sniffed the change in the air and did not like it. The voice of the barracker was heard in the land: ' 'It 'em,' mourned a man in deep travail. 'For the Lord's sake, 'it 'em.' It was frustration's own voice.

Barnes and Tyldesley went their dour Fabian way for ninety minutes and made 65. Then temptation lured Tyldesley to self-destruction. Rhodes tossed him a slow hanging ball, and Tyldesley, visited by the vision of the distant boundary—an oasis in the afternoon's desert—swung his bat at the ball and sent it high but not far enough into the deep. Sutcliffe ran in from long-off and held a charming catch. A few balls after this disaster for Lancashire Iddon walked across his stumps unscientifically and his off stump was knocked out of the ground. Lancashire 114 for five, 63 wanted yet to save the follow-on—thus in a trice the match had turned round again. Ernest Tyldesley must have watched the tide change with unhappy feelings: if only he had resisted Rhodes's simple old trick he might have—I am certain he would have stayed at the wicket for as long and just as untroubled as Barnes himself. But herein is the fascination that cricket has for us: how it does play on the weaknesses of men!

RHODES: TEN OVERS AND ONE RUN

Between half-past two and four o'clock Lancashire scored a mere 47: in ten overs a solitary run was hit from the historic—nay, legendary—Rhodes. Ernest Tyldesley batted one hundred and ten minutes for his fifty; in one hour and a half Barnes stoically refused to make more than 22: Green, too, played patience coolly and cleverly for forty minutes. And in the end all of this scourging of self, all the eating of this bitter dust, all of this more or less noble renunciation by Lancashire of the gaudy vanities that hang on the boundary's edge—all came to nothing. Green was defeated at 136; then the Lancashire rearguard collapsed and the follow-on, with its indignity, had to be suffered.

Could Lancashire have fared less prosperously had the batsmen exploited a normal game? For the persistent policy of not hitting the ball, witnessed today, has been abnormal even for Lancashire. It is a vain ambition to try and wear out Yorkshire's patience. Ernest Tyldesley got himself out, it is true, by chancing a big drive. But must a cricketer never venture a bold hit simply because other cricketers have been known to get caught near the boundary? These questions I ask in good faith: I am seeking to discover whether the canny, risk-equals-nothing method of batsmanship is the wisest in the world to exploit against Yorkshire throughout a warm day. Obviously, a cricketer needs to have his eyes about him and go warily at the outset of an innings against Yorkshire. Today, though, Lancashire did not hit the ball hard even when the Yorkshire attack was palpably failing, and even though the batsmen were frequently in position for ripe strokes. The problem is difficult: most counties in the country have asked these many seasons, 'Can the Yorkshire attack possibly be hit?' Apparently it cannot—at least by batsmen of a definitely modern technique.

THE 'ARTFUL' DODGER

The Bradford wicket today was not, I thought, quite so docile as on Saturday: at any rate, Kilner was able to spin the ball sharply at times. I am afraid, however, that this argument does not help to explain Lancashire's failings against Rhodes, who, truth to tell, seldom turned the ball quickly. His was the conquest of what may be called artful dodgery. Rhodes was at liberty this evening to leave the field saying, like somebody in one of Shakespeare's chronicle plays: 'I have gathered many spoils, using no other weapon but my name.' Macaulay's bowling had a deadly pace from the pitch and a disconcertingly late swing—but only for so long as the ball remained new and glossy. He was a good, hard-working, length bowler with the old ball, and little more than that. The secret of Yorkshire's persistent conquest is an attack that never gives runs away.

The Lancashire second innings ran into further trouble: I have not the heart to tell the sorry tale further. But this much I would like to ask: Why at the critical moment, with the follow-on almost saved, did Lancashire's later batsmen throw wickets to the winds by careless hitting? Bold cricket surely does not mean indiscriminate hitting. The high-class batsman mingles defence and offence in proportion. The Yorkshire fielding was excellent, and Dolphin on North-country grounds is our best wicket-keeper.

THIRD DAY

Lancashire lost this match easily at a quarter-past four this afternoon after letting Bradford witness an exhibition of cricket which, taken in the whole since Saturday, must rank as one of the very worst ever known to have happened in the long history of these games.

The trouble is not that Lancashire have proved themselves not as clever at cricket as Yorkshire; most of us have known this much for a long time and more or less philosophically accepted the truth. The charge against our county in this game is that several of our men played apparently with lack of thought and responsibility, and also that, through seeming not to concentrate overmuch during the crisis, did less than justice to their proper talents. Why did some of the later batsmen in the first Lancashire innings throw wickets away wantonly, just at a point where a little patience would have saved a fatal follow-on? Does every member of our eleven always bear in mind, as he takes part in these great contests, that lovers of the country's cricket everywhere are anxiously waiting for news about the event, taking to heart all that has happened, is happening, and likely to happen—and all the time sending forth their good wishes to Lancashire cricket? We have traditions in our county as superb as Yorkshire's; they ought always to be an inspiration to every Lancashire cricketer whenever he faces the old enemy, good days or bad.

This morning a wet wicket prevented activity; not until three o'clock could Yorkshire get at their prey again. How the weary waiting must have chafed the soul of Robinson! The wicket helped the bowler to spin the ball, but it was not too difficult. Barnes and

Green again let us admire cool and intelligent defensive batsmanship. Between them Green and Barnes batted for nearly two hours of the Lancashire second innings's brief life; the more one sees of Barnes the more one is convinced that if he could play the game regularly he would quickly be known as one of our most reliable amateur batsmen. Even when he is not scoring. Barnes is attractive to watch; with him, slow cricket does not mean dullness. He is always thinking upon the problems of the game as they are presented to him by all sorts of bowling. And he is always seeking to solve them by means of a cultured batsman's strokes. His main defect is one to which I have referred before: sometimes his drives to the off side are made from the back foot, and, as a consequence, his full weight does not go forward into the hit. All in all, though, Barnes makes his runs in a style which rarely fails to please the student of the game.

Green is certain to play a fruitful innings before long. Perhaps he exploits his gifts too diffidently. He possesses far more strokes than ever he has shown us in county cricket. Obviously, he has much command over a real technique: let him trust it freely some fine day. Duckworth also gave a useful account of his batting parts today; the probability is that if he had gone to the wicket on Monday evening, after Green was out, Lancashire would have saved the follow-on. Duckworth can at least play a straight bat—which is more than we can say of some of Lancashire's later batsmen. How is it that any county cricketer, with seasons of experience behind him, is unable to find a little acquaintance with the very rudiments of batting?

Kilner bowled cleverly today, and Major Lupton achieved a good catch. From the evidence of this game, Macaulay is not a Test match winner on a hard wicket.

YORKSHIRE
First Innings

Holmes, c Macdonald, b Watson	53	
Sutcliffe, lbw, b Macdonald	36	
Oldroyd, c Iddon, b Watson	44	
Leyland, c Tyldesley (E.), b Macdonald	29	
Kilner, b Iddon	85	
Rhodes, c Macdonald, b Tyldesley (R.)	21	
Macauley, b Tyldesley (R.)	1	
Robinson, c Tyldesley (R.), b Macdonald		3
Waddington, b Macdonald		15
A. W. Lupton, st Duckworth, b Tyldesley (R.)		28
Dolphin, not out		6
Extras		5
Total		326

44

LANCASHIRE

Makepeace, c Sutcliffe, b Macaulay	18	c Dolphin, b Robinson		0
Hallows, c Sutcliffe, b Macaulay	18	c Leyland, b Waddington		4
Tyldesley (E.), c Sutcliffe, b Rhodes	52	c Kilner, b Macaulay		13
Watson, lbw, b Kilner	3	c Holmes, b Waddington		9
J. R. Barnes, c Sutcliffe, b Rhodes	37	c Kilner, b Macaulay		13
Iddon, b Waddington	0	c Holmes, b Kilner		7
L. Green, b Kilner	12	c Lupton, b Kilner		14
Macdonald, c Holmes, b Rhodes	10	c Holmes, b Kilner		0
Tyldesley (R.), c Macaulay, b Kilner	4	c Holmes, b Kilner		0
Parkin, b Rhodes	0	not out		0
Duckworth, not out	2	c Lupton, b Waddington		7
B 2, lb 1	3	Extras		6
	—			—
Total	159	Total		73

BOWLING ANALYSIS

YORKSHIRE—First Innings

	O.	M.	R.	W.		O.	M.	R.	W.
Macdonald	41	8	110	4	Watson	27	4	60	2
Parkin	23	6	56	0	Iddon	16	7	35	1
Tyldesley (R.)	30·2	13	60	3					

LANCASHIRE—First Innings

	O.	M.	R.	W.		O.	M.	R.	W.
Robinson	10	4	21	0	Waddington	9	5	11	1
Macaulay	27	4	64	2	Rhodes	20·1	12	20	4
Kilner	35	16	40	3					

Second Innings

	O.	M.	R.	W.		O.	M.	R.	W.
Robinson	7	5	7	1	Kilner	15·5	5	19	4
Macaulay	12	2	24	2	Waddington	11	4	17	3

Waddington bowled one wide

THE CASE FOR VOCE

THE body-line rumpus has broken out again, and this time the issue is clouded more than ever. Legitimate fast left-handed leg-theory, much of the same kind as that which was practised by Hirst and F. R. Foster without a protest from anybody, is confused with the questionable method of the right-handed fast bowler who packs his field to leg and persistently bumps the ball about the batsman's head.

The present writer opposed Larwood's tactics in Australia; he was almost the only writer on the game in this country who saw the Australian point of view. Frankly, he is today astonished at the objections which are now being brought against the attack of Voce. The point which is missed in the controversy is briefly this: The leg-side field is as fair and logical to fast left-handed bowling as a four-slip field, with a third man, is fair and logical to the right-handed fast bowler. The right-handed fast bowler's action, with the sweep of the arm from right to left, favours a direction swinging towards the slips; the breakback or inswing is an acquired device to a right-hander. Larwood goes against nature when he packs his leg-side field, and he certainly invites criticism when he bumps the ball from outside the leg-stump. But Voce, being a left-hander, is entitled to a field set almost contrary to that of the right-handed fast bowler. His action sweeps from left to right, and the direction swings from the off to leg—a direction opposite to the right-hander's. Voce therefore must have his leg-side field; they are his slips and third man. This point is crucial, and it has been completely overlooked. Why should a left-handed fast bowler be denied the use of the field which is the right-hander's—changed over for the needs of his left-handedness?

If the objection to Voce is against his three or four short-legs (which, as I say, are his slips), then it is a foolish and ignorant objection. A left-handed fast bowler would be as harmless without a leg-side field as a right-handed fast bowler would be without his slips and third man.

The whole question hangs on the kicking balls. If Voce persistently bumped the ball at the Australians on Saturday, then the objection to his methods might be valid. But he did not, over after over, bump the ball against the Australians at Trent Bridge. He bowled in the way that he has bowled in county cricket for years. No English player has protested against Voce's leg-field. Has it come to this—that Voce must not use his legitimate field against Australians, and use it only against English batsmen? The Australians, with some right on their side, challenged Larwood's leg-trap, in conjunction with the bumper. But nobody is free, in fair sport, to challenge Voce's 'slips' on the leg-side, especially if his bowling rises no higher than shoulder high. Voce can as legitimately bowl to his four legs as Larwood can bowl to his four slips.

The outcry of the popular press that the M.C.C. should make a statement against 'body line' has nothing to do with Voce, or with

46

any other fast left-hander. The M.C.C. have already agreed that 'bumping with intent to hurt or intimidate is wrong'. They cannot make a rule rendering a fast left-hand bowler 'slipless'; in other words, they cannot abolish Voce's four short-legs. Did McLaren, Spooner, and J. T. Tyldesley protest against Hirst's leg-trap? Did the English batsmen of 1921 protest against Gregory's and McDonald's bumpers to their four slips?

No English cricketer is in favour of deliberate bumping by anybody, Voce or Larwood or Bowes or any future successor of Gregory or Cotter. But Voce has for many seasons used, and used lawfully, his leg-side field. No English batsman has protested; the fact needs constant reiteration. Only the other week Iddon was hit by Voce and he went on to score 200 against him. Kent and Woolley the other day routed Voce at Canterbury. Is the objection to Voce's bowling on Saturday an objection to his leg-side field, to his bumpers (which, as all competent observers maintain were never head-high), or to the fact that he took eight wickets for 66?

English cricketers have given Australia a 'fair deal' this year; they must not surrender the rights of every fast left-hander to his necessary field. Bumping the ball is one thing; leg-theory is another. Does Woodfull object to a leg-field and fast left-handed bowling even when it does not bump? That is the whole and only issue.

A. W. CARR

CRICKETERS all over the country will be glad that A. W. Carr (as announced yesterday) has at last been 'officially' appointed to the captaincy of the England XI. Here is a gesture that Collins and his men are likely to appreciate as much as the rest of us; our colours have been nailed decisively to the mast. And if we know our Carr at all, the colours will be those of fearless offence. Carr is a fighter, as cricketers say, with a challenging jaw, a man who knows well that 'he that gets his blow in fust' is thrice blessed. Carr, of course, is England's finest amateur batsmen; he is also an experienced leader of men. Not, maybe, a Machiavellian leader like Fender, but a captain who will get as much out of a team by example as to any conceivable precept. His main claim to the job of England's cricket captain is that he looks the part; there is much virtue in appearances. Not since MacLaren used to stand in the slips, contemplating the face of the earth and his forces upon it; not since MacLaren waved a man here or there with an imperiousness that was in high Roman fashion; not since MacLaren, having looked at the tide of the battle and thought weighty things about the action, plucked up his trousers, squared his shoulders, and then bent down in the slips ready for his will to work its power—not since the time of MacLaren, most majestic of cricketers, has an England XI. ever been led into action by a captain wearing more than Carr's aspect of authority. You need only take a second's impression of him to realise that here is the counter for the craft of Collins; the tall casual poise of him, quick as lightning, though, at the hint of a flying ball through the slips; the slight droop of the shoulders telling of a mind that dwells upon the game's problems as keenly as may be; the bronze on his clean-cut face speaking of much experience in the field; the born cricketer's love of uncovering his head to the wind and sun—surely this is a captain who by sheer spirit, not to say royal temper, will bring the finest parts out of all English cricketers that find themselves this summer living in his by no means mild but magnificent eye.

VERITY'S MATCH

ENGLAND *v*. AUSTRALIA: LORDS 1934

ENGLAND
First Innings

C. F. Walters, c Bromley, b O'Reilly	82
Sutcliffe, lbw, b Chipperfield	20
Hammond, c and b Chipperfield	2
Hendren, c McCabe b Wall	13
R. E. S. Wyatt, c Oldfield, b Chipperfield	33
Leyland, not out	95
Ames, not out	44
Extras (lb 4)	4
	—
Total (for 5 wickets)	293

To bat.—Verity, K. Farnes, Bowes, and Geary

Fall of the wickets:

1	2	3	4	5
70	78	99	130	182

AUSTRALIA

W. M. Woodfull, D. G. Bradman, S. J. McCabe,
W. A. Oldfield, W. A. Brown, A. G. Chipperfield,
C. V. Grimmett, L. S. Darling, T. W. Wall,
W. J. O'Reilly, and E. H. Bromley.

AT four o'clock today Australia were winning again, and Grimmett was this time able to watch the fun from his base at cover-point. He was out of form and Chipperfield caused a collapse of England. I thought I could see a faint smile on Grimmett's face; I thought it was still there, a ghost of humour, so to say, when at half-past six the cricketers walked back to the pavilion through the evening sunshine. For now England were not losing: a grand rally by Leyland and Ames had made 111 runs. But, as I hope to show in this account of a rather pedestrian day, England should never have got into trouble at all. There was a want of resolution until Leyland stuck out his chin and his anatomy in general. Ames, too, must be praised; loads of responsibility were put on his shoulders. Before he left the dressing-room I can hear his captain's, 'Stick to it, Leslie.' He did stick to it, like a proper man of Kent. The prospect for England had he failed would have been desperate.

On a windy, sunny morning, with the flags of Empire fluttering and the trees at the Nursery end making sweet noises, Walters and Sutcliffe began the England innings on an easy wicket. Wall and McCabe attacked with the new ball. In the fast bowler's first over—a technical term which denotes Wall—Sutcliffe edged a stroke to the slips and knew little or nothing about its direction until he saw, no doubt with relief, somebody fielding the ball. Walters lent the bloom of wrist-work to all of his hits, defensive or offensive, but for a long time the cricket was quiet; nine runs came by stealth in half an hour. Then Grimmett began his day's labour, and at the wicket's other end O'Reilly lumbered into action like a carthorse going uphill. Walters drove a long hop from Grimmett to the off for four, and Sutcliffe flicked a boundary to leg from Wall—an exquisite piece of work and the last example of real cricket he showed us in a strangely inept innings.

Walters was charming; he used his feet to Grimmett, and his

strokes were timed to perfection. He leaned over to the leg-side balls and forced them away with a touch so intimate that it was a visible signature, a personal caligraphy of cricket. In an hour 34 were amassed, eight of them by Sutcliffe, who looked himself only when he reclined on his bat between the overs and surveyed the scene and the day like a sort of Sir Willoughby Patterne, convinced he was an England batsman. Walters lifted himself up, thrust forward his front foot, and drove O'Reilly to the off like a king; this was the Test-match style, with the true people in it.

The England innings opened prosperously, thanks to Walters, whose mastery helped us to overlook the obvious mortality of everything done by Sutcliffe. Woodfull employed all his reputable bowlers in vain; they looked fairly impotent, even Grimmett. At a quarter-past one Woodfull was reduced to calling up Chipperfield, and in two overs Chipperfield swung round the wheel of the game, plucked the lion's mane, and, so to say, landed him one on the nose. The score was 70 when Chipperfield got Sutcliffe leg-before-wicket. In his next over Hammond played forward with great hauteur, his mind apparently on other and loftier subjects; he returned the ball condescendingly to Chipperfield, who might well have dropped the catch and declined to believe his luck and eyesight.

The fall of these two wickets was shocking. England had been making comfortable progress, for though Sutcliffe's batting all the time was bad technically, none of us was unduly depressed because of that; Sutcliffe is the best bad player in the world; he often reminds us of those men who have been given up by their doctors and live to be septuagenarians. Hammond's fatal stroke was the kind a cricketer makes in a shop when he is buying a bat, and finding out whether it 'comes up' well. At lunch England were 82 for 2, Walters, thank heaven, not out, 58.

After the interval Wall was brilliantly cut by Walters for four, and Hendren drove Chipperfield's leg-break with the spin to the off. Once again our hopes were mere bubbles of optimism. Hendren, at 99, ingloriously held out his bat to a wide out-swinger and was caught in the slips. Another wicket lost now, and England were 'for it'.

A pretty leg-break by Chipperfield confounded, but did not beat, Walters; then Walters soothed out hysteria by means of a gallant off-drive; he was splendid. Wyatt, grim as death, took up his stand; Wall bowled faster than he did before lunch. A nice state of things—England struggling and sweating, and Grimmett not the bogy this time, but Chipperfield. I do believe that Mr. G. K. Chesterton or Mr. Bernard Shaw would, with leg-spin, bring lines of concern to the faces of England batsmen at the present time.

Wall's pace soon faltered, and O'Reilly came on. He missed a sharp one-handed return catch from Walters when England were 120 for three; the hit was not bad enough to make an end of a beautiful innings. We breathed thankful relief, and we were chastised ironically two or three overs afterwards. O'Reilly sent his best ball to Walters, a slower ball which breaks from middle stump to leg. The flight deceived Walters, who hit precipitately, and though he tried to check the stroke at the last second, he could not avoid sending a catch forward to short leg. For two hours and fifty minutes Walters had been the only England batsman on view. The Australian attack was seen by him realistically; he played a pedigree innings—it was by MacLaren out of F. S. Jackson. His strokes were aglow with style; he made them swiftly and late. His wrists gave lustre to every movement of his bat. This was an innings fit for Lord's and a Test match. It lent distinction to England's innings while it was being made, much as the John Rylands Library lends distinction to Deansgate—it was erected amidst poor, jerry-built slum property. Walters was guilty of only three dangerous hits.

England were 130 for four when Leyland joined his captain, who found his thumb-protector an inconvenience. But Wyatt played solidly, and Leyland hit three loose balls for fours—for all the world as though the occasion were a light-hearted affair like a Lancashire and Yorkshire match. Grimmett was out of form, his spin lacked bite, and O'Reilly always looks a second-rate bowler when he is not taking wickets. He could not break the ball from leg today. England's opportunity to get a big score was golden. Wyatt hung on adhesively while he and Leyland lifted—you could see the heaving, manual labour and you could feel it—England's total from 130 to 182. Then Wyatt went forward to Chipperfield, snicked the leg-spin, and was caught; Oldfield also stumped him to clinch the argument.

The situation was appalling hereabout, and nobody could find an explanation that did not indict the nerve of the batsmen. Tamer bowling could not well be imagined in a Test match; the Australian attack seldom looked capable of getting wickets even when they were falling. The crowd sat in silence, the sun shone, and the wind blew. Father Time, on the Lord's weathercock, gyrated dizzily. I imagined that the old man, in his fuddled-headedness, had mixed two dates for the occasion, arranging for a Test-match crowd but

51

somehow assembling the multitude for an engagement between Middlesex and Leicestershire. The two hour's play between lunch and tea saw cricket as flat as cricket well could be. Sometimes I think of music that would go in tune with cricket: an allegro by Mozart for Woolley; *Tyl Eulenspiegel* for a Bradman innings (as he bats nowadays). Today the English innings for a tome time groaned and moaned like the dreadful music in Saint-Saëns's opera where Samson turns the millstone round.

Leyland at last remembered his county and his relationship to Roy Kilner. He began to discover the bowling as it was in fact, a toiling perspiring business, living on hope and bluff. Ames put his bat protectively to the ball; for half an hour he did nothing but obstinately refuse to get out. Slowly and surely the game was pulled out of the hole. Grimmett could not spin, no matter how hard he twisted his wrist. O'Reilly bowled industriously, and his congested action caused me to feel tired and worn out. The Australian attack looked at its best when Oldfield was throwing the ball back to the bowler with a lovely curve.

At tea England were 194 for five; an hour afterwards England were 250 for five. Then Leyland hit a no-ball for six, off O'Reilly, and twenty thousand people woke up and discovered that Australia had lost their grip on the match. Ames opened out his forward style; the stand came out of the chrysalis. At the last ditch Yorkshire and Kent counter-attacked: just after six o'clock Leyland and Ames had put on one hundred runs. Leyland's strokes cracked over the field with his own jolly broad accent. 'Ah've found thi out,' he seemed to say to the weary Australian bowlers. 'Ah've found thi out, and Ah can't think what our Herbert were thinking about this morning.' He drove and hit to leg with the long handle, yet he was always over the ball when it pitched a decent length. So far Leyland has been at the wicket just over three hours; he has never faltered, never once forgotten that he is the life and soul of the champion county.

SECOND DAY

ENGLAND
First Innings

C. F. Walters, c Bromley, b O'Reilly		82
Sutcliffe, lbw, b Chipperfield		20
Hammond, c and b Chipperfield		2
Hendren, c McCabe, b Wall		13
R. E. S. Wyatt, c Oldfield, b Chipperfield		33
Leyland, b Wall		109
Ames, c Oldfield, b McCabe		120
Geary, c Chipperfield, b Wall		9
Verity, st Oldfield, b Grimmett		29
Farnes, b Wall		1
Bowes, not out		10
Extras (lb 12)		12
Total		440

England first-innings bowling analysis

	O.	M.	R.	W.		O.	M.	R.	W.
Wall	49	7	108	4	O'Reilly	38	15	70	1
McCabe	18	3	38	1	Chipperfield	34	10	91	3
Grimmett	53·3	13	102	1	Darling	6	2	19	0

Fall of the wickets:

1	2	3	4	5	6	7	8	9	10
70	78	99	130	182	311	359	409	410	440

AUSTRALIA
First Innings

W. M. Woodfull, b Bowes		22
W. A. Brown, not out		103
D. G. Bradman, c and b Verity		36
S. J. McCabe, not out		24
Extras (b 1, lb 6)		7
Total (for 2 wickets)		192

Fall of the wickets:

1	2
68	141

We have this afternoon seen the artillery of England—the barrage of fast bowling which for long has been planned and talked of with a strategy so secret that everybody knew all about it excepting, apparently, Bombardier Bowes, who, when the action began against the Australian lines at half-past three, attended to his particular battery for a while as though he had been suddenly called out of a nice sleep in front of the fire in the mess-room. I am afraid that England's heavy guns were supplied with dubious ammunition; I had a vision of spurious shells hitting the earth and burying themselves in the middle of the wicket. They will probably explode in some innocent match in the future between the M.C.C. and Hampshire, and blow everybody sky high, scorers and pavilion-cat and all.

If the Lord's wicket remains fast and firm for Monday, Australia's total might go beyond 500, unless Bowes and Farnes can work up a semblance of pace and also pitch a respectable length. Bowes now and again caused a long-hop to rear sharply today, but as soon as the ball had lost the 'shine', his attack was palpably related to his general deportment as he goes to his bowling place. Why do fast bowlers nowadays walk with a heavy, somnambulistic slowness? Do they hope that by the law of contrast their attack will astonish the batsmen and look really quick? Farnes was a complete disappointment. Brown several times was observed to be patiently waiting to play a back-stroke from Farnes's bowling when at last it arrived at its destination. And Geary bowled as though the occasion were Leicestershire *v.* Northamptonshire; I can say no better than that on his behalf.

The Australian batsmen needed to worry about nothing save Verity's admirable length and spin and 'bounce', Yet the wicket was as amenable to fast bowling as a cricketer could reasonably expect in a Test match on the second afternoon. It was drier than on Friday and firmer. Bowes and Farnes, it is true, contrived to hit Woodfull on the body once or twice, but poor Woodfull's batting just now seems to want spectacles. He stayed in with the boy Brown while 68 runs were made in eighty minutes; all the time his bat groped myopically. It is a shame that this fine cricketer should this summer be afflicted by form too bad to be true. Bowes may be said to have suffered poor luck when Brown hooked under a rising legside ball at 21 and sent a ghost of a chance high up to short square leg, where Farnes, a tall man, could just reach it. Again, when Brown was 68, he hooked another long-hop from Bowes to Farnes at short square leg; this time a good fieldsman most likely would have held the catch. But Bowes would have been flattered in both instances had a wicket fallen. Unless rain comes as an ally, a Blücher out of the blue, England's attack on Monday may go through a terrible massacre.

Let us thank fortune that Bradman got out when he did, on the crest of an innings of terrible power and splendour. He batted forty-five minutes, and though Brown took more than an even share of the bowling, Bradman hit seven fours. The moment he reached the wicket Farnes was put on; propaganda has established beyond doubt that Bradman does not like fast bowling. He hooked Farnes's first ball for four catastrophically; the second was a boundary, too, half-pulled, half driven—a hit of genius, superb in strength and swiftness. The last ball of the over was a glorious cover-drive; in the same over Bradman hit a two to the on off the back foot; no other living batsman could have forced the ball, which was excellent, more than a few yards away, even if he could have stopped it at all. Bradman struck the fire of genius out of the match's honest and rather dull rock; the atmosphere became tense and luminous; we could feel that Bradman was the creative force of the day, that while he was at the wicket the hour was enchanted, that in the forge of his batsmanship rare history was being beaten into shape. Farnes had fourteen runs hit off this first over of his to Bradman. Geary came on in Farnes's place, and Bradman drove him for a sumptuous four to the off. Another fieldsman joined the tight off-side cordon, and Bradman, of course, retaliated by a cut to the place from which the fieldsman had been taken.

Brown was inspired by Bradman; he, too, hooked and cut; fifty runs flashed right and left in half an hour. Verity bowled from Geary's end. His first ball was crashed by Bradman for four through the crowded covers; every fieldsman was stone; not one of them could stir; the velocity of the stroke, all along the grass, thrilled the imagination. I could not take my eyes from Bradman for a second; my heart was beating as I saw his bat go back so masterfully, so grandly. Then, when he drove Verity again for four to the off and, next ball, cut him forward for four—three boundaries in three balls —the lump of pride and affection came in my throat; this was the game of cricket as Victor Trumper knew it, as Johnny Tyldesley knew it, as Macartney knew it.

Bradman's innings came to an end with, for me, a sickening suddenness; mischance brought down the young eagle. This is not to detract from the cleverness of Verity; he sent down an over which contained subtle problems of flight and pace-variation. The third ball almost saw Bradman caught and bowled; he hit too soon, and Verity fell on the ground far down the wicket in his effort to hold a prize worth having indeed. The fifth ball of this over pitched outside the off stump and jumped up unexpectedly; scarcely another slow ball in all the match had misbehaved like this. Bradman could not check his stroke, which, of course, was offensive; he jerked his bat and Verity was a happy, consoled man now—imagine it, two chances of return catches from Bradman in one over! The critics shook their heads as Bradman departed; a flamboyant innings, they said, and they wondered once more what had happened to the consummate technician named Bradman in 1930, the adding machine, the robot that scored 304 in a day at Leeds and never once erred or ventured into the unknown—and never looked at a soul all day, hardly spoke, but went on with his work with the impassiveness of one resigned to everlasting efficiency.

For my part, Bradman's innings of 36 this afternoon was far greater than his 304 at Leeds. Spirit lived in every stroke, beauty that comes out of life at the crown of manhood. It was an innings as safe and perfect in technique as any ever played by Trumper or J. T. Tyldesley. The hits were all in the bat's true middle, along the ground. We have come to a nice point of view of the game when we cast deprecatory looks at a brilliant batsman and say he is not playing with a straight bat and not waiting for the loose ball. The truth is we have for years watched the canny push stroke of the average English batsman. Down the line of the ball, up and down it, like the pendulum of a grandfather clock, telling the weary hours—tick-tack, tick-tack! Bradman did nothing today that Victor Trumper would not have been proud to do. My only doubt about the cricket was whether Bradman really needed to seek a four off every ball. I do not want to see him scoring his two hundreds and three hundreds again. You cannot measure delight and inspiration by the clock or the score-book's arithmetic. But duration does count in genius after all. I want to see Bradman, as I want to see Kreisler, not in small pieces but in long ones, not in a mere 'valse caprice', but in a concerto.

The boy Brown had the honour of scoring a century in his first innings in a Lord's Test match. He has so far been at the wicket three hours, playing with a bat straight as a tall hat, immaculate and calm and old-headed. He is a young man who, I imagine, never gets into a state about anything. His cricket is perpetually keeping an appointment leisurely with moments to spare. Does the bat have an engagement this over with a half-volley? Very well, then, put it down in the book. We'll be there for it. Plenty of time. His strokes are economical and quiet. Now and again he allowed youth its fling at

Bowes. On the whole, the innings was a hundred in runs and in experience before close of play. Brown will be with us when many of us who have applauded him today are ancients of the pavilion. Over the seas, back and forward, he will travel. Lord's and Sydney, Melbourne and Old Trafford, year after year. The amount of trouble for English bowlers concentrated in the compact form of Brown is unmentionable.

McCabe cracked the bowling of Bowes about at his own sweet will—three fours in an over—and at close of play he had a formidable aspect about him, though an exquisite ball from Verity missed the edge of his bat by an inch as it broke away.

England's fielding was mediocre. And why waste Hammond at fine first slip, a position to which on a good wicket not two balls go in an hour?

England's innings lasted until three o'clock. In one hundred and fifty minutes 117 runs were added to Friday's score. Leyland and Ames both deserved their hundreds. They saved the England innings from ruin. Leyland was always his Yorkshire self, enjoying his cricket immensely. Ames is a batsman of talent. He can drive handsomely. He can defend with his head cannily over the ball. He can use his feet. But somehow his superb utility never assumes the dress of art. An innings by Ames is like a splendid article printed anonymously and not signed, even implicitly. Wall bowled manfully and almost fast. But I doubt if ever again England's batsmen will find the Australian attack as harmless as it has been in this game. The windy weather has made a sad mess of Grimmett's spin.

A magnificent crowd watched the play. And when Bradman was batting, thousands of hearts were uplifted. The excitement throbbed visibly. Perfect strangers spoke to one another, the tavern emptied temporarily. Roars of delight went to the sky. And everybody was dashed to earth again when Bradman got out. True and glorious sportsmanship in this our England on a June day!

THIRD DAY

ENGLAND
First Innings

C. F. Walters, c Bromley, b O'Reilly	82
Sutcliffe, lbw, b, Chipperfield	20
Hammond, c and b Chipperfield	2
Hendren, c McCabe, b Wall	13
R. E. S. Wyatt, c Oldfield, b Chipperfield	33
Leyland, b Wall	109
Ames, c Oldfield, b McCabe	120
Geary, c Chipperfield, b Wall	9
Verity, st Oldfield, b Grimmett	29
Farnes, b Wall	1
Bowes, not out	10
Extras (lb 12)	12
Total	440

England first-innings bowling analysis

	O.	M.	R.	W.
Wall	49	7	108	4
McCabe	18	3	38	1
Grimmett	53·3	13	102	1
O'Reilly	38	15	70	1
Chipperfield	34	10	91	3
Darling	6	2	19	0

Fall of the wickets:

1	2	3	4	5	6	7	8	9	10
70	78	99	130	182	311	359	409	410	440

AUSTRALIA
First Innings

W. M. Woodfull, b Bowes	22
D. G. Bradman, c and b Verity	36
W. A. Brown, c Ames, b Bowes	105
S. J. McCabe, c Hammond, b Verity	34
L. S. Darling, c Sutcliffe, b Verity	0
A. G. Chipperfield, not out	37
E. H. Bromley, c Geary, b Verity	4
W. A. Oldfield, c Sutcliffe, b Verity	23
C. V. Grimmett, b Bowes	9
W. J. O'Reilly, b Verity	4
T. W. Wall, lbw, b Verity	0
Extras (b 1, lb 9)	10
Total	284

58

Australia first-innings bowling analysis

	O.	M.	R.	W.
Farnes	12	3	43	0
Bowes	31	5	98	3
Geary	22	4	56	0
Verity	36	15	61	7
Hammond	4	1	6	0
Leyland	4	1	10	0

Fall of the wickets:

1	2	3	4	5	6	7	8	9	10
68	141	203	204	205	218	258	273	284	284

AUSTRALIA

Second Innings

W. M. Woodfull, c Hammond, b Verity	43
W. A. Brown, c Walters, b Bowes	2
S. J. McCabe, c Hendren, b Verity	19
D. G. Bradman, c Ames, b Verity	13
L. S. Darling, b Hammond	10
A. G. Chipperfield, c Geary, b Verity	14
E. H. Bromley, c and b Verity	1
W. A. Oldfield, lbw, b Verity	0
C. V. Grimmett, c Hammond, b Verity	0
W. J. O'Reilly, not out	8
T. W. Wall, c Hendren, b Verity	1
Extras (b 6, nb 1)	7
Total	118

Australia second-innings bowling analysis

	O.	M.	R.	W.
Farnes	4	2	6	0
Bowes	14	4	24	1
Verity	22·3	8	43	8
Hammond	13	0	38	1

Bowes bowled one no-ball

Fall of the wickets:

1	2	3	4	5	6	7	8	9	10
10	43	57	94	94	95	95	95	112	118

Umpires: Chester and Hardstaff

The change in the weather and a glorious bowler defeated Australia today and avenged Trent Bridge. Verity sent crashing to earth early this morning all the castles of optimism built on Saturday by Australian batsmanship. And it was a moist, unpleasant earth, beautiful to bowl on if you happened to be left-handed and born in Yorkshire.

If it was not exactly a sticky wicket, until after lunch, it was as near one as we are likely to see again in this year's Test matches. The Lord's pitch suited that 'bounce' in Verity's attack which Rhodes admires immensely; also it was amenable to the classic left-hander's ball, the curving thing of deceit which comes with the bowler's arm as though anxious to meet the bat's true middle, but whips away at the last second.

Verity was magnificent; his flight and length were exactly right, visible temptation. And his break and rise from the ground were exactly right, too, visible betrayal. He bowled not more than three loose balls while the Australians first innings died the death; his run to the wicket, so loose and effortless, was feline in its suggestion of silkiness hiding the claws. He looked dangerous the first moment he bowled this morning. I shall never understand why Wyatt for a short while disturbed Verity's rhythm by asking him to attack from the Nursery end. This move, as I hope to show later on, almost played into Australia's hands. In the end all was well; Verity's genius prevailed.

Bowes took the three wickets which Verity omitted to take in Australia's first innings. If Yorkshire had been fielding, with Mitchell near the wicket, Australia's runs would have been even fewer. England did not field like a great side, and when Verity was not bowling they were not a great side. It was Yorkshire's victory.

When the cricketers walked into the field at eleven o'clock the sky was gloomy, and before Bowes could emerge from his sweater everybody returned to the pavilion in a bad light. But the pause wasted only a quarter of an hour. Soon the game's pot was on the boil; the fire crackled spitefully for Australia. Rain had come in the night as an ally to our bowlers; the turf, hard underneath and resilient on the top, endowed the attack of Bowes with vitality, while at the other end of the wicket Verity could, as I say, bounce the ball after pitching a length that allured the batsmen farther than they wished to go. Bowes took the first wicket, though; a ball flashed from the earth and found the edge of Brown's bat; Ames, as usual, held the catch. On Saturday, Bowes was no more able to bowl such a ball than he was able to walk the tight-rope or play the B flat Piano Concerto of Brahms.

Darling, in next, played two or three balls from Verity with a bat as distrustful as the hand of a man groping in a carburettor; the suspense apparently upset his customary nonchalance. He desperately swept round and gently skied the ball to fine-leg, so close to the wicket that Ames might have considered the catch his perquisite. Verity then accounted for McCabe with a vicious ball; it was full in flight, yet it jumped straight up after pitching and spun to the edge of McCabe's speculative blade. The Australians were trapped; Saturday's happy hunting-ground was now a place of much evil, with snakes in the grass. Bromley drove a glorious straight four from Verity, only to fall helplessly to a ball that spun across his left-handed stance; he merely helped it round to short-leg and, for a while, stood still dumbstruck.

Australia were 218 when the sixth wicket fell; Australia needed 73 to save the follow-on. At this moment of crisis Wyatt did curious things with his attack. After Geary had bowled a few amiable balls, in place of Bowes, Leyland was put on—a sure sign of Wyatt's opinion of the wicket, but a dangerous experiment, for Leyland is as likely to drop a ball half-way down the pitch as he is to send one smack on the bat. And Australia did not need a heap of runs to send England in again and so elude trouble for the day, in unsettled weather, too. I felt that England's chances of winning the match rested on an Australian second innings straightaway.

Wyatt not only risked Leyland as a bowler; after he had taken him off with an apologetic promptness, he stupefied my senses by moving Verity over to the Nursery end. Hammond bowled at the Pavilion end for a few minutes, and by his breakback demonstrated that this was the end from which the damage could surely be done. Had not Verity himself made the point clear enough by taking three wickets for next to nothing in an hour and by causing two balls an over to kick horridly? From the Nursery end Verity was harmless; so much so, that Wyatt put him back to the Pavilion end with the alacrity of a man caught in the act and wishing to retrieve it before we saw. And instead of asking Hammond, who had bowled beautifully, to go on at the Nursery end, he called back the amiable Geary. Why did Wyatt not leave well alone? Why did he change Verity round, when Australia were in palpable distress and when Verity was winning the game himself over after over? It was Verity's 'job', as they say; all that was needed at the wicket's opposite crease was a steady length; and Hammond could guarantee accuracy.

The vacillations of Wyatt unsettled Verity and played Oldfield and Chipperfield in; both batsmen seized their opportunities, and in an hour they added forty priceless runs. Oldfield was brilliantly caught high up in the slips by Sutcliffe; his little innings was stylish and heroic. Australia needed 33 to save the follow-on when Grimmett arrived. Bowes was bowling with Verity now; at last the English attack had unravelled the dreadful tangle. All morning England's attack should have been Verity from the Pavilion end, with Hammond and Bowes serving in turn as supernumeraries. Grimmett snicked a fortuitous four off Bowes; then in the same over, to prove to us he could do it, he made the most brilliant cut of the match with an entrancing flick of the wrists. But in the last over before lunch, he put forth a bat crooked as a signal-post on Sundays, and allowed Bowes to bowl him. Australia 273 for eight, and eighteen runs the heart's desire of Woodfull.

After lunch Verity settled the issue, like a great bowler. He bowled O'Reilly and tricked Wall leg-before-wicket. Australia this morning lost eight wickets for 92, six to Verity; Yorkshire took all the Australia wickets, in fact, which was very like Yorkshire. The Australians played for the most part like cricketers who had never before seen left-handed spin. They were no doubt unlucky to fall victims to the weather, after the splendid batsmanship they showed us on Saturday's beautiful pitch. But England were just as unlucky to lose at Trent Bridge on a broken ground which might have been 'made' for Grimmett and O'Reilly.

Chipperfield played a magnificent innings, worth many a century on a turf of ease and security. He watched the ball and, like a fine player, he made his strokes late; he got his body behind the spinning ball cleverly; moreover, he jumped to the half-volley with his left shoulder aggressively forward. His innings lasted two hours; it was an example to his colleagues of the way to deal with a difficult bowler and a challenging situation. Before he is much older, Chipperfield will develop into the best all-round cricketer in Australia.

At a quarter to three Australia went in again; they had failed by seven runs to become allies of time and depressions from the Scillies. The enormous crowd, which before lunch had seen the King shaking hands with the cricketers in front of the pavilion, sat in the fitful sunshine and waited. Whenever a ball from Bowes flashed past Woodfull's bat, a thousand voices howled, 'How's that?' Australia were in the corner, fighting for life in an inimical air. Brown hooked Bowes to leg, the bat sent out a gallant crack. And the ball soared to deep fine-leg, and Walters waited, all eagerness, and caught it. The crowd howled ravenously; even when McCabe's wicket was sent flying by a no-ball from Bowes they exulted. Poor Woodfull, captain of a besieged garrison, might well have looked to the heavens for rain, even as General Gordon looked out from Khartoum over the vacant land. Blue sky kept peeping through the clouds, tormenting him.

McCabe, for the second time in the day, found Verity an insoluble problem. He attempted to get out of his predicament by violence. He 'let fly' with his bat, only to be marvellously caught a few yards away by silly mid-off, who tossed up the ball like a juggler politely requesting no applause.

Bradman came now, and the Australian enclosure cried out 'Coo-ee', sad, vain noises of encouragement and hope! He played his first ball to leg prettily for two. He smote a 'bumper' from Bowes savagely. He sent a good-length ball from Verity towering towards long-on—a stroke which announced a lost cause and need for desperate measures. But after that he batted for ten minutes like a cool player. Woodfull all the time defended, patiently and painfully. Sadly he saw the downfall of Bradman, who, as though suddenly goaded by Verity's persistent length, slashed clean across the spin and sent up a hideous skyer over the wicket. The ball seemed to hover like an impending bolt. Bradman had time to see it fall—a long time. Ames's gloves received the ball with a thud, and a sickening thud it must have sounded in Bradman's ears. He departed a sad cricketer—conscious, surely, that he had failed his side when all depended on him.

Bradman's overthrow must have broken all Australian hearts. Darling helped Woodfull to hold the fourth wicket while 37 were scored. Then an exquisite ball by Verity rooted out the hole in Woodfull's bruised armour. The pit yawned before Australia now. Woodfull for two hours conquered by his will-power. He was out of form, technically vulnerable. But he would not surrender his innings. Great spirit overcame for long the fallible machine. When he came back to the pavilion the crowd rose at him. He was the captain, home from the wars.

Australia lost four wickets for one run after Woodfull fell. Hammond bowled Darling at 94; at 95 Verity caught and bowled Bromley off a stupendous drive worth six—a piece of fielding that let loose pandemonium. Then, with consecutive balls shortly afterwards, Verity accounted for Oldfield and Grimmett. The crowd was red-hot as these blows pierced the Australian vitals. Chipperfield again struggled like some dismembered limb that possessed life of its own. He is a splendid batsman, who knows that on a wicket which helps the spinning ball you must hold back your stroke. England would not have beaten eleven Chipperfields today, or tomorrow for that matter.

The end came at ten minutes to six, and Verity performed the happy dispatch, thanks to a catch which sent Patsy Hendren spinning over his own head.

The crowd rushed across the field, cheering. Verity ran as though for his life. A strong cordon of policemen saved him from the mob. All day he bowled with only short rests, and nobody was his equal. Beautiful left-handed spin, there is nothing like it. The click of the finger, the spit of venom on the ground. How does Yorkshire keep on finding these craftsmen—Peate, Peel, Rhodes, Kilner, Verity? I never see a baby in a perambulator in Leeds or Huddersfield or any Yorkshire place without saying to myself: 'There goes another of them!' Verity took fifteen wickets in the match, fourteen in the day; the record-hunters will revel in his figures. And the gods of the game, who sit up aloft and watch, will remember the loveliness of it all, the style, the poise on light toes, the swing of the arm from noon to evening.

Australia's batsmen played the spin, as a whole, too much with their arms; they stabbed forward fatally, and seldom exploited back-play with the body over the ball. Chipperfield must give them lessons.

The crowd at the finish gathered rank on rank in front of the pavilion; there, in the afternoon's soft light, they hailed the victors. And their generous applause buried the fallen in high Roman fashion.

THOUGHTS AT TRENT BRIDGE

Is it possible that in another four or five weeks the cricket season will be gone from us, that the morning is at hand when there will be no match to go to, no cricket scores in the papers, only the burdened news of the outer and perishing world?

As I write, the sun is high over Trent Bridge, and I cannot believe that summer is on the wane. The jolly shouts of small boys, released from school, are in my ears; Trent Bridge is the schoolboys' happy hunting-ground. For Trent Bridge seems always to be in the country; there are green trees and plenty of fresh air, no industry, and lots of space on the field. Boys at Trent Bridge, when they get tired of their county heroes, can pitch wickets themselves at the far corner of the ground; they can themselves play Notts. *v.* Lancashire all over again in miniature—the smallest boy Larwood. And as they do so they can keep their eyes on the real Larwood and, 'monkey' his actions from the life.

A boy at Trent Bridge can get a marvellous seat on a stand for sixpence; he can go to the nets, too, and see all the great men at close quarters. When I was a boy I would have given worlds to get near MacLaren, Johnny Tyldesley, and Ranji as they practised at the nets at Old Trafford. But the Old Trafford nets were (and I believe still are) inaccessible to those who can afford to pay only sixpence.

At Trent Bridge they keep the great covers for the wicket at the far end of the field, just under the scoring-box. I saw a tiny boy sitting under one of them, watching Yorkshire *v.* Nottinghamshire; imagine the wonder and joy of it—to pretend you are in a tent and at the same time to see a cricket match! He sat there solemnly, arms folded, as though a great chief in charge of the entire proceedings.

Trent Bridge is the pleasantest place in England amongst the big cricket fields; I like to go there so dearly that I fervently trust the match between Lancashire and Nottinghamshire, one of the great games of cricket's history for years, will not be given up merely because of some present and transitory discontents. The sense of humour demands that the Lancashire and Nottinghamshire match should not suffer interruption because of an objection to 'body-line' bowling. The country will pour ridicule on the rumpus: will ask the awkward question, 'What about Macdonald?' The country is asking the question already. And Australians are not missing the opportunity of giving us a dig in the ribs. 'And so the Lancashire club agrees with us that Larwood did bowl in that way. . . .'

The M.C.C. must really deliver some ruling on the point sooner or later; they have sat on the fence too long. Larwood apparently is not playing cricket (in England) if he bowls short balls to four slips and one short-leg. But Bowes is quite in order if he exploits 'bumpers' to three short-legs. Fast leg theory, with the ball passing by the batsman's head three times an over, with the field packed on the leg side, is not good sport—and was not good sport even when it happened in a Test Match in Australia. But to denounce fast leg theory is by no means the same as denying a fast bowler the right to send down short balls from time to time to a field fairly set, a right enjoyed by every fast bowler I have ever heard of, excepting Larwood, of course.

The Lancashire *v.* Nottinghamshire match has been one of the greatest in the history of the county championship; common sense and humour will see to it that it continues in good spirit. Shades of Shrewsbury and Albert Ward, Briggs and Flowers, A. O. Jones and MacLaren! I once watched Spooner score 249 at Trent Bridge; an innings I see every time I go to the famous ground, where George Parr's tree grows, where J. T. Tyldesley first played for England. There can be no end to a cricket match that has seen George Gunn walking out of his crease to the hair-raising attack of Macdonald, walking out cheekily, as though asking, 'When are you going to bowl fast, Mac?' There can be no end to a cricket match which brought a ray of everlasting glory to Lancashire on that far-off Saturday before the war when Lancashire were given 400 to win by Nottinghamshire—and got them. I think Wass bowled under A. O. Jones's captaincy that day; Wass has never had an equal on a bad wicket. He was a remarkable curiosity of cricket: a fast bowler who preferred a wet summer. What a team could be chosen from cricketers of Lancashire and Nottinghamshire! All comers might well quail before eleven men picked out of Shrewsbury, MacLaren, J. T. Tyldesley, William Gunn, George Gunn, Ernest Tyldesley, Briggs, William Barnes, R. H. Spooner, A. O. Jones, Wass, Mold, Larwood—to name only a few.

These thoughts were put into my mind by an afternoon at Trent Bridge on Monday. So too was the thought of the happiness that can be given in August to schoolboys. There is no connection on the face of it between the one train of reflection and the other. At bottom, perhaps there is; anyhow I will leave it at that.

FROM THE SUMMER GAME

VICTOR TRUMPER

WHEN Victor Trumper died he was a young man and a cricketer. The death of a cricketer before age has fallen on him is sad; it is even against nature. Well may he look down on our fields from his chill hall of immortality, far removed from the jolly flesh and blood of this life, and cry out 'Another day in the sun and wind and I not there, I not there!'

It is only a score or so of years since Victor Trumper played a great innings at Old Trafford in a Test match and hit a century before lunch. Can it be true he is now part of the impersonal dust—this Victor Trumper we knew so well? All the little intimate delights belonging to cricket, a man's flannels and his bat, his own boyish enthusiasm for a summer game—surely these are things which ought to hold a cricketer to the friendly earth till he is tired of them? You can never speak to an Australian about Victor Trumper without seeing his eyes glisten with pride and affection; Trumper will always remain for your true Australian the greatest batsman that ever lived. But it was in England that Trumper achieved his most wonderful play; every lover of the game will pause for a space in the hurly-burly of the present period's Test matches to spare a moment in which to do homage to Trumper.

> The shadow stayed not, but the splendour stays.
> Our brother, till the last of English days.

In 1902, a season of bowler's wickets here, Trumper's batsmanship was day by day of a brilliance that beggared description. Lest this language be thought overdrawn (I am not above suspicion in my use of words when it comes to writing of a Trumper), I will draw on the restrained vocabulary used in the M.C.C.'s Cricket Scores and Biographies: 'For Trumper the season [of 1902] was one long triumphal progress, and those who were fortunate enough to witness his amazing brilliance will never be able to forget the unrivalled skill and resource he displayed. On sticky wickets he hit with freedom and scored well, often whilst his companions were puddling about the crease, unable to make headway and seemingly content if they could keep up their wickets. . . . He was always to be feared on Australian wickets, but followers of the game in England were privileged to see him at his zenith.'

Was it not genius that made Trumper a master batsman in conditions not common to Australian cricket? Only a few of our own batsmen were resourceful and skilful enough to conquer the English pitch as it was in the old days whenever sunshine and rain got to work on it. Trumper learned his game in the land where perfect grounds are the rule; he came to this country, and in a season that saw the wickets of English batsmen of the highest rank falling like corn before the sickle he was masterful. Trumper in 1902 took our finest spin bowlers by the scruff of the neck, usually from the first ball sent to him, drove them, thrust, glanced and 'carted' them, right and left, for all the world as though they had been schoolboys. Amongst these same bowlers happened to be Rhodes, Haigh, Lockwood, J. T. Hearne, Hirst, Barnes, Trott, Wass, and Braund. In the Test match at Manchester, as I say, Trumper scored a century before lunch; even MacLaren with all his strategy, could not set the field for him. No shibboleth about an 'outer and inner ring' of fieldsmen ever troubled Victor Trumper. He was master of all the strokes, and he could use almost any one of them at his pleasure, no matter the manner of ball bowled at him. He would cut the identical length which a moment later he would drive. It was, indeed, impossible to pitch a length at all to Trumper on one of his great days. 'He would,' says the sober record of the M.C.C., 'get a yorker to the square-leg boundary, and it was by no means unusual to see him cut a ball off the middle stump for four. Some of his biggest hits, which went over the ring, were made without any apparent effort.'

Let me give a few more prosaic facts about Trumper before I squander words over his art (whoever would not be spendthrift of language about Trumper, let him not write on him at all). In our bowler's year of 1902, Trumper scored eleven centuries, two against Essex in the same match; he hit a century for Australia at Old Trafford before lunch, as we have seen. In the Test match at Sheffield in 1899 he scored 62 out of 80 in fifty minutes. For New South Wales, on a bowler's pitch, he made 101 out of 139 in fifty-seven minutes, at Sydney in 1905. He scored in Test matches 17,150 runs at an average of 45·01, an astonishing figure for a batsman who lived so dangerously at the wicket. In Australia he averaged

84·30 (for 843 runs) in 1912–13; 72·10 (for 721 runs) in 1899–1900; and 69·22 (for 1,246 runs) in 1910–11. Facts, as Mr Bounderby would say. And now let us come to the imperishable spirit of the man.

To change the old saying about the strawberry, God no doubt could create a better batsman than Victor Trumper if He wished, but so far He hasn't. Ranjitsinhji is the only cricketer that might be instanced as Trumper's like in genius. But even Ranji was not so great a match-winner on all wickets. Even Ranji never smashed the best attack of his day with the sudden vehemence of Trumper. Ranji did not rout his bowlers; he lured them onwards to ruin by the dark, stealthy magic of his play; the poor men were enchanted into futility. Trumper put them to the sword. . . . Yet it was a knightly sword. There never lived a more chivalrous cricketer than Trumper. I see his bat now, in my mind's eye, a banner in the air, streaming its brave runs over the field. He was ready always to take up the challenge of a good ball; Trumper never fell into the miserable philosophy of 'Safety first—wait for the bad ball.'

And what of the man's style? He had, as C. B. Fry put it, no style, yet he was all style. 'His whole bent is aggressive,' wrote Fry, 'and he plays a defensive stroke only as a very last resort.' Imagine Spooner's cover drive, Hirst's pull, MacLaren's hook, J. T. Tyldesley's square cut, Macartney's late cut through the slips—imagine a mingling of all these attributes of five great and wholly different batsmen, and perhaps some notion of Trumper will emerge in your mind. The grand manner of MacLaren, the lyrical grace of Spooner, the lion energy of Jessop, the swift opportunist spirit of Tyldesley—all these excellencies were compounded proportionately in Trumper. Do I exaggerate youthful impressions of the man? Then let me give here a tribute to Trumper uttered to me by an English cricketer whose name stands for all that is masterful and majestic in our batsmanship: 'In comparison with an innings by Victor at his best, my best was shoddy—hackwork!'

Trumper's winged batsmanship was seen in the golden age of cricket; he was, at his finest, master of some of the greatest bowlers the game has ever known. When he played for Australia, Clem Hill, Noble, Duff, Darling, S. E. Gregory, and Armstrong were batsmen with him. Splendid as the cricket of these men might be, day after day, whenever Trumper got out the light seemed to go for a while from an Australian innings. 'The eagle is gone, and now—crows and daws.' We make an artist's immortality by thinking upon and loving his work; Trumper was an artist-cricketer; let him live again in the mouths of men whenever Test matches are in action. Since he accomplished some of his greatest innings in this land, English cricket owes much to his ghost.

CRICKET AT DOVER

Dover, June, 1926

THE distance from Lord's to the Dover cricket field is farther than the crow flies or even than the train travels. Here we find a different habitation from cosmopolitan Lord's; here is Kent and real England. The Dover field is tucked away in hills along which Lear must have wandered on his way to the cliffs. There are green lawns and terraces rising high behind the little pavilion, and you can sit here and look down on the play and see the cricketers all tiny and compact. In such a green and pleasant place, with June sunlight everywhere, slow cricket by Lancashire has not seemed quite so wearisome as usually it does. The absence of animated play has gone well in tune with the day's midsummer ease and generous warmth. We have been free to watch the game idly and give ourselves up with lazy delight to the June charm and flavours of a field all gay with tents and waving colours; and we have been free to observe the delicious changes in the passing hour—the full light of noon, the soft, silent fall to evening.

The gentle tap-tap-tapping of the Lancashire bats has made the quiet music proper to this gracious Kentish place and occasion. On a perfect wicket Lancashire set a poor prelude to the innings. Hallows was twenty-five minutes getting his first run, and with the total 24 he sent a puny stroke to short-leg and was caught at leisure. Ernest Tyldesley and Makepeace then played the steady Kent attack with a like steadiness. At lunch, after ninety minutes' action, Lancashire's score was 60 for one, and on the whole Makepeace had revealed himself our quickest maker of runs.

Between lunch and tea, two hours and a quarter, Lancashire added 138 for the loss of the wickets of Makepeace and Tyldesley. These batsmen built a partnership worth 109 in 105 minutes. They showed us good cricket enough, but it was always kind to the bowling. Tyldesley was missed in the slips at 15, and got himself out by a half-hit to mid-on. I wish his batting were a little more masculine this year. Tyldesley and Makepeace each persisted for the same period—two hours and 35 minutes. After Watson had let us see half a dozen strokes I chanced with myself a half-crown wager that he would make 50 at least. Watson's cricket, though slow, had always a more certain touch than anything he has done of late. One or two of his cover drives possessed a decisive strength I have not seen him use since last year he played an innings of a century at Lord's and delighted the heart of poor Sydney Pardon, who, alas! did not live to see his dreadful Australians considerably humbled yesterday on the cricket field he loved so dearly. Watson reached 50 in one hour and three-quarters, which apparently is the standard rate of movement nowadays in the making of a cricketer's innings. Watson seemed to give a chance to the slips at 28. Halliday struck too late at a fast medium length, after giving some hint of an ability to get his bat well over the ball. Lancashire's score arrived at 200 in ten minutes short of four hours—Poppy and Mandragora of cricket.

The Kent attack rarely fell from accuracy. Collins, Ashdown, and Wright each exploit the fast to medium length which drops cannily just on the short side. Only batsmen with late, wristy strokes are able to get rapid runs against this style of attack, and, truth to say, Lancashire is not rich in wristy cricketers. Freeman's spin came from the ground with little venom, but his pitch and direction were reliable throughout all his labours. His flight has scarcely the clever variations of Mailey's bowling. To the lovely afternoon's close the Lancashire batting remained true to type.

SECOND DAY

We have had another lovely day and plenty of fascinating cricket. The Kent innings began at noon under a sky that was like a dome of glass all stained blue. On such a morning a batsman is certain to see visions and dream dreams as he comes to the ground eager for the game. And Hardinge and Ashdown started to make runs with easy, confident strokes. In half an hour the Kent score reached 39, and the Lancashire men must quickly have resigned themselves to hours of sweaty toil in the warmth of a sun whose rays of light hit the hard earth like blows from a golden rod. But the chances of cricket hang on a hair's-breadth. Macdonald's first 41 balls were hit for 29 runs, and he did not seem to be in a conquering mood.

Another six balls without a wicket would, I think, have ended with Macdonald going out of action and taking a longish rest. It was at this period of incipient crisis for Lancashire and Macdonald that Ashdown was guilty of a foolish mistake. Macdonald had been trying to bump them—a certain proof that he was not feeling at his best. Ashdown tried to hit one of these bumpers to leg, and instead of standing up straight and to the side of the ball and exploiting the authentic hook stroke, he scooped with a blind bat, ducked his head, and sent a skier to the leg-side, where Duckworth held a clever running catch.

This unlooked-for success obviously caused Macdonald to lift up his heart. His pace became faster immediately, and yet again was he encouraged by thoughtless batsmanship. Hardinge once or twice held out an indiscreet bat to quick lengths on the off-side and was lucky not to touch them. The warnings taught him no lesson: again he put forth a highly experimental bat to one of Macdonald's fast rising balls, and Duckworth caught him behind the wicket, crowing in glee like a cock as he did so. Macdonald realized, in the style of a good opportunist, that he was in fortune's good books: he worked up a lot of his true speed, pitched a length on or near the off wicket. Seymour made a sheer reflex action and sent a slip catch to Richard Tyldesley. Chapman also flicked a speculative bat, though this time the ball was much too close to the wicket to be left alone. Chapman was Duckworth's third victim in ten minutes. The match in this brief space of time wheeled round dizzily in Lancashire's way. Macdonald got the wickets of Ashdown, Seymour, Hardinge, and Chapman in nine balls for three runs. This merciless exposure of Kent's want of acquaintance with authentic fast bowling reduced the crowd to a silence which was broken—at least where I was sitting—only by the emphatic statement of an old gentleman to the effect that modern cricketers cannot cut, and, moreover, that Jack Mason and Burnup would have cracked this bowling of Macdonald far and wide—a strong opinion indeed, announced with much ferocity of tone and addressed to nobody in particular.

The Kent batsmen, no doubt, played Macdonald feebly. Several of them merely thrust out their bats to the line of the ball, using arm strength only, and not getting the body over and into a resolute stroke. Woolley threatened for twenty minutes to stem the onrush of Macdonald. He drove him to the off boundary with rare power and beauty, and then sent a cut past point like the flash of valiant steel. I settled myself down to enjoy a dramatic sight—Woolley and Macdonald as antagonists: Woolley standing at the wicket waiting with his curving bat as Macdonald ran his sinuous run along the grass: Woolley flashing his lightning and Macdonald hurling his thunderbolts. This spectacle of grandeur did not, as they say, materialize outside the mind's eye: Watson suddenly and comprehensively bowled Woolley even before some of us were aware he had begun to take part in the Lancashire attack. The ball scattered Woolley's leg wicket out of the earth: it pitched between the off and middle stumps and went with the bowler's arm. The Australians would gladly pay Watson £100 for the sole rights to that excellent delivery. The downfall of Woolley, fifth out at 74, knocked the decisive nail in the coffin of Kent's first innings. It is true that Hubble batted brightly for a while and also Freeman, but the lustre of their cricket was only like that of a sort of brass plate on the aforementioned coffin. The innings closed at three o'clock for a total which was an insult to the splendid turf. Duckworth was in reliable form: he made five catches and also accomplished a very easy case of stumping. His high-pitched shout of 'How's that' was constantly in the summer air: shall we call him chanticleer of wicket-keepers?

The other day Mr. Warner wrote that English batting has improved vastly since Armstrong beat us in this country. As I watched Macdonald get his wickets today I was convinced that Collins would win the Test matches almost as comfortably as Armstrong did if he commanded the Macdonald and Gregory of 1921. English batting has not improved since then against really fast bowling—a melancholy truth which Macdonald will demonstrate for us on any day that finds him in his strongest form.

Green rightly did not compel Kent to follow on: Macdonald was tired and the wicket perfect. Makepeace and Tyldesley forced the runs excellently after Hallows had got out: 50 was reached in little more than half an hour. Makepeace scored 37 in 50 minutes— furious driving for him. Ernest Tyldesley was brilliant: not for many a long day has his cricket been so powerful, so handsome, so masterful as in this innings. He played Lancashire's proper game from the outset, drove in front of the wicket with a superb poise of body, and reached 50 in 70 minutes. No English innings in the Test at Lord's the other day, save perhaps Woolley's, could compare with this by Tyldesley in point of beautiful and versatile strokes. Moreover, the Kent attack was on the whole as good as the Australians'—at any rate until Tyldesley hammered it off its length. This is the kind of batsmanship we need for the winning of Test matches within three days.

Tyldesley arrived at his century in two hours and five minutes without a shadow of a mistake. Iddon played strong cricket, too, and this time his forcing drives were proportionately blended with strokes of sound defence. He has still much to learn of the art of picking out the right ball for a safe hit, but he is going along nicely. In Lancashire's second innings Cornwallis did not field because of an injury to his leg. Cornwallis, by the way, is a true Kent captain —keen, chivalrous, and always in love with the game. Iddon and Tyldesley scored 122 for the fourth wicket in 90 minutes. We have seen a Lancashire eleven today in which we could take a pride indeed.

THIRD DAY

Green closed the Lancashire innings last night, and Kent had the whole of this cool and pleasant day for the making of 424 needed to bring them a famous victory. Five hours and ten minutes of play were to be gone through. A bad beginning happened to the innings; with only a dozen scored Ashdown tried a leg hit from Sibbles, and the ball seemed to swing in from outside his legs astonishingly, and it clean bowled his leg wicket. Seymour, who is not at all a defensive batsman but needs must play the old Kentish game of chivalry, hit ten runs off three balls from Sibbles, and attempted a stroke to the off from a short bumper sent by Macdonald. He skied the ball high to leg, and Halliday, running from somewhere near mid-wicket on the on-side, made an admirable running catch, taking his prize as it dipped away from him in the wind. Even with this unfortunate prelude, Kent's score reached 80 in an hour—cricket is always a game for Kent, rarely a penitential labour.

Woolley and Hardinge joined partnership at five minutes to twelve, and in ninety-five minutes they lifted the total from 41 to 181—which brought us to lunch. The cricket was never in the least rash or demonstrative; indeed, Woolley batted half an hour for eleven. The runs came by play in which defence and offence were mingled by the most accurate judgment conceivable. The good ball was treated soundly and cautiously; the indifferent ball was seen quickly by both batsmen, and hit hard by means of a splendid range of scoring strokes. On present form Hardinge is one of the best batsmen in the land. Today his cricket was beyond criticism—solid yet antagonistic. He plays as straight a bat as any English cricketer; he can cut, drive, and glance to leg with the best of them. His batsmanship always shows to us the pre-war stamp.

Hardinge made his fifty in ninety minutes: Woolley was twenty

74

minutes quicker over the same score. Just before lunch Woolley in getting his fifty sent a hit to third man that Hallows might possibly have caught had he made ground with some alacrity. Hardinge came to his century after two hours and three-quarters' handsome activity. At twenty minutes to three Kent wanted 224 with two and a half hours still to go. A slight drizzle hereabout damped the grass, and probably added to the hardships of a failing Lancashire attack. Woolley was badly missed by Richard Tyldesley when his score was 82, and Kent's 220—a blunder which must have caused the whole Lancashire side to shudder from head to foot. Woolley got his beautiful hundred out of a total of 239 in two hours and ten minutes; his next stroke, a great on-drive, made the Woolley–Hardinge stand worth 200—hit in 140 minutes. At three o'clock Kent were 170 runs from victory's goal, and two hours and ten minutes remained.

Green rang the changes on his bowlers, but all of them seemed merely so much fuel to the brilliant bonfire of batsmanship which was burning for the glory of Kent cricket before our eyes. Three fieldsmen stood on the edge of the off-side field for Woolley—a rare sight in these days. The Lancashire cricketers looked rather broken in wind now: there was little hurry in their feet and apparently not much hope within their breasts. Every other ball bowled, it seemed, was hit to the distant parts of the ground: it was the fieldsmen near the wicket who had least work to do. At 294 Woolley was leg-before-wicket: in two hours fifty minutes he had shown us his own delectable art and helped Hardinge to make 253 for the third wicket. With no increase in Kent's position R. Tyldesley broke through Hardinge's defence and missed the wicket by an inch: his face, red as a moon of blood, wore the aspect of anguish as he saw Hardinge escape.

It was a bolt out of Kent's blue sky that finished Hardinge's great innings—a lion-hearted quick throw-in by Green from long-on hit the wicket with Hardinge out of his ground. But for this mishap I imagine Kent would have won easily. Hardinge batted ten minutes short of four hours and a half, and he deserved a more fortunate end. The cricket of Hardinge and Woolley taught a lesson which at the moment is needed in our game—the ancient lesson that offence skilfully exploited is the best form of defence. Collins was bowled, fifth out, at 327. Tea was taken at four o'clock—with Kent 341 for five— 20 minutes to be wasted, 85 runs wanted by Kent, and five wickets by Lancashire. Anybody's game and a moment of palpitating crisis in which a tea interval was an absurd irrelevance. Why should there be tea intervals at all on the closing day, on which, of course, stumps are drawn at half-past five? The heady situation challenged the audacity of Chapman, who flashed his bat like a sword at Macdonald's off ball: he cut and carved 49 in fifty minutes, and then, as the game was coming again well into Kent's grip, he was neatly caught at cover by Makepeace, sixth out at 361. The next ball bowled Deed: thus a sudden heave of the game's great wheel landed the laurels at Lancashire's grasp. And Macdonald's next ball shattered Wright's stumps—a hat-trick for Macdonald at the very moment every Lancashire cricketer must have been praying for the miracle which alone could pull our county out of the fire lit by Hardinge and Woolley.

As Hubble and Freeman took up the defence of the Kent ninth wicket the band on the edge of the grass made the mellow music of the madrigal out of *The Mikado*. The moment was too tense, perhaps, for these golden strains, yet their sweetness was in tune with the afternoon's lovely English flavour. To my dying day I shall remember gratefully these afternoons in Kent, afternoons full of the air and peaceful sunshine of England. Macdonald bowled at a noble pace during this last act of a memorable game, and as he ran his silent run of sinister grace the scene was one of those that do cricket honour—the crouching slips, the dogged batsmen, the crowd watching, hoping, and fearing, now dumb and now making exuberant noises as some lightning stroke beats the field. Macdonald bowled Freeman at 390: the little man had shown himself a fighter. Two runs afterwards Hubble was stumped exactly on the stroke of five o'clock. And so a noble match was nobly won and, what is as true, nobly lost by 33 runs. Both sides did the grand old game service on this July day. Every cricketer played hard and passed through his difficult hours. The running-out of Hardinge was the afternoon's turning-point: the splendid feat of Macdonald settled the issue. He bowled finely at the finish, and Richard Tyldesley bowled finely too. A match well worth remembering—the brilliance of Hardinge, Woolley, and Ernest Tyldesley, the changeful hurly-burly of Kent's titantic second innings—and everything done in a beautiful cricket field.

LANCASHIRE

First Innings		Second Innings	
Makepeace, b Collins	71	c Hubble, b Ashdown	37
Hallows, c Freeman, b Ashdown	12	lbw, b Wright	2
Tyldesley (E.), c Ashdown, b Freeman	69	not out	144
Watson, st Hubble, b Freeman	78	b Freeman	3
Iddon, lbw, b Wright	18	b Chapman	39
Halliday, b Cornwallis	13	not out	1
L. Green, c Hubble, b Collins	18		
Sibbles, c Hubble, b Wright	17		
Macdonald, c Chapman, b Freeman	0	c Woolley, b Chapman	13
Duckworth, b Wright	10		
Tyldesley (R.), not out	15		
B 1, lb 12, nb, 1, w 1	15	B 1, lb 3	4
Total	336	Total (for 5)	*243

* Innings declared

KENT

First Innings		Second Innings	
Hardinge, c Duckworth, b Macdonald	27	run out	132
Ashdown, c Duckworth, b Macdonald	19	b Sibbles	6
Seymour, c Tyldesley (R.), b Macdonald	1	c Halliday, c Macdonald	24
Woolley, b Watson	24	lbw, b Watson	137
A. P. Chapman, c Duckworth, b Macdonald	3	c Makepeace, b Macdonald	49
J. A. Deed, b Watson	8	b Macdonald	0
Collins, c Duckworth, b Macdonald	17	b Tyldesley (R.)	0
Hubble, c Duckworth, b Macdonald	20	st Duckworth, b Tyldesley (R.)	17
Wright, st Duckworth, b Tyldesley (R.)	19	b Macdonald	0
Freeman, b Macdonald	14	b Macdonald	13
W. Cornwallis, not out	1	not out	1
Nb 1	1	Extras	13
Total	154	Total	392

BOWLING ANALYSIS

LANCASHIRE—First Innings

	O.	M.	R.	W.		O.	M.	R.	W.
Wright	38·2	9	81	3	Woolley	8	2	23	0
Cornwallis	7	0	26	1	Collins	14	3	25	2
Ashdown	24	4	69	1	Hardinge	2	1	1	0
Freeman	50	14	96	3					

Woolley bowled one wide and Collins one no–ball.

Second Innings

Wright	16	2	51	1	Woolley	11	1	42	0
Ashdown	16	2	46	1	Hardinge	7	0	18	0
Freeman	12	4	34	1	Chapman	4	0	24	2
Collins	5	0	24	0					

KENT—First Innings

Macdonald	17·3	0	81	7	Tyldesley (R.)	10	3	35	1
Sibbles	9	3	27	0	Watson	2	1	10	2

Macdonald bowled one no-ball

Second Innings

Macdonald	30	2	106	5	Watson	16	2	58	1
Sibbles	16	1	75	1	Iddon	9	0	47	0
Tyldesley (R.)	22·4	1	93	2					

Iddon bowled one no-ball and Macdonald three

RANJI, FRY AND SUSSEX

CRICKET teams sometimes are true to the character of the counties for which they stand. The Yorkshire game is obviously different from Somerset's, different in the style which denotes the men, the blood. When George Hirst got down on his knee and clouted a ball from outside the off stump round to the on boundary, you were made to think of North Country humours and the air of the broad acres. And when the Hon. C. N. Bruce poises himself aristocratically and drives through the covers, you are looking at cricket that has blue blood in its veins. Lord's cricket, cricket straight out of Debrett. So, too, with the homely energies and shape of Richard Tyldesley; they tell of little Lancashire towns that have cobbled streets running up and down hill.

Sussex is a side which is full of the warm South. They play, surely, tawny cricket that has lived much in the sun. Think of the Relfs, old George Cox, Brann, and today Tate, Gilligan, and Bowley—all of them brown cricketers. It was right that Ranji should have played for Sussex; warm, brilliant light was always in his batting. His dark, lissome beauty might have seemed out of place day by day at Sheffield.

Ranji and Fry! Let bowlers of the present time thank their stars that they have not any afternoon to tackle the problem of getting these two cricketers out on a perfect wicket. Ted Wainwright used to talk to me about Fry and Ranji, talk with a simple eloquence—years after actual experience of them had lost its sweat and hopeless labour. 'Aye,' Wainwright would say to me, 'Ranji and Fry at Brighton on a plumb wicket. It were t' same tale every year.' In those times the Sussex innings opened with Fry and Vine. Granted ordinary luck, Vine's wicket would be taken at half-past twelve on the first day: Yorkshire, so Wainwright would narrate, 'allus lost t' toss at Brighton in hot weather.' Vine was a good batsman, but within the resources of the science of bowling to circumvent in decent time. Then Killick used to come in first wicket down. He, too, was a good batsman, yet not invincible. 'Every year,' Wainwright would say, 'it were t' same tale. Sussex 20 for 1 at half-past twelve, Vine out. Then Sussex 43 for 2 at one o'clock. Aye, we told oursel's, every blessed year, we're doin' reight well, Yorkshire! Sussex 43 for 2! But, bless your soul, *we knowed there were nowt in it!*' At the fall of the second wicket Ranji came to the middle, swishing his bat like a cane. At close of play the score was, more often than not, Sussex 392 for 2. 'We knowed there were nowt in it!' Ranji and Fry in a long partnership made a fascinating contrast of style. Fry played by the book of arithmetic; his was the batsmanship of the rational mind. If it sent out a light at all it was the dry light of science. Fry's cricket was Fry's mind. He was the acutest thinker ever known to the game; his every stroke was an idea, a principle, and his every innings a synthesis. Even when he drove straight—and few cricketers have commanded a stronger drive than Fry's—his energy was disciplined.

When you looked upon Fry at the wicket you looked upon the schoolman glorifying a system, even though it bound him, body and soul. It was all superb, but of the comprehensible earth. When you looked upon Ranji at the other end, you turned from the known world of law and order to the world of the occult; you turned from the West to the East. Ranji was the most remarkable instance in all cricket's history of a man expressing through the game not only his individual genius but the genius of his race. No Englishman could have batted like Ranji, 'Ranji,' said Ted Wainwright once, ''e never made a Christian stroke in his life.' The light that shone on our cricket fields when Ranji batted was a light out of his own land, a dusky, inscrutable light. His was the cricket of black magic indeed. A sudden sinuous turn of the wrist and lo! the ball had vanished—where? The bowler, knowing he had aimed on the middle stump, saw, as in a vision, the form of Ranji, all fluttering curves. The bat made its beautiful pass, a wizard's wand. From the very middle stump the ball was spirited away to the leg-side boundary. And the bowler, a good believer in the true faith, crossed himself at the sight of it all. 'Ranji,' declared George Giffen. 'Call him a batsman? Why, he's a bloomin' conjurer!' Well, do we not associate the East with conjurers, flying carpets, rope-climbers, and all manner of enchantment? When Ranji came to cricket it was a thoroughly English game, thriving in a thoroughly English period. Grace, Shrewsbury, Gunn, Attewell and the rest were eminent Victorians, who gave to cricket the period's direct, firm, and rather complacent outlines. It was the age of the straight bat and the honest length ball. And at that time, English and Victorian through and through, this miracle of Ranji happened in our land. The ancient ways of doing things were subverted. This cricket, born of old Hambledon, and open as the day—it was changed into something rich and strange whenever Ranji batted, for, as I say, he played the game as no Englishman ever played it, or could play it. When Ranji passed out of cricket a wonder and a glory departed from the game for ever. It is not in nature that there should be another Ranji. We who have had the good luck to see Ranji, let us be grateful. Did he really happen? or was he perhaps a dream, all dreamed on some midsummer's night long ago?

WEST COUNTRY LADS

MEMORY has to reach beyond 1911 to discover Somerset cricket's heyday. It was, I fancy, at the beginning of this so-called twentieth century that S. M. J. Woods and his team were a great power in the land—so much so that the very mention of the name Somerset caused strong men in Yorkshire to turn pale and tremble.

In one gaudy week in July, 1901, piping-hot history was written by these West Country gallants. At that time Yorkshire, as ever, were champions. And they were invincible. Leeds, Sheffield, and Bradford had watched Yorkshire man and boy for a summer and a half and not once had they seen their darlings beaten. To say the

truth, all England outside Yorkshire was sick and tired of Yorkshire's ruthless ride over our cricket fields. Imagination pictures
Yorkshire in 1900 and till July, 1901, moving rough-shod over our
green and pleasant land, leaving red ruin in her track. The day-by-
day story was always the same: 'Another Yorkshire victory; great
bowling by Hirst, Haigh, and Rhodes.' Let it be freely confessed
that in Lancashire we grew especially weary of the 'damnable itera-
tion'. There seemed to be no way of putting an end to the conqueror's progress; this Achilles seemingly had no heel. July came,
and on a sunny morning at Leeds Somersetshire went into the field;
more lambs to the slaughter, we all said. The first news of the match
was tiresomely 'as usual'—Somerset all out 87. 'More superb
bowling by Hirst and Rhodes.'

The next day at lunch saw Yorkshire bloated with impregnability;
to Somerset's 87 they answered with a boastful 325, and Schofield
Haigh hit 96. Manchester let the match drop out of mind; our
mouths tasted sour grapes; we mumbled vain words about the use
and abuse of giant strength. It was towards three or four o'clock in
the afternoon of this second day at Leeds that, far distant from what
all of us thought in Manchester to be the sacrificial field, we first
sniffed in the wind some strange hint of trouble marvellously brewing for Yorkshire. Rumour ran through Lancashire with a hundred
tongues; for a while no definite facts emerged; there was merely a
stirring in the air. The writer in those days was a boy at school; he
recollects that during a change of lessons he was told Somerset was
making a fight, that at long last Yorkshire's attack had been tied
into strange, complicated knots. There was, as I say, no telling
whence came these tidings of comfort and joy; the news was whispered on the summer air.

Imagine the spiritual torment of this same schoolboy as the prison
walls of the classroom closed on him once more. Today he can live
again through the long-drawn-out hour of that afternoon's last
lesson, suffer again the rack of intolerable waiting for five o'clock
and freedom to dash out into the world and seize the latest paper.
I can see yet the classroom, confined and silent, with sunshine
gleaming through the windows. I can see the blackboard, and globes,
and pyramids, and cones—all absurdly irrelevant—and the stony
form-master apparently absorbed in teaching the Fourth Declension
of German Nouns (der Tisch, des Tisches, dem Tische, den Tisch),
oblivious that at that very moment, in a furnace of sunshine at
Leeds, Somersetshire cricketers were holding Hirst and Rhodes at

bay! And yet—so it now seems to me in the wisdom of years—even the form-master may have suffered private agonies, and under his front of rock may have ached as much as the rest of us for sure and certain news from Leeds. Evening brought in great consternation and delight—Somerset 549 for five. The night was spent in mid-summer dreams—of Somerset victorious—slightly disturbed by nightmares of Hirst and J. T. Brown accomplishing the usual York-shire fight. To cut short a story more marvellous than words can tell, Somerset won by 279. Their second innings total reached 630; then on a broken wicket Braund and Cranfield skittled out the Invincibles for 113.

During this great game Braund and Palairet scored 222 (in two hours and twenty minutes) for Somerset's first wicket in the uphill second innings. Tears of joy may well come even now at the thought of the skill, the pluck. But there was a joke, a mighty joke, about it all. To this day Yorkshiremen maintain that Braund was caught at slip by Tunnicliffe when he had reached 55. The umpire at the one end could not give a decision, the bowler getting in his way; the umpire at the other end 'decided in Braund's favour'. Years after-wards I met and came to know Ted Wainwright, who played in the match. ('One for 'undred and seven—that's what happened to me!' he used to say.) Poor Wainwright never got over this 'decision' of Walter Wright's. It was a wound in his mind that remained un-healed to the end, quick to bleed again at the slightest prick of memory. 'Aye,' he would say, not in anger but in sorrow, 'Len Braund were out, reight enough; Walter Wright lost us t' match. Ah s'all never forget George Hirst that day; he *were* upset, Ah can tell thi. He never trusted himself to speak to Walter Wright all through t'afternoon. At t' last, Somerset sent up t' 500 (all in a few hours!), and poor George listened to t' cheering, looked hard at t' scorin' board, and then, as he walked to his place in t' field, he passed t' umpire, and said to him, reight from t' bottom of his heart, "Hey, Walter, tha knows; tha art a foo-il!" '

Somerset cricket never will outlive the glory of the match at Leeds, July 17th, 1901. Palairet's score was 173, Braund's 107, F. A. Phillips's 122. Sammy Woods hit right and left for 66—a West Country breeze of an innings from a West Country man. Do you remind me here that S. M. J. Woods was an Australian? My reply is that he was Australian only by the accident of birth; at any rate, the West Country assimilated him, took him to heart, made him grow up after the image of Somerset cricket—fresh, gusty, smacking of the land. Why, Sammy Woods was a very Squire Western of Somerset cricket! Is it not sinful that such a man as Woods, with his love of cricket and the sun, should ever be taken out of the light into the shadow of age! Of all the men who played at Leeds in this most notable match only Rhodes remains a cricketer today. The others are—where and what are they?

SHASTBURY AGAIN

AND while these interminable Test matches have been going on in the heat and dust and mud of Lord's, Leeds, and Old Trafford, far away at Shastbury the school's wide playing fields have remained, as ever, haunts of ancient peace. A memory of Shastbury's greenness, its country calm, visited me the other day even at the moment the crowd at Old Trafford during lunch pressed all around, a babel of confusion. My mind's eye saw the place as it was standing at this very moment, right across England, at two o'clock on a July day of sunshine. A delectable hour at Shastbury, two o'clock in mid-summer. The school tower sent out its chimes; then all the jolly activity of the noon net practices finished; the fields were swiftly deserted. At one moment the air would be full of the noise of crackings bats, of thudding feet, of voices shouting 'Heads! Heads!' as the ball went sky-high. But with the first stroke of two o'clock every boy went into his house for lunch, and Shastbury was left, stretched in the burning heat. Over the vacant playing fields you could look now to the meadowland beyond, gleaming in the light. Here was the richness of open-air England; great trees in their immemorial sleep and the low sound of summer making its throbbing music on the earth. At this hour, summer seemed to stay awhile in its movement onwards and poise itself over the bountiful scene. Everywhere was quiet, still as the hour glass. Lord!—I could shed tears today as I think of all the happy hours I lived through at Shastbury in the wind and sun of the old years.

When two o'clock had come and cricket was over for a space, William and I used to sit in our flannels on the little pavilion's balcony and rest ourselves from our scorching work in the nets.

William would light his pipe, put his feet on the balustrade in fron
of our seats, and sigh contentedly. His famous career with Notting
hamshire and All-England never brought him greater happines
than the summers he spent at his life's end down at Shastbury. And
I am glad to believe he always knew this was the truth, knew it in
his every Shastbury hour, and never more so than during the littl
pauses from work which we sat through on the school pavilion or
these golden days. As he rested himself there and cooled prodi
giously, I would sometimes look at his fine old face—brown no
only from his present warmth but from the warmth of his ancien
years in the sun on this side and on the other side of the world.
would try to find in the white hair of his head, in any of his wrinkle
lines, some mark clearly made by the man's history. So far behin
him was his period of renown. His name had become legendary
he had himself grown older than his memory's power to keep hi
past warm and alive. His notable summers had gone over him lik
the wind of his many days. 'Ah can't say as Ah exactly remembers,
was often his simple remark when I tried to get him to tell me o
some achievement of his at the game—some achievement writter
down for posterity's admiration in *Wisden*. William was not mock
modest; he had played his cricket in unsophisticated heart, playec
it because he liked it and because it was, in his language, his 'living'
I doubt if ever he understood that either time or fame was layin
hands upon him.

On half holidays Shastbury was crowded with cricketers agair
at three o'clock; the grass flashed green and white in the sun. Yo
could play fifteen matches on Shastbury's fields at one and the sam
time. There was a little congestion, true, but it only made for mor
and more fun. A bowler in one match would frequently need to pul
himself up in the middle of his run as some fieldsman from anothe
match dashed over his wicket, across his line of flight. Whereupor
the bowler vowed in his heart that the ball he was about to bowl bu
never did would have been most deadly and unplayable; he felt i
in his bones. Once I chased a ball, driven hard, picked it up anc
threw it in with one action (you remember Pellew), and threw dow
the middle stump—only to find I had run out a batsman in th
wrong match. Mid-on in one engagement and cover-point in anothe
stood back to back frequently, and each would ask the other to mov
up a little and how was the state of *his* game. Our umpires usuall
were the two next men in; they stood and dispensed law leaning or
their bats; it sometimes happened that your chances of surviving ar

appeal for leg-before-wicket depended considerably on whether a fast bowler was on and making the ball bump unpleasantly.

The animation did not wane as the afternoon flamed to its end. I see it all yet, and hear it all too—cricket at life's springtime, the game of youth. 'Play up, Mosers!' 'Oh, well hit, sir!' 'Run, you silly ass, run!' 'Quick—this end, this end!' All the merry noise of cricket and all of cricket's rosy health. Everybody played for all he was worth, and round about him alarums and excursions made the scene dizzy. Over there Rhys was getting another century; Oldham's were actually winning against Chance's! Suddenly in the teeming field a pitch would become vacant; Pickering's had finished their match, and the place on which they had been playing was now a smooth still spot, lying like cut grass in a field of high-moving corn; the stumps remained with one of them flat on the earth, eloquent of somebody's devastating and match-winning ball.

Then, at twenty minutes to seven, the school bell began to ring. Play was over; from far corners of Shastbury came hot, happy cricketers, going back to their houses. Again the playing fields were left to the sunshine, now falling aslant from beyond the quiet meadows. It was my job sometimes to go over all the ground and bring in the stumps. If I live a hundred years I shall never forget the sense of walking in the falling afternoon's soft light, moving alone across the grass, my face burning and a soft wind running through my flannels and touching the body deliciously. And in the pavilion William waited for me, and at last we would go home, across the ferry, to the little room in which he lived, and William would remove his coat and take his tea. (He always ate and drank at home in his shirt sleeves.) . . . Later we would go back to the playing fields and sit under the big tree near the pavilion and watch the sunset.

Everybody else was in school, and in the evening's calm the chapel seemed to huddle closer under the shadows of the trees. Far away the low hum of the world went on, while the red glow died out of the sky and some old crow flapped his slow, comfortable way to his high nest. The long day's end—'Let's be goin',' William would say. 'It's gettin' a bit chill; Ah s'll be ready for bed 'fore long. It were hot work bowlin' today; Ah'm none so young as Ah used to be.'

85

FROM GOOD DAYS

ERNEST TYLDESLEY

ERNEST TYLDESLEY is, and has been for years, one of the North of England's most courtly batsmen. Had he played for Gloucestershire he would have batted like Barnett's twin spirit. Even the strain of service in a team which, until recently, was perpetually winning or trying to win the championship—even this burden of duty has not caused the iron to enter the heart of Tyldesley's play. He, of course, has many times been compelled to scorn delights and live laborious days for the cause and the crown. But the heavy armour of stern battle, though grim and a hindrance to lightness of movement, has seldom made his spirit hard and cold; he has worn his rue with a difference. Years ago, when Lancashire and Yorkshire matches were given over to attrition long drawn out, to subterranean trench warfare hidden and ruthless, Ernest Tyldesley once turned the cockpit of Bradford into a tournament of princely challenge. His batsmanship that afternoon lives in the memory like the batsmanship of Trumper and Macartney; it was triumphant and strong, yet it was modest and without savagery. There is in Tyldesley's style a certain graciousness, a touch of what the French call *politesse*. He is never brutal, not even when he is driving and cutting at his fastest and best. He reminds me of the stupid old verse:

> 'He kicks you downstairs with such infinite grace,
> You'd think he was handing you up.'

Tyldesley is at the point of his career when energy is compelled by nature to cultivate economy. The years go by like breath on the pane; it seems but yesterday that I saw Ernest Tyldesley score two hundred runs in an innings at the Oval when Lancashire were a beaten side, score them with tremendous power and swiftness. Hitch began the morning using four slips, and he bowled as fast as any Larwood. In half an hour the four slips were moved over to the leg side to try to stop Tyldesley's hook. Few cricketers have hooked fast bowling with more than Tyldesley's grandeur. He has put this vanity behind him now, but it will still have its fling. Last summer at Trent Bridge he sent ball after ball from Larwood hurtling past square-leg, most of them off his left eyebrow.

But Tyldesley is not, as I say, warlike in the mailed fist manner; he is the 'gentil' knight. Can anybody see his leg-glance and not adore it? The body leans forward and then a turn of the wrists flicks the ball round off his pads; it is a bonny stroke and a winsome one. In the gallant period of McLaren, Tyldesley would have played day by day as J. T. Tyldesley played—a hundred in one match, none in the next, and a hundred in the next but one. His immortal brother did not many times attack the bowling of Australia as Ernest Tyldesley attacked Armstrong's terrible men at Old Trafford in 1921. None of the heroes of the present moment ever dreams of batting in that d'Artagnan strain. Ernest Tyldesley at his best was given few chances to show his quality for England. He played at Nottingham in 1921, was knocked almost senseless by a bumper from Gregory, and was dropped by the Selection Committee until the Manchester Test match; he achieved his death-or-glory innings then, and at the Oval a few weeks later he scored 39. That was his last chance for England for several years; but in 1926 his consistent form forced Lord's to give him his due. He again played at Old Trafford, just missed a hundred—and was dropped once more. He was taken to Australia a year or two too late; Hendren was never his equal as a batsman against good bowling.

Does some purist whisper that Ernest's bat has never been quite straight? A family failing; Johnny's bat was never academically straight. Was Abel's, or Denton's, or Duleepsinhji's? Is Bradman's bat straight? Too much straightness of bat, as we have agreed, can spoil fullness of life, and richness. Not many of the great strikes can be made with the conventional straight bat. And Ernest Tyldesley learned his cricket in the period of A. C. McLaren, who was his first county captain. When he was a boy he batted for Lancashire with his brother or MacLaren or Spooner at the other end. In the presence of these great players, learning must have been easy. Example is better than precept. When Ernest Tyldesley began his career great strokes were considered an essential part of the game; it was considered as natural for a county batsman to make great strokes as it is for a steeplechaser to take all the jumps. Even the stonewallers made strokes: Quaife, for example. One of Ernest Tyldesley's first innings in a county match began just before lunch: J. T. Tyldesley was batting at the same time. Ernest took the last over and played a maiden. He was only a boy, and of course he wanted to be not out at the interval. As the cricketers walked from the field, J. T. Tyldesley spoke to Ernest: 'Why didn't you hit that half-volley?' Ernest shyly murmured something about not wanting to get out in the last over before lunch, 'But,' said J. T. T., 'a half-volley's always a half-volley; you must always hit them.' Imagine this counsel given to a young cricketer of the present day. Strokes are discouraged; if a lad is caught at deepfield he is severely chastised; if he is out leg-before-wicket for none, no hard words are hurled at him—he is developing on the right lines then.

Look at Ernest Tyldesley; look at his style, how it is organised for strokes. He makes all the other Lancashire batsmen seem pedestrian, anonymous, unfinished. He has scored more hundreds than any other Lancashire cricketer. What is more, he has honoured cricket all the time while scoring them. The pleasure given to us by a great batsman is above the score-board's comprehension. R. H. Spooner would have delighted a man from another planet where two and two made five or triangles. Cricket, more than any other game, can rise above contention and the race for a prize. Its beauty is a thing in itself, sometimes an unconscious grace, not known to the players —the great players, I mean. The cricket of Ernest Tyldesley has always been the man himself, with modesty in its manliness. I have seen almost a blush on his finest hits.

180 FOR NONE

'O MY Hornby and my Barlow long ago!' I suppose they were the best men that ever opened an innings. Poets do not write lovely and immortal songs about mediocrity. I was too late in the world for Hornby and Barlow, but once I met Hornby at his Nantwich house when he was near his end. I tried to call back to his mind great days of the past; he could not remember many a glorious deed; time had gone through his mind as though with the swiftness of breath on a glass. But his eyes twinkled at the mention of Barlow's name. A humorously assorted pair: 'A. N.' all impatience, Barlow solid and immovable, apparently, as a rock. Yet he ran 'A. N.'s' short runs like the wind.

A. N. Hornby was obviously a man disappointed with life whenever a bowler succeeded in sending a maiden to him; what in his heart did he say about Barlow's stonewalling? No doubt he perceived in his simple way that in this world it is not affinities but opposites that achieve the happiest marriages. The opening parnerships of old usually made a combination of offensive and defensive properties; at one end the bowling was attacked first ball of the match, while at the other some canny fellow kept watch. Hornby and Barlow; Brown and Tunnicliffe; A. O. Jones and Iremonger; A. C. MacLaren and Ward; L. C. H. Palairet and Braund, Hobbs (in his young days) and Hayward; Holmes and Sutcliffe—aggression and resistance, twin-souled and mated.

Now and then this classical rule of the division of play and labour was 'honoured in the breach'; the most magnificent of all opening pairs were Victor Trumper and R. A. Duff, each of them a Don Quixote, neither of them willing or made by nature to play Sancho Panza to the other. I thank all the gods of cricket that I was privileged to see Trumper and Duff. It was in the epic Test match played at Manchester in 1902. I played truant from school to see it, and to my dying day I shall feel the sensation on my forehead of the iron bar that ran round the sixpenny seats. For on that day of Trumper's and Duff's daring, I pressed my head hard against the iron bar and prayed that Trumper or Duff or both would get out next ball. Oh, the folly of a boy's patriotism. I used to petition Heaven for a quick end to an innings by Ranji. Now, in the middle way of life, I would that I were with Trumper, whether in heaven or hell. I have listened to great music since Trumper played cricket (which I grant is only a game); I know and love well the gorgeous bannered beauty of the music of *Die Meistersinger*. But never have I felt the pride of life to open and to flower more grandly and sweetly and graciously than I feel it today as I call back to mind the batsmanship of Victor Trumper.

At Old Trafford, in the 1902 Test match, Australia won the toss on a soft wicket. Soon, after lunch, the wicket would become vicious under the heat of the sun; MacLaren knew it, and Trumper and Duff knew it. On the England side were great bowlers; the duty of MacLaren was to keep Trumper and Duff quiet while the wicket remained easy before lunch. After the interval, cunning spin and pace from the evil earth would settle Australia in an hour. MacLaren, greatest of strategists at cricket, concentrated upon the job of keeping Trumper and Duff quiet from noon until two o'clock;

he set his field protectively, and commanded his bowlers to pitch where the batsmen could not drive or hook or pull. And at lunch Trumper was 100, and Duff was 78, and the total was over 180 for none. At three o'clock the pitch was a 'glue-pot', and Lockwood unplayable. Trumper and Duff won the rubber of 1902 in two hours of cricket fit for any knights' tournament ever known, and fit for the fairest of all the old-time ladies.

Trumper and Duff attacked from the word 'Go!' In 1902 Trumper was, I think, twenty-four years old and Duff twenty-three. The following winter, in the Australian season of 1902–3, Trumper and Duff one day sallied forth to open a New South Wales innings against South Australia. In two hours and a quarter they scored 298. Ten days afterwards Trumper and Duff set about the bowling of Victoria, and in the same time, two and a quarter hours, they scored 267. Trumper had three strokes for every ball. I can see him now, as he was when the bowler began his run, the bat moving up behind him, the feet advancing—the picture of menace, yet with nothing brutal in it. Trumper's bat was a lance of chivalry, never a lethal instrument. Duff was the obviously belligerent one; he reminded me of a pikeman, savage and terribly strong, just as Trumper reminded me of the knight-at-arms. Duff's hooking was positively vicious; he hit the long-hop with a short-armed blow of the bat which said, 'Die and be damned!' And before Triumper and Duff had been in action ten minutes the best attack in the world was sending down long-hops. 'Heaven help me!' muttered the bowler to himself, 'Where can I pitch this one?'

Trumper and Duff are both dead now, and they were young men when they died. When Trumper was buried, the whole of Sydney stood in silence in the streets as the funeral procession passed by, and there were few eyes not moist or wet. To this day I can hear the grand thunder of Trumper's and Duff's cricket, and a lump comes in my throat.

Brown and Tunnicliffe were also amongst the heroes of my youth —'Long John and the study 'J. T.', who could cut late with a sweetness beyond compare. In the same golden period R. H. Spooner began to play for Lancashire, and he went in first with MacLaren. Here were the two handsomest batsmen that ever opened an innings for any county. Then there were the young Hobbs and the matured Hayward, the comet and the fixed star. Hobbs in those years was like Trumper again, a batsman on winged feet. We have seen him achieve the sunset touch; his cricket today is ripe and quiet and no longer concerned with vanities. Could Trumper have grown old—could Shelley? Hobbs and Sutcliffe will go down in history as the most reliable opening batsmen of all, but we must not forget Hobbs and Rhodes. Even before Sutcliffe, Rhodes was. I imagine that A. N. Hornby would have revelled in Hobbs and Rhodes, for they, too, loved a swift, short run. Posterity will cherish these two cricketers, and will love to look back on them and see the silent, shadowy host as the run-stealers flicker to and fro.

There are, at the moment, no great opening batsmen in the land, though in Worcestershire, which once knew the rampaging brilliance of H. K. Foster and Bowley, there are C. F. Walters and Gibbons. To go in first is to go in at the most romantic place of all. As they walk into the field, we give a heartening cheer to the first-wicket batsmen; we see them as two companions of adventure, pioneers daring the unknown, opening up paths for the others to come.

LOCKWOOD

RANJITSINHJI thought that Lockwood was the most difficult fast bowler he ever played against, not because of Lockwood's pace but because of his slow ball. 'I don't think it is a slow ball at all when it comes,' said Ranji. 'He does not seem to alter his action in the slightest. I can generally tell at once when other bowlers give me a slow . . . but Lockwood's a mystery to me.' And herein lay the difference between Lockwood and Tom Richardson, surely the two most beautiful fast bowlers ever seen in action at the same time, for, of course, both men attacked for Surrey many days and often, scattering wickets magnificently. Richardson was a simple-hearted giant whose energy passed naturally into fast bowling; the rhythm of his beautiful body needed no spur from mind or will-power. Momentum was everything in Richardson's attack. Richardson's bowling had in it something of the man's own frankness; it contained no subtleties. His speed was as open and honest as that of a wind which upsets apple carts and seems to laugh as it does so. There was no frankness about Lockwood's attack. His bolts seemed to come catastrophically out of the sullen air bred about the field wherever Lockwood moved. Temper was required to stir

Lockwood to greatness. Nobody ever called Richardson's breakback spiteful, unplayable though it could be on the hardest ground. He felled your wicket as the next woodman fells his tree, regretfully, maybe, but as part of the bright day's work. Lockwood's bowling was vicious, and, as we have seen from Ranji's comments, it was not to be trusted. Richardson's action told you unambiguously that he was going to send along a fast ball. Never did he let cunning of mind go counter to the honesty of giant limbs in galloping motion. 'I will not deceive you,' he seemed to say to the batsman, like the dear old lady in Dickens. 'Here's a fast ball; it will break back on to your leg-stump. Try and stop it, sir; I'm sure you are clever enough. Well tried, sir! I think you played it on!' Lockwood's action would advertise as fast a ball as ever Richardson bowled, and lo! energy was suddenly masked, bewitched, transformed; and a ball came along hanging in the air, hovering over the wicket like some circling evil thing. Richardson always bowled well; the loveliness of his rhythm made it impossible for him to bowl ill, for his action, so to say, 'went by itself', as though uninfluenced by anything so capricious as sinful human will. Lockwood's bowling was as sophisticated as Richardson's was open-hearted, which means that Lockwood was the more rational bowler of the two. Reason will sometimes waver and tell the body not to work in vain, whenever the facts announce a lost cause. Richardson bowled by faith, not by reason, and for him no cause was ever lost. At Old Trafford in 1896, in the Test match against Australia, Richardson bowled throughout a long day when England was losing all the time. He bowled till reason in every onlooker was astonished; he bowled till even his own great nature was abused. When the game ended and Australia, despite all his efforts, had won, Richardson simply shook himself like a superb animal, and walked from the field. He had tried his best, and the attempt had been worth while—so did his spirit console his weary limbs.

Lockwood's energy would blow hot and cold. At one hour he was a bowler becalmed; the next hour a whirlwind possessed him. Whenever Lockwood bowled badly, batsmen could not believe their good fortune; they had an uneasy feeling that they were enjoying some fool's paradise on the pleasant slope of a volcano. Any minute an eruption might take place and consume them.

In the winter of 1894–5 Lockwood and Richardson went to Australia with Stoddart's team. The season was terribly hot; day after day the sun fell upon the hard earth, making a fiery ordeal for bowlers to pass through. Richardson achieved wonders of endurance and skill, but Lockwood was found wanting. He bowled in the Test matches only 124 overs, and he took 5 wickets for 340 runs. Richardson bowled 309 overs for 849 runs and 32 wickets. He quite lacked the horse sense that sniffs in the wind trials and torments beyond a thoughtful man's power to tolerate. In England, and on the occasion of his own choosing, Lockwood was the cleverest fast bowler since Spofforth. He had something of Spofforth's genius to combine with speed certain crafty tricks of spin and flight. 'There was something in his action,' said C. B. Fry (who at one time wrote on cricket like an Aristotelean), 'which made the ball sometimes behave as though it were a slow ball bowled very fast. Although his off-break was considerable, there is no doubt that he more often than not beat the batsman before the ball pitched.' Lockwood swung his arm over on high with a proud poise of the body. He ran along the grass with a springing stride, and attacked from the extreme edge of the crease, and so caused the ball to travel diagonally to the wicket. Nowadays we would have talked of Lockwood's 'in-swinger', but in his day the language of cricketers was plain and modest.

All the honours came his way; no Players team or England team was possible without him. In his career he took 1,376 wickets at an average of 18 runs, wonderful work considering the marled excellence of the Oval. He could bat and hit hard; twice he reached 1,000 runs in a season, and in first-class cricket he scored 10,673 runs at an average of 21.

He touched the heroic heights in the Oval Test match of 1899, when on a hard unflawed pitch he bowled fifty overs against one of the greatest of Australian batting sides and took seven wickets for 71. Three years later, in the unforgettable Old Trafford Test match which Australia won by three runs, Lockwood, on a soft pitch, took eleven wickets for 76. On the opening day, when Victor Trumper scored a century before lunch, Lockwood did not attack until after the interval, because, it was said, he could not find a foothold. During the summer of 1898, at the Oval, Lockwood and Richardson bowled Yorkshire all out twice in a single day. Can it be wondered at that such an epoch is now thought of by old players and lovers of cricket as an age of giants?

GOOD DAYS

(JULY 1931)

IN a day or two the cricket field at Shastbury will be empty and the boys gone home for holidays. I used to watch them go, happy as only boys can be when they have weeks and weeks of fun and freedom before them. But I did not like the end of the summer term at Shastbury; it meant that for me cricket on green grass was over and done with for the year; it meant that I had to go back to a noisy, dusty city. Sometimes I would stay on at Shastbury a day or two, and at evening-time I would walk over the playing-fields in the sunset. I shall never forget the peacefulness of those solitary hours, with the little chapel huddled in the trees. The crows came home one by one, flapping their way overhead. It was good to sit under the great oak and watch the light leave the sky and hear the hum of the town in the distance.

I see those years at Shastbury now as years full of the thoughtless happiness of youth. When we get older our pleasures no doubt gain subtlety and fineness, but the habit of criticism sets in; the middle-aged temperament places every precious moment against a moving background of time—and no longer is it possible to live a life of pure sensation, every pulse of it deliciously to be felt for its own sake, with no bitter-sweet sense creeping in of the onward movement of life and of the bloom that makes the hour blessed, maybe, but fugitive.

When you have lived in a lovely place until, at the time, you were part of it, and could feel every day the fragrance of it going into the texture of your being, it is hard afterwards not to get a sort of resentment that the place still goes on and exists complete as ever, though you yourself have left it and have not seen it for years. Many a day in recent summers I have sat on a crowded county cricket ground and sent my thoughts far away to the school over the river. And I have seen in fancy the field white with boys playing cricket, hundreds of them, the bat cracking noisily—and I not there. Old William is not there any longer, either. Yet in his day he seemed as permanent at Shastbury as the ancient oak tree near the wooden pavilion. Year after year he came at the springtime and I with him. My first summer at Shastbury happened when I was young enough to retain the boy's hero-worship for great cricketers of the past. I had seen William play for his county in my schooldays, and now I was at Shastbury on a fresh May evening, eager to meet him in the flesh and next day to begin bowling with him in the nets. I remember walking up the hill in the narrow High Street (it is changed nowadays—a noisy habitation of motor-cars). And I remember going into the small house where William was, as he called it, 'lodging'. I introduced myself, and he shook hands with me while still lying on a sofa, his shirt-sleeves rolled up. I wanted him to know that I knew all about the splendour of his first-class cricket, and I spoke of a day at Brighton when he bowled Ranjitsinhji and Fry with consecutive balls on a perfect wicket. He did not remember it, not until I had prompted his memory. Then it all came back to him, and he reflected for a while and said, 'But it were a long time ago.'

When I knew William he did not often talk of his great days at the game; he even seemed to regret that he had given his life entirely to cricket. Once I was writing a letter in the sitting-room we shared, and he watched me carefully. I dashed off my note home in a few seconds. William, when he had to write a letter, gave up a whole evening to it, and took off his coat. He gazed at me as I wrote rapidly. 'By Gow,' said he (avoiding what he would have called blasphemy, for he was religious in a simple old-world way), 'By Gow, if I'd 'a' been able to write like that I'd a'a never wasted my life at a game.'

Then he spoke of the blessings of education, and asserted that his own son, thank the Lord, was doing well in the 'Co-op.', and might some day become a head cashier. Bless you, old William, wherever you may be today; it never occurred to you that playing for England at Lord's and Melbourne was achievement proud enough. No; he believed, at the end of his life, in 'education'. One evening, after net practice, we walked into the park of the township and listened to the band. William was moved by the 'Brightly dawns' of Sullivan. He listened intently, and at the closing cadence he said; 'By Gow, that were beautiful. I'd give all my cricket to play music like that.' It was William, as I have written before, who laid his head on his hands one evening at the end of a long afternoon of bowling, and asked, 'What have we done today? We've bowled and bowled and bowled—and for what good? We've prodooced nowt.'

He was one of the old school of professional cricketers; I cannot see him in a Morris-Cowley, as any day I can see many contemporary Test match players. And I cannot see him in suède shoes, or any sort of shoes. William wore enormous boots which had some sort of metal protection built into the edge of the heel. You could hear him coming up the street miles away. 'I pays a lot for my boots,' he was fond of telling me, 'but they lasts!' I am glad that he loved Shastbury and knew it was a beautiful place. Often he sat with me in term-time under the big tree, at the day's end. He would smoke his pipe and talk about the time of the year and of weather-lore. 'The swallers are high tonight; it'll be fine tomorrow.' Or 'Red at night's a sailor's delight, Red at morning's a sailor's warning.' And something about the oak and the ash and a summer of 'wet and splash'. He was very fond of that one, because the rhymes brought it within his view of poetry. We would sit there on the darkening field until the last red bar in the west had gone. Then we walked home to our room, and William would have his supper, a glass of beer, a chunk of bread, and an onion. As the lamplight fell on his fine old face I used to think of all the sunshine that had burned on it in his lifetime, here and at the other end of the earth.

I wonder who has taken William's place at the school up the hill, across the ferry. Perhaps a cricketer of the age that succeeded William; perhaps somebody who does not sit on the seat under the big tree at evenings, but goes about the countryside in a car. As I say, I cannot think of William in a Morris-Cowley. He was fond of telling me how he and Bill Lockwood and Tom Richardson often came back on a late train after a cricket tour and walked at midnight three or four miles to their villages. But next morning they were at practice on the county ground at half-past ten, and no doubt ready if not anxious to tackle W. G. Grace on a good wicket. Does the 'cotton' tree drop white blossoms yet at Shastbury? Is the little grey master of mathematics still there, with his passion for the game keen as ever? He lived for cricket every summer, kept a huge set of ledgers in which he entered all his runs. He loved to come to the school nets on quiet Monday afternoons, and ask William and me to bowl him into form. He was always depressed when he was out of form. He had a peculiar way with him while he was batting in a match. After he made ten he gave the umpire a batting-glove; after he made fifteen he gave the umpire his other batting-glove. When his score was twenty he took off one pad and gave it to the umpire. When he made thirty he took off the other pad and gave that to the umpire, too. He wore sleeves to his shirt that were divided at the elbows by buttons, so that the lower half could be detached. When his score was forty he would take off one sleeve like a glove; when he had reached fifty he would take off the other.

William acted as umpire once in a match while the little master of mathematics batted. Without comment he received the various articles of wear as they were handed to him. But at last William found a chance to say to me quietly: 'I sh'd like to see him someday when he's got a hundred!'

Good days, indeed, long drawn out in the heat, with all Shropshire stretching away in the distance, while we bowled and bowled, William and I, sometimes until we were fit to drop. Often I walked hopelessly over to him as the field was changing positions, and said, 'What a wicket, William; there's not a spot on it anywhere; we'll never get them out.' And this is how he would reply: 'Don't worrit; somebody'll make a mistake. And all's one; it'll come half-past six long afore t'day is over.'

'YOUTH'S A STUFF . . .'

BY remembering the day of my first county cricket match, I can easily make myself feel like the oldest inhabitant, because it happened when Queen Victoria sat on the throne; when the free-wheel on a bicycle was a remarkable invention; when a motorcar was the sign of the idle rich; when the newspapers were full of Kruger and the Uitlanders; when there were no loud-speakers. It was a morning in June 1899. I hesitated outside the ground at Old Trafford, a small boy again absent from school. Dull clouds came up the sky as I grasped my sixpence; I looked at the terrible warnings about 'entering at your own risk' and 'no money returned'. I looked again at the forbidding clouds, then plucked up courage, paid my money, passed through the turnstiles, ran into the ground and was thrilled to my bones as I saw the green field sweeping in a circle.

I saw MacLaren the moment I got a seat. He drove a ball from Paish, of Gloucestershire, for four, to the off, right away at the Stretford end. His bat swept down and, after his stroke, it remained on high, and MacLaren stood still, as though fixed by the magnificence of his own stroke. Then it began to rain, and it rained all day. I waited patiently for more cricket, until at three or four o'clock we were all sent home. But I was not sorry; I did not regret my sixpence. For I had seen a wonderful sight, and when I met my companions that evening I told them all about it: MacLaren standing there, his bat resonant with one majestic crack.

There really was wind and air at Old Trafford in those distant years. You could sit in the pavilion and see miles of countryside all round. At the top of Warwick Road, or near, were the Botanical Gardens—beautiful Victorian name. Well-brought-up little boys were taken there, possibly to contemplate botany. I saw William Gunn in the Botanic Gardens one evening, but I do not think he was studying botany. He looked an enormous man in his ordinary clothes; I preferred him in flannels. If I were a county cricketer, I would take care never to be seen by boys unless I was wearing flannels; without them the greatest hero of batsmanship can appear disappointing in the eyes of the young. William Gunn made a hundred in the first match that I ever saw between Lancashire and Nottinghamshire; he kept putting his left leg down the wicket until I thought it would stretch to the other end. Arthur Shrewsbury also played a long innings the same afternoon; he went back on his wicket very cool and tidy, and I knew he would never get out, so I hated him, as I hated all the cricketers who stayed in a long time against Lancashire.

They say that we who saw cricket in the Golden Age have given it a sentimental glamour which really it did not possess. But I certainly never wanted to enjoy Gunn and Shrewsbury and Ranji; my boyish love of a Lancashire victory must have blinded my eyes to many excellences. Until we are grown up we are not artists savouring the game for the sake of its skill and personality. The old cricketers stamped themselves upon young minds prejudiced against them. They achieved renown by sheer force of character. And the point of their appeal is that in those days we had no screaming headlines in the newspapers to help us into credulous acceptance of our heroes. They asserted themselves simply and convincingly. When a newspaper photographed Tom Richardson it was a stiff artificial picture showing him reduced to eternal immobility with his right hand held up vaguely in the air. But we had only to see him actually bowling to know of the unparalleled glory of his action —running to the wicket in long strides, ending with a great leap off the grass.

He was a dark, handsome man, with shiny black hair and a moustache. There are no cricketers today as big physically as Richardson, Gunn, Ulyett, Grace, Trumble; they all came out for a world more natural than ours; none of them could have put his feet into feminine shoes of patent leather; none of them could have looked like a personage from Hollywood. Their cricket was an unconscious flowering of the game's own genius at the high noon of its growth. For we must remember that county cricket in the 'nineties was almost a new event in the nation's life. Twenty years earlier it had only just emerged from the round-arm period of bowling. Grace had discovered cricket's modern scope, but it had yet to be explored. The 'nineties saw county cricket's manifold parts exhibited for the first time by men who, though masterful enough to be superb technicians, were themselves unstaled and were perpetually delighted at the handsome deeds the game stirred them to perform. Boredom was not dreamed of; we were the first in the field and there was such a lot to do. I remember how we were all thrilled to hear that R. E. Foster had scored two centuries in one match; a phenomenal piece of work then. And I remember the day on which Johnny Briggs took all the ten wickets against Worcestershire at Old Trafford in 1900; the miracle had been done before, but not frequently. It was still a miracle, and after the ninth Worcestershire wicket fell we suffered agonies while Mold bowled outside the off-stump; we trembled for fear some inept 'rabbit' would defeat Mold's kindly self-abnegation and get himself out, and so deprive Briggs of his glory.

Today the scope of cricket seems to have been worked out; nothing is left for our amazement. We watch Bradman making his two-hundreds in Test matches and we are merely interested. Yet only thirty years ago even Ranjitsinhji staggered belief if he maintained a batting average of eighty. I see cricket of the 'nineties now as a game played in a sort of morning of achievement; the players were explorers in a land unhorizoned. A Test match was an event of magnitude; since the war there have been countless Test matches. The bloom has been rubbed away by usage; the schoolboy of the present time sups full of records in every edition of the newspapers, and he cannot easily be astonished.

But of course it was not the feats and the figures which stirred us in the distant years. W. G. Grace did not score centuries more prodigiously than your Bradman or Hobbs scores them. S. M. J. Woods did not keep up the average of Hendren as a batsman, or the average of Larwood as a fast bowler. He looked a man of immense character, though, tall, tawny, alive with enjoyment of the game. I met George Hirst at Sheffield the other day in a pavilion crowded and congested

He at once sent out the flavour of nature, broad, homely, humorous, fine. I thought of Dr. Johnson's saying about Burke—that if you met him for a few minutes in a shed while sheltering from the rain you would say, 'That is a remarkable man.' So with Hirst; chance contact with him would draw you to him. As a cricketer he came straight down from Hambledon and the pastures.

We must all try to believe that our cricketers of today are as rich in character and as earnest in their play as the masters of the Golden Age. Perhaps they would strike us as really heroic if they wore whiskers and moustaches. The hairiness of the old players was somehow suggestive of strength and manly endeavour. The 'nineties, of course, were a 'manly' epoch; we were discovering the open air. Look at the ancient family albums and you will see men sitting on chairs, legs astride, with the backs of the chairs to the front, and their arms leaning on them; there was masculine nonchalance for you! There used to be matches between Smokers and Non-Smokers; and the Smokers often were photographed either with their pipes stuck out of their mouths boldly or with cigarettes dangling negligently from their fingers. Sometimes the Smokers won— and then there was confusion amongst those who regarded cricket as a mode of Victorian morality. The age was simple, which was the beauty of it. You cannot do anything greatly if you do not approach it rather like a greenhorn. The proper hero must be without self-consciousness; he must risk seeming a little absurd. Perhaps the hero has gone out of cricket for the same reason that he has gone out of the tales and novels we read—we do not any longer believe in the heroic. But, as I say, it is hard to strike the hero's attitude if the background and all the deeds that can be done are familiar. Grace and his immortal company were lucky to be first in the field while the cuts and drives and the new-fangled spin were so many splendid toys which nobody had yet grown tired of. . . . Do I suggest by all this that some of us are tired of cricket nowadays? Let me see Bradman batting, or Woolley, or Hobbs, or McCabe, or let me see a Rhodes bowling, or Larwood, or Robins—and I will gladly pay more than sixpence and wait for as many hours as I waited years ago when that I was a little boy, and the rain it raineth every day.

THE SENSITIVE PLANT

No game is more sensitive than cricket to the environment, to the material conditions in which it is played. A night of gentle rain will change a harmless slow bowler into the terror of all batsmen. A fall of the barometer usually means a fall of even Bradman's batting average.

We can understand, then, that if, in one and the same county, a great player's form is much at the mercy of variations in the climate, there is bound to be some difference between the cricket of one part of the world and that of another. Hirst in England was a great winner of matches; when he was in Australia his power lost all true edge and menace. Not only is the style the man, it is also the country, the race itself. Ranjitsinhji played as only an Indian could play; Emmott Robinson was obviously Yorkshire in all that he did, whether batting or bowling or telling the batsman, from a position at silly-point, 'to get on with thi lakin'.' If we take two brilliant artists, one an Englishman, the other an Australian, we shall at once see a difference in colours which are at first glance equally dazzling.

There is a hardness somewhere in Bradman's cricket which we never felt in the cricket of R. E. Foster; it is the difference between the sword of war and the lance of tournament. The Australian temper is at bottom grim; it is as though hot sun has dried up nature. I do not mean that Austalian batting is not as attractive to watch, not as rapid in its runs as English batting. As a fact, the Australians invariably score faster than we do in Test matches. But at the centre of the Australian game, let it be as vital and active as cricket well can be, there is a hard-bitten something, a realism that has no use for decoration. There has never yet been an Australian Palairet or an Australian Woolley. When the superb team of Armstrong scored runs in England in 1921 at the rate of over eighty an hour throughout the summer, there was all the time the hint of a ruthless policy in all the swift and flashing boundaries; here were Roundheads dressed up as Cavaliers.

During the golden age of English cricket, the public school flavour could be felt as strongly as in any West End club. When Spooner or K. L. Hutchings batted on a lovely summer day you could witness the fine flowerings of all the elegant cultural processes that had gone to the making of these cricketers; you could see their innings as though against a background of distant playing fields, far away from the reach of industry, pleasant lawns stretching to the chaste countryside, lawns well trimmed and conscious of the things that are not done. English cricket has usually reflected the social scene or psychology of the country at large in any given period. It was prosperous and middle class in the 'nineties; in the period of Squire Osbaldeston it was like fox-hunting, an evidence of a nation balanced nicely because of the compromise between the old landed gentry and the new-rich.

Just after the war, when the spirit of jazz became rampant, cricket saw the advent of the one and only great jazz cricketer ever known—Cecil Parkin. At the present time the game is off the gold standard, like everything else; there are as many splendid men still playing as ever, maybe, but we have a new way of reckoning values. The values, indeed, achieve remarkable flunctuations month by month: for example, fast leg-theory was 'booming' here only the other day. At the moment we are all announcing that fast leg-theory is a doubtful investment, almost a ruinous one.

A national game is as good a means as any other of exhibiting the character and outlook of a people. Most of us are our honest selves the moment we find ourselves exposed in the 'middle'—with a Larwood after us. Today, quite a number of peoples are attending the confessional of Test cricket. Not only England and Australia and South Africa are fighting for international honours; the West Indies, India, and New Zealand have put forward ambitious if youthful challenges. In this farther-flung battleground we may well be able to get a view in brief of the biological history of cricket. We may well see the game reliving its various stages of growth, from infancy to age. The West Indians, at any rate, may be said to show us cricket in its impulsive boyhood, naïve, if clever; not callow and not bored by too much success. Nearly every West Indian bowler seems to want to bowl fast, which is a proper ambition in life for all young cricketers. And they all hit the ball hard, or at least they would like to hit it hard. Many English and a few Australian batsmen do not care to hit the ball hard on principle.

Watch Constantine, and you are aware that he is more than a cricketer of astonishing dexterity. He is as much a personification of the West Indian racial psychology as Paynter is of Lancashire psychology. India, too, revealed to us recently the game in its fresh years; but contact with British influences in India lent an occasional sophistication, a flavour of the Army and Navy Club. The New

Zealand style and technique belong to the early manhood of cricket; their cricket is keen, accomplished, but not yet too clever by half. You could not confuse New Zealand cricket with Australia's; not only is it less mature in aim and outlook; it has a refreshing air; it is not so sun-dried that nature has departed.

Where do the South Africans come in our family tree of the game? They do not represent youth or middle age or ripeness. I should say they come somewhere in the thirties—just out of the tentative stage that lives mainly on high spirits and hope, but not yet arrived at the maturity which begins to conserve as well as to adventure. The South Africans developed to a rare pitch of reliability the googly ball; mere precocity could not have refined the trick, and maturity is usually content to wait until a trick has been tested. True, an Englishman, B. J. T. Bosanquet, first discovered the possibilities of the googly; but not until Vogler and Faulkner had demonstrated the lasting value of the device did we hear of the English D. W. Carr, of Kent, and the Australian, Hordern.

Test cricket is likely to be all the better for the new blood that has come from the West Indies, India, and New Zealand. For a number of years the atmosphere of international matches between England and Australia has been that of repletion and fulfilment; we have felt that the combatants were rather like two great houses arriving at the end of their lines. The glamour was all behind, and some of the new scions seemed shaky in blood. Even a Bradman does not come to us young; the head on his shoulders was old from the beginning. English cricket at the moment is definitely burdened by the discreet years; Jardine's team a year or two ago beat all records in slow-scoring in Test matches. Fast leg-theory was a sudden spurt of new life in the old dog; gland treatment sometimes works well. The old dog will be little the worse for a shaking now and again, administered by one or two of its own puppies. None of us would regret a defeat of England (or Australia) by the West Indians.

FROM DAYS IN THE SUN

THE FIRST MATCH

THE first match of the cricket season has been played. It happened the other evening on a stretch of earth as virgin of grass as the African veld. Behind the bowler's arm was a block of tenement houses. Now and again from the doors of these houses a Mrs. Jones or a Mrs. Carruthers would emerge, and after looking closely into the heart of the conflict would shrilly inquire: 'Where's our Willy? Come in, you young divil; yer farther wants yer.' Thereupon some inglorious, but by no means mute, Hobbs discovered himself foiled in the hour of triumph. He might at this point be wanting only a beggarly four past cover to complete his century, and now out of the gaudy light of glory Fate was snatching him. He had to surrender his militant bat, pass from the scene, go home and fetch the coals up. 'Yer can't have yer innin's out when yer gets back,' was the fiat that was sure to come to his ears as he put his coat on. 'Yer've given yer bat up!' There's where the canker gnawed.

This great game was not arranged by Lord's, and sometimes it was conducted not so much under the rules of Lord's as under Queensberry rules. A batsman while playing the ball would miss it, and it would thud against a huge brick wall on which three wickets were drawn in chalk. 'Out!' would howl the bowler, who if he were big enough was also the umpire. And the field was invariably with him to a man. 'Yer out! Give yer bat up!' Expostulation stared from the batsman's face at this. 'Out be blowed! It didn't never 'it no-where near th' wickets!' If he chanced to be a small batsman the bowler showed no inclination to bandy words. Down the pitch he would move to administer justice by strength of his right arm. 'Give yer blinkin' bat up else yer'll cop it.' The batsman, name of Jenkins (*soi-disant* Hendren), had to go. Maybe he would depart not only from the crease but from the field altogether, announcing to the world as he went, and setting the tidings to a chant in the Lydian mode: 'Bill Brown's a cheater—can't bowl for nuthink.'

The wickets in this Olympian game were, as I have said, drawn in chalk on a wide wall. Whoever designed them, plainly was a bowler himself. In the olden times at Hambledon the bowlers used to get up early in the morning and mark out the pitch on the 'nobbliest' pit of land they could find. In this match between Union Street and Summer Place the bowler had exercised a privilege not unlike that of the Hambledon men. He gave his chalk freely to the erection of his wickets, which possessed immense height and width. Whenever the ball hit them it would be made white on one side. Batsmen who owned mother wit and the muscle to support it would parry the bowler's aggressive 'Out!' flung at them each time the ball beat the bat by demanding with implicit irony; 'Wher's the chork mark on the ball? Garn, that's not a noo mark. It 'it them wickets wot we was usin' for practice larst night. 'Ere's the noo wickit, my lad. Carry on. We've got yer licked this time. Play up, Union Street!'

The match passed through widely different moods. It began with every combatant armed to the teeth, so to say. The bowler, before going into action, swung his arm round furiously. 'Get ready, lads,' he declaimed. 'Goin' ter bowl fast ternight; chuckin' googlies fer good.' Meanwhile the batsman was seeking to get himself into an attitude he had once seen assumed by greatness at Kennington Oval. 'Andy Sandham,' he said, and then he made sundry wonderful curves through the air with his bat, playing an imaginary ball wherever it was his fancy to direct it. The fieldsmen drew a tight net round the bat—the nearest man to the wicket, it seemed, was the one most likely to get the bat, and in consequence an innings, at the fall of the first wicket. It so happened, though, that tonight Andy Sandham was in great form. He drove powerfully, and the match was stopped while Horace Wilkinson, the youngest combatant, climbed over Moggridge's wall and threw the ball back. There was a little further hot disputation here between bowler and batsman. 'Yer out. It's allus "out" over Moggridge's wall.' Apparently this ruling had been rendered necessary by experience, Mr. Moggridge in the past having retained every ball that had disturbed his reflections on Form and Weights as he sat in his retreat in the summer evening's sun. But Andy placed himself beyond the law tonight. 'It's my ball, and if I'm out yer can orl put yer coats on and 'op it.' And thus he persisted in his mastership at the crease. And as he did so a strange lethargy fell on the fieldsmen. Point and cover-point went in for wrestling, as a *divertissement*; long-field met Miss Auriol Tompkinson, and, after a few courtier-like addresses to the lady as she went by, he shouted after her, 'Cedar mop!'—which, one inferred, was an oblique reference to the way her mother had decreed she should wear her hair, in an ambitious moment, some months ago.

Once the batsman hit the ball far across the brickcroft, and the parson happened to be passing. 'Thank yer, sir,' howled the bowler. 'Leave it—leave it, sir,' howled the batsman, starting his fifth run. The parson hesitated, then threw it back to the bowling crease. 'Interferin' old ——,' murmured Sandham. He was defeated at last, and the bat taken from him despite his assurances that he 'hadn't been ready'. The game woke up here. ' 'Ow many are yer?' inquired the captain of Summer Place. 'Thirty-eight,' responded Sandham, dropping the 't' in 'thirty'. 'Yer've been putting 'em on,' came the accusation from all over the field. Batsmen, it seems, are in Union Street League cricket trusted to keep their own scores. 'I mean twen'y-eight,' admitted Andy, feeling the weight of evidence dead against him.

As the light faded it was difficult to follow the contest to its crisis. Mrs. Carruthers or Mrs. Jones or Mrs. M'Dermott did great damage now from their respective doorsteps. Even those spared to fight on got a little confused. 'Yer've 'ad your innin's onst. Get out of it!' This cry went up time and again into the darkening sky. Then suddenly over the field flashed rumours of the first importance to those that had no coals to fetch up. 'Chips and fried fish is ready at 'Uddleston's.' This indeed meant the end. (It was, at any rate, usually chips and fried fish that caused play to be abandoned for the day amongst boys of a score or so years ago; in our times perhaps the second house at the pictures serves the same purpose—but what a poor substitute! Memory still holds that whiff of vinegar, the squelching noise as one shook the bottle, and the hailstone rattle of the salt out of those capacious tin castors.)

Union Street and Summer Place now went their opposite ways, but as they did so the ancient feud broke out again, with derision the weapon, and continued till the strongest lungs could not penetrate the distance and the houses between foe and foe. The more or less Parthian thrusts were: 'Call yerself Andy Sandham—wait till we get yer on our middin.' 'Our Willie, come and get the coal up!' (Very mocking this.) 'Summer Place? Garn! Ours is a nice 'ouse, ours is!'

J. W. HEARNE

HEARNE, of course, is one of the great men of cricket today. More than that, he is one of the few men in the cricket of our time who would have been great and looked great at any period in the history of the game. First and foremost he is a batsman. And unmistakably he is a Lord's batsmen. Nature has a happy way of giving to the art of some master cricketers a spirit that nicely expresses the different counties and setting in which they pass the bulk of their days. Hirst was Yorkshire through and through; Bobby Abel's batsmanship had the perky, Cockneyfied air one expects round about Kennington; even Ranjitsinhji's cricket was out-and-out Sussex 'by absorption', as Harry Lauder used to say the tawny colour of Ranji's batsmanship was in its right place in sun-brown Sussex. Even S. M. J. Woods was only an Australian by the sheer accident of birth; essentially his play had the breeze and vigour of the West Country; he gave us Somersetshire cricket; he was the Squire Western of cricket. So with Woolley; he is ever telling you of the gracious fields of Canterbury and Tonbridge, even when he is on the blasted heath of Bramall Lane.

At any rate Hearne is definitely of Lord's; the *hauteur* and the polish of the place are in his batsmanship. And to see him at his finest and truest you must go to Lord's on a June afternoon. The spirit of Lord's is incarnate in him as he moves an unhurried and elegant way there to a century. Let the afternoon be hot, with the austere pavilion ashine in the light, and the trees beyond the Nursery End incredible still. On such an afternoon think well upon your own sweaty condition, poor mortal that you are, compact unmistakably of flesh and blood. And then behold Hearne and your senses will go cool as though in the presence of marble. Aristocracy transcends the common need for perspiration, and Hearne's play never perspires. It is eternally as glossy as any top-hat in the pavilion. Refinement has expelled workaday nature out of Hearne the batsman. There is about him, as he makes his runs, something impersonal—that detachment which we have come to associate with the classic style. His face is a mask and his movements are so deliberate that you might well imagine there is no nerve or muscle in him not utterly subject to the will—the will to be as divinely formal as in this rude world a man may. Never does he seem to get surprised into an

108

unpremeditated step—for him there surely is no such thing as reflex action. One, indeed, might ask, watching him bat: 'Has this inscrutable cricketer really got in him none of the moist and variable humours known to the rest of us?—is there in his blood not one of those animal spirits which, as Tristram Shandy tells us, stir themselves suddenly like hey-go-mad and drive men to excess?'

His technique is a triumph of conservation of energy. Rarely does he need to use vulgar force for the making of a boundary hit. The main portion of his strokes suggests he has thought deeply about what might be called the geometry of deflection. He seems to know exactly from which point he must bring his bat to direct most balls to the farthest edge of the field without aid of energy of body. He steers, or persuades, a ball along a course predestined, so to speak, by its flight through the air after the bowler has let it go. Rarely do you see Hearne *forcing* a ball—sending it in a direction that flatly contradicts the direction given to it by the bowler. As one has said, he is a master of deflection.

This is a science which has its weaknesses. For happy exhibition it depends on true wickets, where a man can reasonably foresee what course a ball will ultimately take after leaving the bowler's hand. On sticky wickets, where bowling behaves as though some capricious imp were inside the leather, this science of deflection stands a good chance of getting confounded. When the turf is full of guile, the quick-footed drive which hits the ball on the half-volley is the specific—and Hearne is no master of the quick-footed drive. A stroke so clearly belonging to primitive batsmen, to the rude elements of cricket has, quite properly, no place in the equipage of Hearne, immaculate son of Turveydrop that he is. But we are not bound to insist on this limitation in Hearne's art; as we have agreed he is definitely of Lord's. And Lord's, understood rightly, means a smooth lawn of turf on a golden day. Let the sticky wicket be relegated to Bramall Lane or Old Trafford, for the sticky wicket is like a return to nature—'nasty, brutish, horrid', in the philosopher Locke's language. At Lord's nature is expelled, not by so coarse a weapon as a pitchfork, but by the chaste bat of Hearne. (Yet even at Lord's nature *will* come out—in any of Hendren's cricket when he is faithful to himself.)

And, after all, Hearne is himself human at bottom. He has plainly found that his superbly bred batsmanship tends to become much too fine and good for daily food. A revolt from chastity has happened in him—as we can tell as soon as we consider him as a bowler. Does he bowl as he bats—in terms of clean, balanced outlines? He does not. His bowling, in truth, is in mood and technique at the extreme of the mood and technique of his batsmanship. Heaven bless us, he is a googly bowler, flagrantly upsetting the principles of the classic bowlers' craft! Here's a paradox!—as Edward German sings in *Tom Jones*: a cricketer who walks by reason when he bats and by faith when he bowls. He must be a first choice for an England XI for a considerable time to come, because of his skill, and because he stirs the imagination in the way a Test match cricketer ought to do.

HOBBS: AN APPRECIATION

(May, 1920)

THAT the first century of the season should usually come from Hobbs is, as Mr. Square in *Tom Jones* would have said, in accordance with the eternal fitness of things. For Hobbs is indisputably our leading batsman; moreover, he is an out-and-out product of the modern game. Were a Martian to come upon us, wanting an introduction to the science of batting as we know it today, he need go no farther than the Oval some morning when Hobbs is at his best. And, truth to tell, Hobbs is always at his best, even if he fails to put up a big score. This is no paradox. There are cricketers who can give a glimpse of their mettle even in the very process of getting clean bowled, just as a tyro may hit a ball to the boundary time after time, yet only to convince us of his total lack of art. Whoever saw MacLaren act in any way unbecoming to a great cricketer? I always think of him today as I saw him once playing forward to Blythe beautifully, a majestic rhythm governing the slightest movement. He was clean bowled on the occasion I have in mind, for none, but nobody other than a giant of the game could have made a duck so immaculately. He played cricket as some proud Roman might have played it.

Hobbs, without possessing MacLaren's magnificence, can similarly convince us even on his unfruitful days. Rarely does he lose his wicket through incorrect or, rather, inartistic play. He does, of course, deviate from the conventions; that is because, like the artist he is, Hobbs cannot go on from day to day just scoring runs in the way that comes easiest to him.* No artist is happy moving along the lines where resistance is least, and Hobbs is for ever seeking to widen the scope of his craft—experimenting, creating obstacles for the sheer joy of overcoming them. So does a Chopin choose to write a study for black notes only, a Chardin paint a white tablecloth against a white background! Any green boy fresh from his coach at a public school may hit a ball on the off stump past cover; Hobbs often prefers to get it round to the on with a daring hook shot. Of course it is risky, and now and again he pays the penalty.

At the beginning of a certain bygone summer an amount of gloom set in at the Oval because Hobbs failed several innings in succession. Was his day over? asked the Jeremiahs. And then, just before the Lancashire match in London, Hobbs decided he had been playing a little too confidently, trying his on shots before getting the pace of the wicket. In this match he promised himself he would take no undue risks. As a result he got a century. And he would get a century every time he batted if he chose to 'sit on the splice' and wait for the inevitable loose ones. Fortunately for the glory of modern cricket, Hobbs sees in the game more of art than of science. Like Peter Pan, he is ever out for 'an awfully big adventure.'

I have said that Hobbs in himself would provide an ample idea of the scope of modern batting technique. And I should say that the great batsman of today differs from the great batsman of yesterday in his fuller command over back play as an offensive factor, and in his ability to combine it easefully with forward play. Men like Hobbs have worked out a method of back play such as few cricketers of the 'eighties dreamt of, though there have, of course, always been geniuses who 'builded wiser than they knew'—wiser, that is, than the law taught them. Such a one was Arthur Shrewsbury, whose back play was faultless, no matter how bad the wicket. But how far cricketers of yesterday were, in the lump, from realizing the full scope of back play we may understand from this sentence in Grace's book on cricket:

'Whatever you do, do not get in front of the wicket when you play the ball. . . . My experience has shown me that by keeping your right foot firmly in its place and drawing back the left until the heels are almost touching, one can resort to what is called the glide stroke and place the ball to leg.'

The G. O. M. was, of course, laying down a canon taught by

* This was written of the Hobbs of 1919.

experience of the bowling of his day.* But other times other manners. Bowling is not as accurate now as it was in the Shaw and Attewell epoch, but it turns more than it did in those times and is distinctly shorter. Two conclusions emerge if we consider these changes. The 'classical' forward stroke was, from its very muscular action, slightly speculative; that is to say, one did not actually see the ball at the moment the bat met it. The stroke assumed that the ball on pitching would follow more or less along the line of flight. In that case the stationary right leg as a *point d'appui* for the lunge forward was a sound enough rule. If the ball turned out rather shorter than you had at first calculated, you could, as the G. O. M. instructs, play back at it simply by drawing in the left leg.

But latterly we have had scores of good bowlers (I am speaking of bowling on the average during the last dozen years) whose deliveries you could not trust to follow along the line after pitching. Some of them—Vogler, Faulkner, Bosanquet, Hordern—did not even break the way their finger and wrist action indicated; they were 'googly' men—bowlers of 'wrong 'uns'. To cope with these, the more or less speculative lunge forward was suicidal. Better to run out, if it was a case of forward play at all. Most of these men, however, bowled rather short of a length, so that if your right foot was grounded stiff just behind the popping crease, you met the ball as it was turning and, what was more dangerous still, taking an upward trajectory. In 1912 the South Africans went to pieces in the Triangular Tests mainly because of immobile play on the right foot. This defect, as Mr. E. H. D. Sewell once shrewdly pointed out, was probably due to the fact that in South Africa cricket is played on matting, and that a batsman tends to ground his right foot behind the edge of the matting and keep it there. Whatever the cause, fast-footedness was the South Africans' ruin against Barnes.

Batsmen like Hobbs (but today there are few!) meet the 'new' bowling mainly by using the feet as batsmen never used them before. They go back right on the wicket, when they cannot jump to the pitch, thus giving the ball time to work off its spin and devil and so become more playable. They simply have to move the right leg across the wicket (to the horror of the old 'uns!) so that it may be used as a pivot on which to swing the body for the hook stroke to

* Grace himself did not always obey his own rulings; see the portraits in Mr. Beldam's book on *Great Batsmen*.

a break-back—the pads quite legitimately protecting the stumps. Hobbs has this stroke to perfection.

Old cricketers may argue with some force that modern batting—even that of Hobbs—is not as delightful to watch as batting was when it was three-parts forward play. The grace of forward play comes from the longer swing that can be got if you move your left leg fairly well out. But a flowing rhythmical movement is not the only way in which great batting may titillate the aesthetic emotions. If Hobbs, for instance, finds the wicket or the bowling rather against a free forward game, then he makes the main factor in his back play take the form of wrist-work. And who will deny the fascination of wrist-work? Why, the most stylish bat of the last twenty years, and that is R. H. Spooner, appealed to us less by his forward play than by wrist action used in conjunction with back play.

With Hobbs, when he is on a bad turf, back play is made positively dramatic. He times his strokes so beautifully that you catch your breath as you see the ball on the very wicket. Then he gives you that wonderfully quick swing round, the right leg as pivot, and you have the finest on-side shot of recent years! The drive through the covers is sweet, but Hobbs on the on-side is majestic. Besides, given a fast wicket, Hobbs can play the conventional forward game with the best of them. How superbly adaptable is his style we can understand from his success in this country, in South Africa, in Australia, against all conceivable sorts of bowling. The modern batsmen may have the good fortune to play on better wickets than those which fell to cricketers of yesterday, but, to be just to them, let us realize that they have bowling infinitely more diversified to tackle.*

Hobbs has mastered great bowlers in the 'classical' manner, and Rhodes, Blythe, Noble, J. T. Hearne will compare with any of the bowlers of the 'eighties and 'nineties; he has also mastered the greatest of the modernists—Hordern, Schwarz, Faulkner, Barnes, Hirst, F. R. Foster, 'googly' men, leg-break-cum-off-break, swerve or what you will. He learnt all the well-tried tricks of the trade from Tom Hayward, and he has added a few of his very own.

* Again, let me make it plain that I refer to bowling during the Barnes–Vogler–Foster period.

ON A FRESH CRICKET SEASON

THE beginning of cricket was fixed by Lord's for round about the 1st of May, and ostensibly it began then, and was duly reported in the newspapers. But here and there a cricketer of spirit was made to understand that the season was upon him before this; it came, for him, a day sooner at least than the rest of us were aware; the very instant, in fact, that a spring light woke him one morning and stirred in his mind a solitary thought: 'Today we leave for the South; today we set out on the summer's first tour.'

Nothing can go wrong with him on this blessed morning. He packs his bag blissfully, beholds the faded labels on it, eloquent of many a golden Odyssey. Lovely, sequence of names—Canterbury, Taunton, Worcester, Horsham, Tonbridge! It was at Horsham, our happy cricketer tells himself, he saw the season die last August. How far away did May seem on that afternoon when the sun burned out and he packed the bag for the last time and said 'Good-bye' to his companions! Did he not wish then with all his heart for Maytime back again? Did he not then ask himself why, when the season's beginning was with him, he had not shouted for joy the day long? Well, a spring morning is here for his delight again. Let him hang on to every minute of it, revel in a delighted sense of the time of the year, tell himself over and over: 'I am getting the best out of the day as its passes; I am missing nothing!'

Observe, happy man, from your bedroom window, at this moment as you prepare yourself for a journey to the South—observe the passers-by along the road opposite. They are going to work, going to the city, there to live stuffily in one dingy spot, while you—while you are going away for the beginning of cricket. Tonight these poor souls will pass by your house again, back from the city, but you will not be there to see them return. By then you will be at the other end of England; perhaps you will have just been taken by the hotel porter to your room, just have unpacked, washed, and gone out into the delicious streets, to ravish yourself in them with the feeling of the miles you have covered that day, and also with the feeling of romantically settling down now in a new place.

Does it matter that as the tour begins our cricketer finds a train crowded as it leaves London Road Station behind, with its mile's view of slate roofs on every hand? Not a bit of it. The other people in the compartment are plainly the veriest birds of passage; prosaic shortness of distance is to be their portion. They must depart at Stockport, or at the most at Crewe. When Market Street and Deansgate are at their crisis of unloveliness and congestion, our happy cricketer is moving through green fields; he is getting intimate glimpses into country life, as from the spacious rolling view outside the carriage window his eye detaches a thatched cottage with a postman knocking at the door, or a village street lazy in noon warmth—it is underneath him now, for the train rattles thunderously over a bridge. And now it is gone!

At Wellington, or in some such place deep in the garden of our land, the journey is broken; there is a change here. The Manchester train goes out, leaving you exquisitely aware that you are now quite out of touch with Manchester. Your connection arrives—a train that obviously has never been in Manchester. The people on it have just as obviously never been in Manchester. Here, unmistakably, you are in a fresh hemisphere, entering on the journey's last lap through a drowsy landscape. And how peaceful the closing hour of a day's railway travel is! The mild agitations of the morning—felt even by a happy cricketer— have spent themselves. The senses are tired at last of responding to new scenes, new sounds, new odours. Through too much unfolding of strange life about him our pilgrim feels an agreeable tedium; he drops into a reverie. . . . After Oxford, Cambridge, and then Leicester—always lots of fun at Leicester. Must look out for Astill's swinger, though. Yorkshire after that; suppose they'll give us the usual hot stuff. Where do we play Kent this year? Good Lord, at Gravesend! Why not on the Angel Ground at Tonbridge—glorious place! Wonder if my off-drive will be better this year. Must get my foot to it more. That's a nice piece of wood Smith picked for me; must get it going tomorrow at Oxford. Might easily pick up runs for nothing at Oxford; always a few green bowlers there this time of the year. A good start's everything. . . .

On the carriage seat he notices a newspaper, and there is a paragraph in it giving the County XI for its first match. He sees his name and is thrilled. After the winter's obscurity he is to become an item in the public news once more. In a day or two from now men in Newcastle and Woking, men he has never seen or heard of, telegraphists, sub-editors, and compositors by livelihood, will be bandying his name about. 'Blank drove Benskin and completed his fifty in sixty-five minutes.' This will be read on the Manchester

115

Exchange, in the Reform Club even, in Back George Street among the grey cloths, in Gorton, and in Westhoughton.

Will he run into form quickly? But he has no use for misgivings in this hour of May content. He is master of his fate, captain of his break-back. He sees, in his splendid vision, a hundred moments that the summer holds for him—the yellow stumps standing upright as he reaches the crease at the fall of the first wicket, with the white line of the popping crease just broken in the middle where Smith took his guard; the fieldsmen moving back to position as he gets his bat ready; the trees away in the distance behind the bowler. He sees the bowler coming towards him, face set; he feels his bat circling in the air, feels the ecstasy that comes with a hit clean in the blade's middle; he sees a fieldsman on the off-side boundary picking up the ball after it has been thrown back into the field from the crowd. He sees Lord's again, basks in the sense of walking to it on a June morning down the St. John's Wood Road; he sees himself 'going on at the Nursery End,' the while the score-board announces 'Bowler 7' and the pavilion bloods look at their cards and pronounce his name. He sees all the lovely cricket fields in England beckoning to him; he sees the sun mellowing on an afternoon somewhere in brown Sussex as cool drink is brought and bowlers slake their thirsts, while away on the field's edge a man in white lies prone on the grass even as he, our happy cricketer, stands erect at the wicket, 86 not out. And, best vision of all, he sees himself 'not out' even to the close of play, privileged to remove his pads, to change from his warm flannels, to leave the ground, to go here, there, and everywhere that evening, to go to bed, to get up in the morning; privileged to pass through all these spaces between one day's play and another and to remain not out all the time! Moments of vision indeed. Tomorrow and tomorrow—days in the sun, luscious grass to walk on, wind running over the body. Happy man, this is the time of the year for you; August will never seem so far away again.

The train's whistle blows; pace slackens. Here you are, and the others, cricketers all, with the season well and beautifully launched. No runs yet, maybe, and no wickets down; but a paradisal day already lived through.

M. A. NOBLE

THE general law which divides human mentality into two contrasted types—making of us Liberals and Conservatives in politics, classicists and romancists in the arts and literature, Platonists and Aristoteleans in philosophy—would seem to operate even in our sports and pastimes. In cricket, at any rate, we have our Frys and our Ranjis, our Trumpers and our Nobles. M. A. Noble was in the classic school through and through, and that much can be said without contradicting the view that also he was definitely a player of today. For it is possible to be classic without being pedantic. Noble's style scrupulously observed all the principles which long experience has sanctioned, but with him these principles had, so to speak, developed naturally, and the ease with which he was able to adapt them, especially in his batting, to every change in the technique of the game, was a striking justification of their undiminishing utility.

As a bowler he was far enough advanced to cultivate the swerve, but even here he never forgot the time-honoured axiom about good length being the basis of good bowling. Too many of our 'swervers' can only bring off their effects by over-pitching, and indeed the very conditions which are required to induce the swerve, render it difficult not to over-pitch. Before a ball will curl, obviously it must be in the air for a longish time, and take an uncommonly spacious curve in its flight. The trouble, therefore, is to swerve without presenting the batsman with the full toss or half-volley which can so easily be hit to the boundary. Noble solved the problem like the thoughtful student he was. He got the necessary addition to his curve in the air at his end of the pitch—not at the batsman's. This he managed by going down rather low on his right knee in the act of delivery, and by releasing the ball from the hand farther back in the swing over than is usual. The ball thus was impelled from a conveniently low altitude, and as a consequence, the upward trajectory was a little higher than the average bowler's, and so the ball gained the extra air in which to lose its spin— and this must happen before the swerve will take effect—all of which operations happened well away from the batsman's reach. His swerve was done so subtly that the batsman hardly saw it at all, for it was less a curve in from the right or the left than a vertical swerve. There was perhaps a

117

slight swing from leg, but the chief danger came from the ball that dropped suddenly down just when it appeared certain to be a delightful half-volley. There was, however, nothing sensational in Noble's swerve; even a purist like Alfred Shaw might have cultivated it had he played the game today. As has been said, Noble always tried to keep his length classically correct. He also had the conventional off-break of the fast medium bowler. But, first and last, it was his generalship that gave the quality to his bowling which made it difficult on all wickets. He was a master of deceptive flight, as, indeed, most great Australian bowlers invariably are. They need to be, too, playing as they do in a country where the hard, fast grounds so often make break almost impossible.

Noble's batting was in all its details quite classical; here no notably modern characteristic entered at all. His play did not fire the imagination of the crowd, like Trumper's; rather, it compelled admiration. There was thoughtfulness in his very stance at the wicket, and every action pointed to a deliberate and studiously cultivated method.

The art of a Trumper is like the art in a bird's flight, an art that knows not how wonderful it is. With Noble there was always a sense of effort; we did not feel, as we did with Trumper, that batting was for him a superb dissipation, a spontaneous spreading of fine feathers. He gave us the impression, always, that there was some difficult obstacle in the attack, to be overcome only by hard work and untiring determination. His was the skill that comes not exactly 'to the manner born', but through diligently scorning delights and living laborious days. He played back to an extent uncommon among Australians. But it was back play of an extremely graceful and polished kind. He did not dab at the ball, bringing the bat from just behind the right leg with a cramped wrist action, as some batsmen do. His bat, even in his very late defensive strokes, came down from above with a full swing; it was as free and as rhythmic as in a forward shot. He combined caution with enterprise in a way that is typical of the average Australian cricketer. In his brilliant moments his off-drive was worth a day's walk to see.

P. F. Warner has described Noble as the wisest of all Australian captains, and though this is high praise, remembering Giffen and Darling, it must come very near the truth. On the field he was the picture of concentration. His temperament inclined him naturally towards the more scientific aspects of the game, and he usually wore the expression of a mathematician tussling with a stiff proposition.

He played the game for all he was worth—as though, indeed, a kingdom depended on it. It will be best to remember him as a long-limbed and tense-featured giant standing abstractedly between the overs at point (where, by the way, he was one of the finest fielders of them all) knitting his brows and letting the whole world go by, save the particular scene of the moment—the warm sun and the grass, the silently moving men in white, and the dire necessity of another wicket before lunch.

A CRY FOR A JESSOP

THE other afternoon as maiden after maiden over was being wheeled up to the wicket in a country match, a spectator cried out of his soul: 'O for another slogger like Jessop!' The sentiment was excellent, but the terms it was expressed in did injustice to a great batsman. One is constantly hearing Jessop discussed nowadays for all the world as though he achieved his wonderful deeds by sheer 'slogging'. It has even been written of Jessop that he 'reduced rustic batting to a science'. All of which is so fallacious that it would be excellent to name it as such once and for all. Let any cricketer who has ever in his life been called on to tackle first-class bowling ask himself how a hitter 'pure and simple' could possibly have played the innumerable long innings Jessop played—the bulk of them against some of the finest bowlers of all time. We may understand straightway the distance Jessop was removed from the 'slogger' if we think of him, only for a moment, with Alletson or Barratt in mind. Here we have clear cases of batsmen who out and out are of the slogging order—hearty, elemental thew-and-sinew fellows, beating the wind with hammer-like bats. Now and again a Barratt, an Alletson, brings off a miracle—actually finds the ball every time he lets go at it in a headlong primitive foray. Most days in a summer, though, he is easy game, blind as a bull at a fence, and a Rhodes or a Trumble will ensnare him in quick time—a wink to deep long-off, a tempting half-volley, a convulsion at the batting crease . . . and somebody on the boundary is tossing the ball from one hand to the other as our 'smiter' walks to the pavilion, feeling rather ineffectual. Jessop never was easy game; he was a batsman in

119

the strictest sense, with a technique not only calculated and polished, but fundamentally grounded in reason.

Of course an innings by Jessop was invariably a sort of cyclone of batsmanship. Well, at the centre even of the wildest cyclone there is a 'point of rest', a calm pivotal spot. So in a Jessop innings: round and over the field would its fury sweep, but deep in the heart of all the motion was the mind of Jessop, cold and rational—a mind making decisions, weighing chances, as judiciously as a Shrewsbury or a Gunn. It was the quickness of Jessop's batsmanship that deceived. Because his pace was faster by far than that of any other batsman of his time, one was always likely to jump to the conclusion that an innings by Jessop was speculative and dangerous. Had we been able to look at a typical Jessop innings with the cinema's 'slow motion' vision, we should have seen that the majority of his hits were, as Harry Lauder used to say, 'sure as death'. What if Jessop *was* fond of a cut from the middle stump?—the stroke was scientifically done, true to the ancient law. The fact that Jessop's cut frequently was accomplished from a straight ball proves simply that he was more than commonly clever at it—not that the cut itself was unorthodox *qua* cut. Jessop's cut from the middle stump was in technique exactly as it was when he cut legitimately from the off-side ball. 'If my cut is correct in mechanism when I use it to a ball *off* the wicket,' we can imagine Jessop saying, 'then it must be just as correct in mechanism when I use it to a ball on my middle stump, because it is the same stroke as far as my share in its performance is concerned. I can't help the position of the wickets going wrong now and then!' And what a gaudy hit this cut of Jessop's was; how the bowler, after thinking he had broken clean through the 'Croucher's' defence, would throw up his hands to high heaven and then cross himself piously as he saw Jessop's bat flash at the last second and crack the ball to the boundary at a pace blinding the slips! Jessop, of course, got out from time to time through this wonderful cut from the middle wicket, but that proves nothing against the essential science that went to the stroke's making. Quaife gets out from time to time when playing forward—and you wouldn't accept that as evidence that Quaife was wanting in orthodoxy.

If you will glance at the splendid action-portraits of Jessop in Mr. Beldam's book, you will see that most of Jessop's hits were modelled on first principles. Even the huge pull with which he would take a ball from a foot or so outside the off wicket and drop it in the heart of the crowd at the on-side boundary—even that gargantuan stroke did Jessop perform much as W. G. Grace performed it. 'Ah, but,' you say, 'Jessop was unscientific, because he would cut and pull good-length balls.' And what might a good-length ball be, anyway? 'They say Jessop hits good-length stuff,' said an All-England cricketer to me once, 'but I'll defy anybody to bowl much good-length stuff at the "Croucher" when he's on the bust!' The whole point about Jessop's methods is in that remark— he did *not* cut and carve good-length bowling. The bowling would have been good-length stuff to other batsmen; Jessop, by his marvellously quick and plastic foot-work, made it into bad-length stuff. He taught a lesson in batsmanship that surely needs to be pondered by cricketers of today. For though we must not lay down from the deeds of a genius like Jessop rules for smaller men to follow, we can at least grasp at the broad, sensible basis from which the genius of Jessop started to work. That good length in bowling is relative to a batsman's reach, footwork, and style of strokes, is at least one great lesson Jessop taught—a lesson which every county batsman worthy of the name should strive to put into practice today. For we are getting too much cricket at the moment in which the bowler is permitted to decide what shall be considered a good length; the bowler is permitted also to pitch much the same length to *all manner of batsmen*—tall, short, thin, and fat. And few batsmen will even try to demonstrate that this good length is illusory; that there is no such thing as a length absolute; that the pitch of a good ball must vary with nearly every batsman that comes to the crease, according to his height and general style of play. In Jessop's day a good length was bowled, so to say, only 'by permission of the batsman.' Cricketers like Jessop, F. G. J. Ford, MacLaren, Ranjitsinhji, Trumper, Spooner, R. E. Foster, A. O. Jones time after time would smash up the scheme of the so-called length bowler and remould it closer to their hearts' desire. These batsmen, consequently, were match-winning batsmen. How many cricketers today possess the ability to 'knock the length bowler off', make good bowling into bad by aggressive, mobile foot-work, and so win a match? I can think only of Hobbs, Woolley, Hammond, Carr, and Fender—the last two cricketers chips from the workshop that shaped the astonishing Jessop.

FROM CLOSE OF PLAY

WALTER HAMMOND

WALTER HAMMOND was one of the truly great cricketers in the game's history; it would be hard to leave him out of any recorded England XI, though blasphemy might be committed if we altered a single name of the magnificent membership of the England XI which played at Birmingham in 1902; who of these could with justice and decency stand down even for Hammond—A. C. MacLaren, C. B. Fry, K. S. Ranjitsinhji, F. S. Jackson, Tyldesley, Lilley, Hirst, G. L. Jessop, Braund, Lockwood, Rhodes? Do I hear a whispered suggestion that Tyldesley was not greater than Hammond as a batsman and no bowler at all? But I cannot argue reasonably on behalf of J. T. Tyldesley. In his heyday he was the only English professional player who by batting alone could retain his position in the England team. I flatter Hammond by bringing his name into contact with Tyldesley's, even as I honour Tyldesley by the same verbal conjunction. Hammond indeed was the complete cricketer in his superb physique, which combined power and lissome movement; his batsmanship attained in time classic poise and the habit of long domination. He was a dangerous medium-paced bowler who, given the ambition, might have vied with George Lohmann in all round and elegant skill; for I doubt if even Lohamnn was Hammond's superior as a slip fields-man.

He looked the part too, even as Lohmann looked it. His shoulders were broad; the physical frame as a whole maybe at first hinted of top-heaviness somewhere, and there seemed a tendency of his legs, as he stood in the slips, to go together at the knees. At the first sight of a snick from the edge of the bat his energy apparently electrified the shape and substance of him; he became light and boneless and down to the earth he would dive, all curves and balance, and he would catch a ghost of a 'chance' as if by instinct; quick though it moved, the body no doubt lagged behind the born gameplayer's intuitions. He could take a slip catch as the ball flashed rapidly away, wheeling on the ballet dancer's toes and not so much gripping or seizing the ball as bringing it back, so to say, with time to spare.

Only A. P. F. Chapman of Hammond's contemporaries equalled Hammond at catching close to the wicket.

I first saw Hammond in 1923 playing against Lancashire at Gloucester; he was an unknown youth, and he batted low in the innings, amongst the tail-enders. He drove one four to the off, then got out; but I had seen enough. I wrote half a column in the *Manchester Guardian* about the boy and ventured a prophecy of greatness to come. It was easy to look into his future; there is no mistaking the thoroughbred. We needn't look for hours at quality. The scoreboard and the statisticians must wait for results; and mediocrity needs the proof of print and percentages before it is recognized even as mediocrity. Hammond was born to distinction on the cricket field; before he had been playing for Gloucestershire long most of us knew that here was one of the elect, the chosen few. But not everybody knew; in 1924 I argued with John Sharp of Lancashire, then on the England selection committee, that already Hammond was worth his colours. But Sharp thought he lacked discretion; 'He's a bit of a dasher,' he said. In fact Hammond's career as a batsman can be divided into two periods, much as the career of Hobbs can be divided. First he was all swift aggression, even to the verge of recklessness. Then followed the illness which in 1926 nearly put an end to his cricket. And now he merged into maturity just as Test matches were changing in temper and attitude according to what I shall herewith call the Jardinian theory, the theory taught by the strongest-willed of all the captains of England Elevens, the theory of the survival not so much of the fittest but of the most durable. The great batsman for the purposes of Test matches, according to this theory, was he who stayed in for hours and compiled large quantities of runs, not necessarily by commanding and beautiful strokes but by the processes of attrition. Hammond remained to the end a batsman handsome to look at, a pedigree batsman, monumental and classic. But I shall continue to try to remember well the young Hammond who in 1927 when the Gloucestershire cause seemed lost beyond repair, hooked the pace of Macdonald with a savage power I had seldom seen before and have never seen since. At this point I imagine the eyebrows of most of my more experienced readers are going up questionably—'Hammond hooking? But Hammond didn't use the hook. If he had a weakness at all it was lack of resourceful strokes to leg. O'Reilly could keep him quiet by bowling on his leg stump.' On the morning of Friday, 20th May, Gloucestershire, with two wickets down in

124

their second innings, were only 44 ahead. The Lancashire professionals planned to get the match over quickly, so that they could go
to the Manchester races. From the first over of the day, bowled by
Macdonald with the velocity and concentration of a man determined to get to Castle Irwell in time to back a certain winner at
5 to 1 against, Hammond drove five fours from five consecutive
balls. The sixth ball would also have counted for four, but it was
fielded on the boundary's edge at the sight-screen behind Macdonald's arm. A straight drive from the first over of the most
dangerous fast bowler of many decades! Hammond punished Macdonald so contumaciously that short 'bumpers' soon began whizz-
ing about Hammond's head. He hooked them time after time as
ferociously as they were discharged at him. I watched this death-or-
glory innings standing in the dusty earth near the Manchester end
of the ground, near long leg. Several of Hammond's hooks crashed
into the earth, sending gravel flying about us like shrapnel. In some
three hours Hammond scored 187, with no chance, four sixes and
twenty-four fours.

In August 1924 at the age of 21 he wrecked the Middlesex attack
on a dreadful wicket at Bristol. Gloucestershire, in first, scored 31,
then dismissed Middlesex for 74. In Gloucestershire's second innings Hammond scored an unbeaten 174 out of 294 for 9 (declared),
in four hours, winning the match. It was cricket of this dauntless
kind, with strokes blinding to the eyesight, strokes of controlled
power and strokes of controlled imagination, all kaleidoscopic and
thrilling to the romantic vision, which impelled me to a column
article I sent to *The Observer*, then edited by J. L. Garvin, who also
became convinced of young Hammond's genius. But we couldn't
convince yet the England selection committee that here was the
greatest England batsman since the high noon of Hobbs. The
philosophy of 'safety first' was at this time in full swing and sway.
By the by, when Hammond first got married, Garvin wrote to me:
'For the next few months he'll probably not do very much—but
afterwards, better than ever.'

Because of illness Hammond did not play for England until 1927.
Then as one of Chapman's team—in Australia in 1928–29—Jardine,
the vice-captain, he scored 905 runs in the rubber, with an average
of 113·12. He began modestly in the first Test Match of the series,
played at Brisbane: 44 and 28. Next at Sydney he scored 251,
followed by 200 and 32 (run out) at Melbourne, followed by 119 not
out and 177 at Adelaide (two hundreds in the same game), followed

by 38 and 16. The world of cricket was staggered, not realizing of the wrath to come from Bradman. So far in cricket's history no one human batsman had amassed runs in Test matches with this insatiable appetite and with Hammond's austerity of purpose and disciplined technique. For he had now put childish things behind him, at least while playing in Test matches. The glorious uncertainty of cricket was a term no longer to be sensibly applied to Test matches between England and Australia; the wickets all this time were anaesthetic, somnolent couches stuffed with runs. We must bear these wickets in mind as we make an estimate of the bowling of W. J. O'Reilly, who was doomed to go to work on them and to toil on them for hours, if he could not spin. In the circumstance his record of performances well bears comparison with that of the unparalleled Sydney Barnes. Hammond fitted himself into the new economy and the new ethic of sport; and he lost nothing of the grand manner while making the adjustment and the ordered concession to the mathematical and the mechanical. He cut out all but his safest strokes; he became patience on a pedestal of modern concrete; Phœbus Apollo had turned fasting friar. He reserved for matches of lesser importance flashes or flickers of his proper brilliance. His stately and pillared centuries and double-centuries were as classic as the Elgin marbles and about as mobile and substantial. With the ease of absolute mastery he batted maiden over after maiden over, his body bending to the ball almost solicitously, making strokes of cradled gentleness. For the Cause he clipped his own wings; but there is something majestical in wings in repose. He played henceforward mainly off the back foot. His terrific punches to the offside received their strength from a propulsion or a swift thrust of the body beginning at a bent right knee then steely wrists directed the energy, so that none was wasted; it all ran like a current of power into the bat and through it into the ball.

At Lord's in 1938 his greatest Test match innings may be said to have added to the ground's lustre and history. When he went to the wicket England had lost Hutton, Barnett and Edrich to the alarming pace of McCormick, and not many more than twenty runs had been scored. Hammond at once took charge of the game and after due scrutiny and circumspection he hammered McCormick and Fleetwood-Smith and O'Reilly to shapeless helplessness, never seeming to hurry himself or use his strength combatively; no; he went a red-carpeted way to 240, his cover-drives thundering against the rails under the sign of Father Time. This innings announced that for Hammond ripeness was all that mattered now; the early and dazzling shooting-star had by some astronomical decree changed into the benign satisfying and fulfilled harvest moon. His batting at Lord's this day was marmoreal; an appeal against him for leg-before-wicket, a raucous appeal at that, sounded so incongruous that I was there and then strangely inspired to a satire, in the form of Meredithian parody:

Hammond leg-before-wicket—has anybody noticed that he *has* a leg? Usually the leg of the modern batsman is ever before us, obscure it as you will, dressed degenerately in pads of breadth and length, inordinate unvaried length, sheer longinquity ageing the very heart of bowler on a view. Most cricketers have their legs, we have to admit. But what are they? Not the modulated instrument we mean—simply legs for leg-work, legs of an Emmott Robinson. Our cavalier's leg—our Hammond's—is the poetic leg, a valiance, a leg with brains in it, not to be traduced by the trick they ken of at Sheffield. . . .

After Hammond put an end to his innings this day in June 1938, everybody stood up as he returned to the pavilion, stood up to render tribute to a cricketer who had ennobled Lord's. After the second war, Hammond again visited Australia, this time as captain. He suffered physical ailment and mental worry, so could not make a good end. But during the 'Victory' Test matches in England, not regarded as official, the original Hammond was seen, riding on the crest of his youth; or, to drop the metaphor, he attacked as of yore, the bat swinging free of care again, sure of aim, and, best of all, a source of enjoyment to himself as well as to all others. One of his more remarkable innings was played on an absurdly difficult wicket at Melbourne, during the 1936–37 rubber; the ball broke most known laws of geometry, trigonometry and suchlike. Now it shot along the earth like a stone thrown over ice; now from the same length would it rise upward at an acute angle threatening batsman's skull or thorax. On this turbulent pitch Hammond maintained his customary poise and calm; his innings of 32 came like oil in raging waters. He stayed in easefully for an hour and a half, never once obliged to hasten a stroke. The irony of it all was that all this mastery was really a service to Australia; much more good would have come England's way had Hammond driven and hooked, defying every tabulated principle of science, and scored his runs in a quarter of the time—so that Australia might have had to go to the wicket and face the music. J. T. Tyldesley in 1903, also on a foul pitch at

Melbourne, made 63 out of England's total of 103, and by brilliance and versatile if sometimes indiscreet strokes, won the match, or at least brought victory within England's reach.

Hammond in his pomp occasionally suggested that he was batting lazily, with not all his mind alert. When he at times scored slowly on a perfect wicket he conveyed to us the impression that he was missing opportunities to get runs because of some absence of mind or indolence of disposition. He once said to me after he had made a large score on a comfortable wicket, 'It's too easy.' He preferred a worn dust-heap at Cheltenham, where he would put the most dangerous attack to the sword, and where fielding in the slip he was Nijinsky and a myriad-armed Indian god at one and the same animate time. His career had its pungent ironies, apart from the disillusionment of the curtain's fall. When he first met Fleetwood-Smith, a googly bowler of rare and enchanting art, Hammond nearly knocked him out of cricket for good and all. Then in 1937 at Adelaide, when the rubber was at stake, Hammond and Fleetwood-Smith came face to face; and we knew that the decision rested with one or the other. On the closing morning, England needed 244 to win, with 7 wickets in hand, Hammond not out. It was the fourth match of the series, England had won two, Australia one. All our eyes were riveted on Hammond as he took the bowling of Fleetwood-Smith in a gleaming sunshine. To the third ball of the day Hammond played forward and was clean bowled. Australia won, drawing equal in the rubber; they also won the fifth. As Hammond's bails fell to the ground, Fleetwood-Smith danced, walked on his knees, went nearly off his head. And I heard Duckworth's voice behind me: 'We wouldn't have got Don out first thing in the morning with a rubber at stake.'

'Too easy.' He was an artist of variable moods. But he was greater than the statisticians suspect. Perhaps all of a beautiful batsman's innings should be of brief duration—as Edgar Allen Poe said all poetry should be short. At least no innings by a master and artist should seem longer than any ever played by Trumper, Woolley or John Tyldesley. There were more things in Hammond's cricket than are dreamed of in the scorebook's economy.

MAURICE LEYLAND

MAURICE LEYLAND played his first innings for England and scored 137, at Melbourne in March, 1929, for Chapman's conquering team. He batted for England against Australia 33 times and in 29 completed innings he scored 1,605 runs at an average of more than 53. At one period, against O'Reilly, when O'Reilly was the greatest medium placed bowler cricket has known since S. F. Barnes, Leyland made four centuries in seven innings. One morning at Brisbane in December, 1936, on the eve of the first Test match of that Australian summer, one or two players were taking light refreshments in the Belle Vue Hotel; and Leyland and O'Reilly were present. After some conversation naturally concerning the rubber about to begin, Leyland said to O'Reilly: 'Well, Bill, nobody can say who'll win, it's a foony game's cricket. But Ah can tell thi one thing now for certain. . . . Ah's got thee where Ah wants thi, Bill—and Ah thinks tha knows it.'

In 1938 Leyland was not chosen to play for England until the Kennington Oval match in which Hutton amassed 364 and England's total reached 903 for 7 (declared), after dreadful and deliberate hours and hours of stone-walling, according to a ruthless plan. Even Leyland, though he scored 187, seldom ventured an uninhibited stroke. I saw him during one of the intervals for rest and surcease, when his score would be round about 100 and his life's record for England already well beyond a thousand runs. 'And even you, Maurice,' I complained, in sorrow not anger, 'even you won't hit the ball and give us some cricket.' 'Hey, wait a minute, Mr. Cardus,' expostulated Leyland, as though pained at my protest, 'wait a minute—tha must remember that Ah'm playin' for me place in team.'

He was in the line of those humorous Yorkshiremen which the broad nature of his county produces from time to time as a contrast to and leavening of the generally dour lump. There was a twinkle in his eye and there was a twinkle in his bat, no matter how grimly and straight it may occasionally be obliged to defend a difficult situation in Yorkshire; for not always was his bat scrupulously straight. He came into the England team as left-handed batsman in the train of Woolley, which was enough to make him think of trying his right hand. Leyland was not a stylist in the decorative

129

sense; he was a sturdy cricketer, not tall, but his sloping bottle-neck shoulders seemed to add inches to him and he had long arms of impressive thickness, veined with strength at the wrists; also he was broad in the beam, with a rubicund smile on his cheerful open countenance. His eyes looked straight at whoever happened to be talking to him, exactly as they looked straight at who ever happened to be bowling at him. He could defend with as much as Emmott Robinson's vigilance and subtly-mingled bat and pad play; but he saw the humour of it all. I do believe that in his heart he thought that a defeat of Yorkshire was really enough to make a pavilion cat laugh. His driving on both sides of the wicket was lusty and free; he would waste no energy, just a quick placing of his feet, and the bat swung from a fairly high 'lift', right leg beautifully to the ball in a cover-drive. Then he would suddenly stand motionless, long arms down by the sides of his body, the bat as though rendered lifeless and out of action. And he would look into the distance, to the direction of his hit, as if contemplating the perspective of it. The hint of a cross bat, which came out of his cricket from time to time, caused the purists to shake heads, until the bowlers assured them it was an illusion and that few players 'middled' the ball with Leyland's accuracy. He was temperamentally, physically and geologically related to George Hirst and Roy Kilner, all bonny fighters who played even Yorkshire cricket for 'foon'. As often as Hirst himself did Leyland come forward in a crisis and save an English innings from breakdown; at Adelaide in 1933 after Sutcliffe, Jardine, Hammond and Ames had fallen for less than 20 at the beginning of the third game of the rubber, with each team a victory to its credit, Leyland and R. E. S. Wyatt saved the day. At Brisbane, the same rubber, he won a match at a moment of incipient collapse. In the face of Australia's total of 701 at Kennington Oval in 1934, he scored 110. He changed the tide England's way at the outset of the Test match at Brisbane in 1936; three wickets, including Hammond's, had gone for about twenty runs. Leyland made 126. On the fearsome 'sticky' wicket at Melbourne, also in the 1936–7 tour, he held England's third wicket with Hammond, frustrating the flying gyrating balls mainly with buttocks and shoulder-blades. His position in the batting order of England was usually as late as No. 6, so powerful was the advance guard. When Grimmett saw him emerging from the dark cavern of the players' pavilion at Kennington Oval in 1934, carrying his bat under his arm and fixing his gloves, he called to O'Reilly, saying: 'Cripes, Bill! This innings seems to me to be starting all over again!'

There are batsmen whose command over technique is so complete that it evokes a sense of a classic impersonality; we admire an innings by Hobbs as a musician admires the music of Bach; that is, he listens to it *as* music and not for revelations of Bach's private emotion. An innings by Leyland was as true to his character and told you as much of his many humours as his speech and countenance. He put his nature into every stroke, and as soon as he had 'got bowling where he wanted it,' he didn't merely hit or drive it—he walloped it. Nothing could shake him out of his Yorkshire citadel of nature. At Sydney, when he was retrieving a dangerous position, the crowd on the Hill 'barracked' him. ' 'It 'em!' they howled without originality. After he had once again frustrated O'Reilly, he came back to the pavilion very contented. 'Hey,' he said, 'just fancy. Them poor chaps on t' Hill; Ah could hardly hear 'em—they should come and have some choir practice at Sheffield next August Bank Holiday.' At Brisbane in 1936 Australia's second innings began in a shocking light. Fingleton at once appealed but, strange to say, an Australian umpire replied in the negative; whereat Voce clean bowled Fingleton. The next batsman also appealed and again the umpire turned him down. By now darkness had fallen over the earth and a third appeal was allowed. As the players walked towards the pavilion, Leyland spoke to the umpire who had rejected Fingleton's appeal. 'Tha's got good eyesight,' he said. (Imagine, as I tell this story, that all the time the players are getting nearer and nearer the pavilion.) 'I don't want any sarcasm,' replied the umpire. 'Nay,' continued Leyland. 'Ah'm not bein' sarcastic. Ah'm only complimentin' thi on thi eyesight. It's not everybody as can see in dark like a cat.' (They are within a yard or two of the entrance to the dressing-room.) 'Hey,' asked Leyland, addressing the same umpire, 'is that where t'gate is?'

He belonged to the happy breed of cricketers which in a properly ordered universe would be permitted to go on playing the game until the spirit in them was tired and the fount of their fun was dried up; it is all wrong that they should have to submit to a physical test of endurance and toe a line of constant technical efficiency. When they leave us they leave behind a vacancy in nature. Fortunately in Yorkshire these vacancies are usually filled by a man of the right kind and blood, so that Bobby Peel succeeded unto Tom Emmett, George Hirst unto Bobby Peel, Roy Kilner unto George Hirst,

Maurice Leyland unto Roy Kilner and now, Johnnie Wardle has walked in the ways of Maurice Leyland, larding the more or less green earth of Yorkshire's cricket fields.

BARNES AND O'REILLY

UNTIL a few years ago, all cricketers who had played contemporaneously with S. F. Barnes agreed that he was the greatest bowler of his century on all wickets. C. B. Fry found him less problematical on a good turf than he found George Lohmann the only other qualified opinion about Barnes's bowling was that of 'Sammy' Carter, the Australian wicket-keeper, who once told me that he seldom was worried overmuch by Barnes; and he spoke thus strictly as a batsman. It is a fact of history that Carter batted 25 times against an England attack containing Barnes, scoring 591 runs, average 27 and over; and Barnes got him out only seven times But the batsman who came closest to mastery over Barnes was H. W. Taylor, the South African; moreover this partial mastery was established on matting in South Africa. Barnes on the mat was probably as unplayable as mortal bowler has ever been; everybody except Taylor were helpless before him in the South African season of 1913–14. No South African batsman except Taylor could survive Barnes's attack except momentarily and by the skin of his teeth. Yet Taylor in ten Test match innings scored 508 runs average 50·80 playing Barnes by means of wonderful footwork. If it is logical to assume that the test of the greatest batsman is his performances and style against the acknowledged greatest bowler, then H. W. Taylor at his best must be reckoned a master comparable in versatility and resource to Hobbs and George Headley.

Bradman one day argued with me that O'Reilly was probably Barnes's superior as a bowler of the medium pace order. O'Reilly bowled on the whole on wickets which match by match were more favourable to batsmen than wickets were day by day in Barnes' period. We must remember that Barnes bowled in three-day Test matches in England; and the wickets for these short-lived games were not especially prepared. Bradman's principal point in this O'Reilly and Barnes comparison was that O'Reilly controlled all the tricks known to Barnes—length, spin, flight and so on—and also he could bowl the 'googly', which Barnes couldn't. Not long ago I met Barnes and put before him Bradman's argument. 'It's quite true,' he admitted, 'I never bowled the "googly".' Then, after a pause and a twinkle in his keen steely eyes, he added: 'I never needed it.' Barnes in Test matches against Australia took 106 wickets for 2,288 runs in 958 overs and one ball, average 21·58. O'Reilly in Test matches against England took 102 wickets for 2,616 runs in 1,228 overs, average 25·64. The main opposition to Barnes was from Trumper, Hill, Noble, Armstrong, S. E. Gregory, Bardsley, Kelleway, Macartney and Ransford. The main opposition to O'Reilly was from Hammond, Sutcliffe, Leyland, Paynter, Hutton, Jardine, Hendren, Walters and Compton. On paper there is little to choose between the two bowlers, but it cannot be insisted on too strongly that O'Reilly had to get his wickets on pitches which were consistently more favourable for batting than those of Barnes's period, notably in England. But when we examine Test match performances we find that of the 106 Australian wickets falling to Barnes in his careet, only 29 were taken in England, average 19·67. In Test matches played in Australia Barnes took 77 wickets at 22·03 each. O'Reilly obviously needed to labour with more patience than any suffered by Barnes, for the simple reason that Test cricket in Barnes's day had not yet developed into a dour war of attrition between bat and ball. Cricketers bred before 1914 were always prepared to take a fair chance to exercise a favourite scoring stroke. Trumper, Macartney, Hill, Armstrong, Ransford, S. E. Gregory— all of them were as eager to hit a ball at all loose in length as they were to defend sensibly against a good ball. I think most of us possessing any historical sense would prefer to bowl at Trumper and Macartney and Hill than at Hammond, Sutcliffe and Hutton.

It is, of course, useless to compare cricketers of different periods, each a master in the material conditions in which he was nurtured. But technique is not everything, even though it is probably three parts of the job. Temperament has its sway. Barnes sometimes allowed his fires to burn without flame—like Lockwood. He was prone to moods wilfully unproductive. Sometimes he bowled like a mercenary. As Mr. H. S. Altham writes in his classic history, Barnes was liable to vary 'between days of irresistible success and others, when his temperament got the better of him, with disastrous results.' This criticism applies most to Barnes as he bowled during his brief experience of day-by-day county cricket when he was in the Lancashire XI. He preferred the easy and not less economically profitable life of a league professional. There was something Mephistophelian about him; he did not play cricket out of love of the game or any idealism. He was the living image in flannels of the 'Spirit of Denial'. He considered that his talents were worth paying for in cash. Those who never saw Barnes on the field of play will get a faint impression of his inimical personality from the painting of him now on view in the Long Room at Lord's—though it is not so much a portrait as a study in still-life. The artist has none the less caught, even though faintly, the suggestion which Barnes always gave of a man aloof, sure of himself, whether planning to do his best or his second best. Barnes seldom seemed one of eleven fellow cricketers: it was a case of Lancashire 'with Barnes'; or of England 'with Barnes'. In his old age he has mellowed. The battle is over for him; there are no spoils for him. I spoke with him not a year ago: he is wonderfully preserved, tall, upright, not at all octogenarian in physical appearance or in his view of man's existence. His humour is, as might have been expected, pungent and cynical. In the Trent Bridge pavilion in 1948 he looked through the long wide windows while the Test match between England and Australia was going on. For half an hour he watched without uttering a word, sucking at his pipe. Then he broke silence: 'Why do these bowlers send down so many balls the batsmen needn't play? I didn't.' Somebody bowled a full-toss. 'Did you ever bowl full-tosses?' he was asked. 'I never had the strength,' he replied.

In Barnes's heyday his best ball was known as the 'Barnes ball'. It pitched on the stumps between leg and middle, and then turned to threaten the off-stump or find the edge of the quickest bat. We must now consider this 'Barnes ball', in the light of historical criticism. When Barnes began to arrive at mastery, the main direction of English bowling was towards the middle and off-stumps and, as a snare for a slip catch, outside the off-stump. There was not much leg-spin in circulation then; Braund and Vine were pioneers. Most of the other leg-break bowlers were used as a last resort to break a long partnership; the stuff they bowled was called 'donkey drops'. 'Wisden' actually found fault with Barnes when he played first in county cricket regularly; apparently, objected 'Wisden', 'he has no off-break'. For any bowler of medium pace to lack an off-break in and round about 1900–02 was as though an army of the period lacked infantry. Indeed it is easy to understand that any bowler who seemed often to pitch the ball near the leg-stump would fall under critical suspicion half a century ago. And it is possible that until Barnes had thoroughly brought his master ball under control it was often severely thrashed and made to look as thought related to that very kind of leg-side bowling disapproved of by the pedants. We can without effort imagine the immediate effect of the 'Barnes ball' on batsmen educated in the left foot forward principle, batsmen brought up to believe that it was sinful to cover the wickets deliberately with the pads, batsmen who had seldom had occasion to play back with the right foot first of all moving towards the off wicket. Whether Barnes caused the ball to turn from leg to off by spin or, to use the strange language of the present day, by 'cutting' under the seam, is a matter of academic conjecture. Barnes himself has told me that he actually turned the ball off the pitch by 'finger twist'. In any case, I have never been able to understand the modern theory of 'seam' bowling; how it is possible to cause a ball to break or have bias 'off the seam'; how could it be possible to manipulate a ball in motion in such a way that the 'seam' remained in a certain desired position? Spin is as comprehensible theoretically as it is workable in practice. A schoolboy is able to understand that given a twist by the hand or finger in a certain way, the ball will on pitching turn accordingly, observing a principle of rotation. Neither metaphysics nor mathematics can explain how a ball can purposely be made to turn off the seam, with the break or bias controlled to go one way or the other.

A. C. MacLaren, on the strength of half an hour's personal experience of Barnes in the nets at Old Trafford, invited Barnes to accompany the team going to Australia in 1901–02 under his captaincy. Barnes had made a name already in the Lancashire league; but several years earlier, sometime in the remote late 1890's, he had bowled with little distinction for Warwickshire. Barnes was from his first overs in Australia a man to be feared. He caught and bowled Trumper for 2; and took 5 for 65 the first time he played in a Test match. The ground was Sydney. England won by an innings and 124. In the next and second Test match, Barnes took 13 wickets for 163—6 for 42, and 7 for 121. Then he broke down at the knee and took no further part in the rubber, which MacLaren's team lost by four games to one. For a variety of reasons he was not chosen to play in the Test matches in England in 1902 until the third, at Sheffield; and now he took 6 for 49 and 1 for 50. It is as certain as anything conjecturable can be about cricket that had he played in the fourth Test match in 1902, England would not have lost by 3 runs.

His preference of the rewards and indolences of League cricket is the reason why the greatest bowler of the age did not reappear in the England XI between 1902 and 1907. He did not go to Australia with Warner's team of 1903–04; he did not play for England in the 1905 rubber in England. He remained aloof from the International scene until December 1907 and suffered a set-back in reputation by taking 1 for 74 and 2 for 63 at Sydney. In this rubber —1907–08—he was third in the England Test match averages, J. N. Crawford and Fielder above him. Yet Barnes's figures were impressive enough: 24 wickets at 26·08 each. When Australia visited England in 1909, Barnes played in the third, fourth and fifth Test matches, and henceforward until the war of 1914 ended his first-class career, the Australians were never rid of the bowler whom they all agreed was the world's greatest, since their own Spofforth.

His supremacy was established for all time at Melbourne in December 1911. The England XI should have had Warner as captain; but 'Plum' fell distressingly ill and J. W. H. T. Douglas was leader. The first Test match had been lost at Sydney; Barnes sulked, with some point, because he was not asked to open England's bowling, Douglas beginning with F. R. Foster. At Melbourne, Australia batted first and Barnes opened with Foster. He staggered the entire world of cricket; he reduced the contemporary giants of Australian cricket for a while to a pitiful smallness of stature and insecurity of tenure. Australia lost six wickets for 38 on a perfect pitch; Barnes bowled as marvellously as anybody since Spofforth bowled in the 1882 'Ashes' match at Kennington Oval; his analysis at one stage of the incredible proceedings was;

11 overs; 7 maidens; 6 runs; 5 wickets.

The batsmen he devoured were Kelleway, Bardsley, Hill, Armstrong and Minnett. Clem Hill, who was bowled Barnes for 4 first innings, and caught by George Gunn off Barnes 0 second innings, spoke with feeling to me about Barnes's attack this day, years after the event. 'Some of us carried blue and yellow bruises on our thighs for days. He made them come faster from the pitch than Foster did and Foster was faster through the air.' At least so it seemed to Hill. The destruction by Barnes at Melbourne in his finest hour was done by length and spin, the ball sent down from a height, with the

'Barnes ball' artfully concealed. In Australia, Barnes usually bowled slightly slower than in England; all the more impressive then is the opinion of Hill, suggesting deceptive pace and sudden accelerations.

Barnes remained a dangerous bowler long after he was obliged to give up first-class cricket. The West Indies team of 1928 played against him in a club match, and they thought he was the best they had encountered all the summer; Barnes was well beyond 50 then. His hatchet face and his hint of a physical leanness and an unsentimental mind were part and parcel of his cricket, which is perhaps best described by the word 'unrelenting'. In the depth of an English winter I ran into him in a Manchester street and fog. He was wearing the lightest overcoat and during a brief talk he, as though by habit and not knowing what he was doing, brought from a pocket a cricket ball and began instinctively to fondle it, twist it, roll his long sinuous fingers round it. 'Keeps me in practice,' he explained.

W. J. ('Bill') O'Reilly, though known to his Australian colleagues as 'The Tiger', was really a genial soul, off the field. He would readily admit that he counted many a batsman amongst his friends, and was always willing to share a drink and a chat; but 'out there, in the middle, on the field of play, they were my enemies, and I hated the sight of them.' There was nothing about O'Reilly of the sinister reserve-power of Barnes. He bowled with obvious effort. He ran to the crease as though up the slant of the deck of a ship tossing in a heavy swell; his arms as they flailed the air seemed likely to upset all accuracy of aim. He ran to bowl as though in the face of a wind; yet in spite of an action not at all classical he was, in certain fundamentals, a classical bowler. He had the classic precision, the classic firmness of purpose; for at the last convulsive moment in his arm's swing over, all his energy became concentrated into the classic forms; length and direction. The fact that he bowled a 'googly' did not lead to impurity or unsteadiness of style. Technically, the bowling of O'Reilly was a constant tribute to and justification of the old-time gospel: accuracy, persistence, integrity. Now and again the strong, steady outlines of his craft would seem to shake and shudder. Down would bend his head and an abrupt fast ball of temper would be hurled at the wicket: the 'Irish' of O'Reilly was coming out now. A straight drive from a good ball from him—a smack in the face—sent him into a regular 'paddy'. Adversity and opposition did not weaken but toughened his character and spirit. Of all his fine performances as an Australian bowler, none was more to his credit, as man and cricketer, than his 59 overs

137

at Old Trafford in the rubber of 1934; he took 7 wickets for 189 in an English innings that amassed 627 runs for 9 wickets, innings declared. The weather was hot. In Manchester the thermometer achieved nearly 90 degrees. One or two Australians, including a Queenslander, were indisposed because of incipient sunstroke. The match began, as it ended, in a furnace of sunny heat. England won the toss and on a wicket which was a batsman's couch of sensual indolence, a wicket stuffed and cushioned with runs, C. F. Walters batted with the magnificent arrogance and authority of MacLaren himself. Sutcliffe at his best followed in Walters's imperial course, holding his train of robes, so to say. Sixty-eight runs were made at will; then O'Reilly in one over dismissed Walters, Wyatt and Hammond for four runs. O'Reilly's 'tail' was seen, by the eye of imagination, to stick up gleefully and avariciously. But Hendren and Leyland frustrated him in a long stand; Hendren scored 132, Leyland 153, and after O'Reilly broke the partnership Ames hit brilliantly for 72. O'Reilly never lost heart or vigour or tenacity; under the sweltering sun he rolled, lumbered, cartwheeled to the wicket, over after over. His balding head shone in the heat; he sweated and cursed, yet all the time he was the personification of Bacchic indulgence, paradoxically mingled with a Spartan austerity and devotion to a laborious toil and duty. At Kennington Oval in August 1938 he was again obliged to carry the cross of affliction and ineffectuality. Hutton scored 364, England closed the innings at the aggregate of 903 for 7; O'Reilly bowled 85 overs, 26 maidens, 178 runs for 3 wickets. He played no more in Test matches. Would Barnes have borne as much impotent servility as this? Can a master ever submit to the enforced labour of a galley slave? Barnes, like Achilles but in different circumstances, might have sulked in his tent. So—which was the greater of the two, as cricketer and man and uncompromising spirit—Barnes or O'Reilly?

MY IDEAL TEAM

My ideal cricket team is one which presents or sums-up all of the game's resources of skill and variety of style, the sort of team of which you would say to somebody fresh to cricket and willing to love it: 'There, now watch these players, and in turn they will reveal to you the game's full and ripe content, with every department functioning: brilliance of strokeplay, solidity of defence, fast and slow bowling, swerve with new ball, spin with the old, expert and beautiful fielding everywhere—and everybody a character living and expressing himself by and through bat or ball.' An artistic team, an encyclopædic team!—and England has never known one which as closely answered to this description as the one assembled at Birmingham in May 1902: A. C. MacLaren, C. B. Fry, K. S. Ranjitsinhji, F. S. Jackson, Tyldesley, Lilley, Hirst, G. L. Jessop, Braund, Lockwood, Rhodes. Could omnipotence improve on this XI as a Platonic idea or representation of all the known parts and attributes of cricket, a perfect synthesis? The most majestic of batsmen is there, the most scientific batsman is there, the most magical of all batsmen is there. One of the most aristocratic batsmen in his outlook and manner is there, the Hon. F. S. Jackson, who was also a superb off-spinner. The most incisive stroke player of the period was there, J. T. Tyldesley himself. Lilley was a wicket-keeper who could truly be called an organised batsman. George Hirst, one of cricket's greatest all-round players, was also one of the greatest men Yorkshire has so far given to the world. There was Jessop, too, the most astonishing of all cricketers ever born, a scientific quick scorer, a whirlwind of strokes which revolved round a point of calm ruthlessly punitive judgment. There was Braund, a leg-spinner and a sound batsman, and also one of cricket's most lithe and remarkable slip fieldsmen. There was Lockwood, whom Ranjitsinhji maintained was the greatest of all fast bowlers in his experience. And, in last, was the legendary Rhodes, the finest slow left-hand bowler alive in 1902, excepting only Blythe of Kent, and already a batsman good enough secretly to say to himself 'one day I shall open an England innings,' which he one day truly did, to the extent of sharing a first wicket partnership with Hobbs amounting to 323.

The England XI at Birmingham in 1902 was, I say, a kind of image or reflection of cricket's essential and finest attributes; every technical excellent was represented by a cricketer whom in his particular capacity God Himself would find it hard to improve upon; for each of them seemed the fully consummated technical exponent and natural apogee of his particular method.

In more recent years I have seen only one other England team which approached this Birmingham one; bear in mind I am not discussing these ideal XI's according to competitive values alone.

England lost the rubber in 1902. I am putting forward combinations of cricketers which revealed the ripeness and variety of cricket at a given period, and revealed the ripeness and variety in a representational way fit to be laid up in heaven, so that after all flesh shall have returned to dust, the angels would be able to understand why, amongst games of the open air, cricket stood first for beauty, skill and the revelation of English character. And here is my contemporary XI to vie with the classic contingent of 1902: Hobbs, Sutcliffe, Hammond, A. P. F. Chapman, Hendren, D. R. Jardine, Geary, Tate, Larwood, J. C. White and Duckworth, a team which played at Melbourne in December 1928. It is not, on paper, as authoritative and convincing as the Birmingham XI; but I can think of no other that sets off to better advantage the qualities of English cricket of a later day. I am therefore tempted to throw in the England XI's at Lord's in 1930, and at the Oval in 1938: (1930)—Hobbs, Woolley, Hammond, Duleepsinhji, Hendren, A. P. F. Chapman, G. O. Allen, R. W. V. Robins, Tate, J. C. White and Duckworth; (1938)—Hutton, W. J. Edrich, Leyland, W. R. Hammond, Paynter, Compton, Hardstaff, Wood, Verity, K. Farnes and Bowes. Maybe these comparisons are odious, but they will illustrate my point; there are more things in the game of cricket than are dreamt of in the economy of the scorers.

A game, like anything else, loses in health and vitality when any part becomes greater, or is made to appear more prominent, than the whole. At the present time, 1955, it is possible to watch a first-class cricket match all day and see little bowling that is not quick or dependent on 'swing' or swerve. It is possible to watch batsmen all day and not see a cut or a full-shouldered straight drive. It is possible to go to a country ground a whole week and not see a really clever leg-spin bowler, unless you are a Kentish man. In the early decades of first-class cricket there was not much to admire aesthetically except the pendulum push forward of the bat alongside the left foot, to pace and off-spin. The game had not yet been subtilized and fertilized by the invention of the 'googly' and the development of leg-spin. Cricket was at its greatest between 1902 and 1930; for during these years every known department of play and skill was practised and brought to the point of fine individual art. Since 1946, decadence has set in, the decadence that occurs whenever specialism elaborates one particular trick or trait to the hurt of the balance of the whole. Until the other day there was hardly a fast bowler in England of unquestionable rank; there is still only one or two slow left-arm spinners. It is all 'swing' the ball 'that deviates from the seam' to use the phraseology of the hour. We hear of green wickets. What was the colour of the Old Trafford wicket in the 1900's, when Tyldesley one summer scored 3,000 runs, average nearly 60, with half his innings played on turf so peculiar in texture that small pebbles came to the surface?

I am not one of those who praise the past and neglect the joys of the present. Much in life nowadays is more happily adapted to human needs than ever before. In the realm of imagination progress is a word with no meaning; none the less it is fair and rational to say that in the technical distribution and ordering of artistic pleasure there has been a vast improvement since most middle-aged folk today were in their twenties. Orchestras play more correctly and musically than of yore. Taste in all directions has lost much of crudity. Books are better written in general than in the recent past. Acting in the theatre is less unnatural and spurious. The Vienna Opera in its palmiest days could not produce women singers as lovely to look at and as lovely to hear as the contemporary Seefried, della Casa, Jurinac, Grünig. I shall not be suspected, then, of the sentimental backward-glance that cannot appreciate quality under one's nose, if I confess that there are only two cricketers of today whom *I* would wish to see in, or could imagine surviving contrast amongst the company of, the immortals of the England XI at Birmingham in 1902. Their names are Compton and Evans. And how could we fit them in?—who throw out for them? MacLaren, Fry, 'Ranji', Jackson, even for Denis? *Who* could choose rightly and happily between Tyldesley and Compton? For functional reasons Compton could not take any of the places held by Braund, Hirst, Jessop, Lockwood and Rhodes. I am not sure, even, that MacLaren or any other England captain of the period would willingly agree to the substitution of Evans for Lilley as a safe experienced wicket-keeper and a really sound batsman into the bargain. If the reader asks why I select Compton from all present day cricketers as the only batsman we could conceivably squeeze into the Birmingham XI, at risk of injustice to a recognized immortal, my answer is, 'Try any other name of today,' and remember that we are dealing with an England team which, second to none, exhibited the multifarious attributes of the game, and enshrined cricket's technical genius fully and proportionately, every player a master in his own way, and an artist. Moreover, bear in mind that this XI was picked to win, if possible, a three-day Test match and to lose it at no cost to cricket's

141

pride in spectacle, its gusto of enjoyment, and its scope for the free play of character. If anybody, properly jealous of individual performance of today or the latest hour, imagines that Tyson or Statham might adequately wear Lockwood's boots as fast bowler he will be chastened to learn that in 1902 Lockwood was not only England's greatest fast bowler but also in the same summer scored a century for the Players against the Gentlemen at Lord's.

It is of course vain if fascinating to compare in the abstract great players of different periods. The environment, technically and psychologically, changes; the tools of the game, as we have seen, change also. The modern sceptics argue that W. G. Grace was never called on to cope with the 'googly' or elaborate leg-spin. But he was able to cope with fast 'shooters' on rough pitches; in fact he was easy master of every trick of the bowler's trade known in his day. We must assume that once he had scrutinized the 'googly' he would have found the right answer. It is the fact, none the less, that batsmen of the so-called 'Golden Age' were on the whole called on to solve fewer problems of attack than those presented nowadays in first-class cricket. Grace, Stoddart, Shrewsbury, MacLaren, Hayward and other 'Old Masters' needed only or mainly to deal with speed and off-spin on good wickets. Moreover methods of defensive and offensive field-placing were not then as flexible and tactical as now. No leg-traps for Ranji's glance; none for an off-spinner even on a turning jumping pitch. Seldom did off-spin bowlers, as I have pointed out elsewhere in this book, attack from round the wicket. No swerve, or very little deliberate swerve, except from Hirst, who was perhaps a more dangerous bowler when he was bringing the ball back, left-hand, from leg-stump to off. No new ball until the end of the longest innings, unless, as John Gunn has said, 't'owd 'un coom in two.'

Extraordinary talent will in all circumstances find its way; a Hutton will assert his superiority over average ability in any period. But I am not sure that all the old-time dashing batsmen, trusting to long-lengthened hits at the pitch of the ball, would survive for long against ordinary new ball bowlers of today, such as Gladwin, Jackson, Shackleton. They lacked organised defences; they played the game more by faith than by reason—and faith is not certain to move an outswinger out of harm's way. Cricketers nowadays may be too theoretical: many of the swashbuckling amateur batsmen of the past lacked fundamental brainwork. Look at the photos of them, in their pretty blazers. There is no speculation in their eyes. When

142

Richard Tyldesley saw them coming in to bat, after hours of sweaty labour spent getting rid of the Meads and Hendrens and Whysalls and Gunns, he would go to his captain and say: 'Let's have another bowl at pavilion end, skipper. Coloured caps is comin' in.' The advent of the 'googly' was a death knell in the ears of rabid adherents of the left leg forward method of batting, the majestic sweep to the pitch of the ball. A. C. MacLaren and R. E. Foster both expressed apprehension upon the influence of the new bowling and feared it would ruin 'style' and free play to the offside. Several fine players, notably Rhodes, changed stance and moved the right foot over towards the off-stump as a means of providing a second, sometimes a first line, of defence against the last-second gyration of the 'wrong 'un'. It is a mistake to suppose—and I make this point again for the sake of emphasis—that all the master-batsmen brought up in the Golden Age were at a loss to deal with the 'googly'; even a stylist as beautifully poised as R. H. Spooner scored happily enough against the South African spell-binders. But Spooner, like Tyldesley, played a good deal from the back foot; both these swift scoring batsmen were at bottom sound in defence. I spoke once to A. C. MacLaren about J. T. Tyldesley. 'It is amazing,' I said, 'that he can keep it up on all sorts of wickets, scoring thirty or forty an hour, taking risks.' MacLaren replied, 'But Johnny is as sound as a rock to a good ball; he is really a very correct player.' This view of the D'Artagnan of cricket was not orthodox, but I could see the virtue of the exaggeration. George Gunn also found the 'googly' an easily soluble problem. He simply walked out to it and, as he says, 'played with tide'. 'There's a lot of nonsense said about battin',' he has often told me, 'and really there's not much to it. If it's a straight ball, no matter how fast, play it with straight bat. If it turns from off, play it with break to on; if it turns from leg play it with break t'other way. Hey, dear, batsmen have always made two serious mistakes, always have made 'em as far as I know; and I began playin' when Doctor Grace were still in game. First of all, they take too much notice of state of wicket, pokin' and proddin'. Then—and I thinks this is more serious still—they take too much notice of bowlin'.'

The influence of the 'googly' has not been at all to the bad. On the contrary it has enriched technique all round; it has, so to say, added to cricket's orchestration. It certainly helped to develop on-side strokes and encouraged close study of direction and flight, making for the delayed stroke. (All great batsmen play the ball

143

'late'.) Besides, 'googly' bowling when practised by a master is in itself a pleasure to watch. To see a Grimmett at work, a Dooland, a Fleetwood-Smith, is stimulating to the imagination of all lovers and students of cricket; here are personal skill and guile in excelsis. 'Swing' bowling is different and boring to see because it is more or less a mechanical exploitation of tools of the game, the seam of the ball, the 'green' of the turf, and all the rest of the jargon. The great leg-spin and 'googly' bowlers were artists and so much in love with the work of their own prehensile fingers that they would bowl for the delight of observing their own handiwork, whether it was being hit or whether in the materialistic eyes of the scorers it was being 'successful'.

To what extent has 'googly' and swerve bowling been responsible for the decline (if any) of great stroke players? I saw nearly all the renowned batsmen of the 'Golden' or pre-'googly' age—MacLaren, Trumper, Ranjitsinhji, Fry, Tyldesley, Spooner, Palairet, Hayward, R. E. Foster, Jackson. I am not prepared to swear on oath that these players were vastly superior in range of strokes or more fascinating to watch than the following, all of whom had to tackle the new bowling, 'googly' and 'swing' at its best: Hobbs, Headley, Hammond, Woolley, Macartney, Donnelly, Merchant, Kippax, Bradman, Duleepsinhji, Compton, McCabe, Worrell, C. F. Walters, Harvey, not to mention Bakewell of Northamptonshire. Technique in cricket must alter when it alteration finds; it evolves by cut-and-thrust, check and checkmate. Now the batsman is on top, now the bowler. In the development of technical tricks of the trade, action and reaction are equal and opposite. When I was a boy off-theory was supposed to be spoiling the game. Today leg-theory is the bane. The genius of great players will lead the way out of every apparent technical cul-de-sac.

My own view is that cricket can be spoiled temporarily and rendered tedious only by a wrong mental approach on the part of players, spectators and press. If imaginative sport is demanded, with the exponents free to give full play to their natural gifts, the right atmosphere of inducement will be produced in consequence of that demand. If the rewards of competition are the *main* desire, victories in rubbers and county championships, then cricket will respond to materialistic stimuli and incitement. It is as simple as all that.

THE YOUNG MEN TAKE OVER

THE intense blue of the sky over Sydney and the glare of the sunshine have always seemed to me as alien to the English spirit of cricket as the city of Sydney itself seems somehow foreign to an Englishman, even to one who like myself has lived in Sydney for years at a stretch. It is not a sky of soft shades or changes; it is not a sunshine that is often yielding or genial. Sydney and Australian cricket in general are seldom soft, yielding or genial. There have been of course many Australian batsmen of brilliance and daring—Trumper, Macartney, McCabe, Bradman, Ransford, Kippax, Jackson, Harvey, Miller; but there has never been an Australian Spooner or Woolley or Palairet. The brilliance and gallantry of Australian cricket at its gayest is aggressive and hard and inimical at bottom: no art for art's sake about it. The most beautiful shot of a Trumper is meant to kill. Yet there was some graciousness about Trumper as there was charm in an innings by Kippax.

When I saw the M.C.C. team at Sydney taking the field against New South Wales in the first weeks of Hutton's campaign, an odd feeling or impression came back to me, an impression that these cricketers from England were in a strange element, not to say dimension. Frankly if I were a gifted young batsman—Colin Cowdrey for example—I confess I might suffer at least a twinge of nervous discomfort to find myself exposed in the middle of Sydney's field, exposed to sun that strips from you your natural shadow at high noon, exposed to the unsmiling presence of Australian cricketers—for if they do smile from time to time there is as much of satire and grimness of intention in the humour as there is amiability. There is the crowd, too, variable of mood, very vocal, sometimes hysterical when women scream if a batsman is nearly run out.

A great game responds to the environment in which it lives and finds being, as during this book we have once or twice agreed. In Australia there are not as many variations in topographical atmosphere, psychology or type as in England. The Adelaide character is quieter than Sydney's. Melbourne looks down its nose on the social scene of the rest of the continent. Yet even in Australia cricket changes in style according to pressure of environment and habit of living. Nearly all the brilliant Australian strokeplayers, the buccaneers and conquistadors, have come from brash garish Sydney.

145

From Victoria and Melbourne have emerged the solid safe, usually reliable and temperate Woodfulls, Ponsfords, Armstrongs; and the educated not to say refined Ransfords and Harveys. Deviation from type naturally happens from time to time. It is easy, for instance, to forget that Keith Miller was born in Victoria. He now lives in Sydney, and is the personification of the casual 'Sydney-sider'. Sydney has assimilated Miller and whipped Victorian suburbanisms out of him.

I was especially struck by contrast of the English flavour and the Australian setting of brittle brightness and toughness, when I saw young Cowdrey batting for the first time at Sydney. He came to the wicket at a moment of incipient crisis; four of the M.C.C.'s batsmen had been got out for less than 40 by New South Wales. He at once began to play with assurance and composure, body over the ball. But all the time there was in his cricket and his demeanour a suggestion of modesty. In Cowdrey's first innings at Sydney he scored a century and hit sixteen boundaries; and not once did he make an ill-bred or boastful gesture. Next day a young Australian name of Watson, playing his second innings in first-class cricket, also scored a century, with a cocksureness as unmistakable Australian as the voices which over the radio speak the praises of the newest sewing-machines or the most glamorous of procurable wedding-rings.

Not since the period of A. C. MacLaren and R. E. Foster has a young English amateur batsman come to Sydney and straightway attained to Cowdrey's power and reputation; he scored two hundreds in the game of his baptism to this great cricket field, happy ground once of Victor Trumper. I have for some time past held the opinion that Cowdrey is a thoroughbred batsman likely to go even beyond the scope of P. B. H. May. He plays extremely close to the line of the ball and in a period of cricketers of peculiarly lightweight brains he is capable of concentration. He proved the firmness of his nerve in all the sudden challenges made to him in Australia, at Sydney against New South Wales, at Brisbane when he was obliged to go out to bat for the first time for England against Australia with wickets already falling and Hutton amongst the slain; at Sydney in the second Test match, where with May he coped with advancing odds and turned bankruptcy into a going concern once more; then at Melbourne where he scored 102 out of England's 191 all out, after he had gone to the wicket when the score was 21 for 2. In three consecutive matches introducing him to the ordeal of Test cricket in Australia, Cowdrey had to face the music of these scores and situations: 11 for 3, 147 for 3, 58 for 3, 55 for 3, and 21 for 2. I cannot remember that any young cricketer has been subjected to more severe strains on nerve and character than these faced calmly and almost confidently by Cowdrey. At Melbourne, while he cleared the air for England of crisis and took charge of the two ends of the wicket, safeguarding colleagues far older than himself in years and experience, he moved towards his century as though unaware of the scoreboard's existence. It is, in fact, a curious feature of Cowdrey's batting that in the middle of an innings, after he has been on view some two hours and apparently has solved all the problems contained in the bowling and has got it at his mercy—he will then inexplicably lapse into a sort of sulky inactivity. His strokes lose animation; they merely defend ball by ball; it is as though a quick-minded conversationalist had become wilfully monosyllabic. There is probably a certain want of elasticity at present in Cowdrey's psychological and physical make-up; time will bring freedom here, then he will—or should—develop to true greatness. Already he has batted against Australia with a mastery not shared by merely talented players; also he vindicated the classic front foot forward method. W. J. O'Reilly described Cowdrey's 102 at Melbourne as 'one of the finest centuries I have seen in Test matches.' It was made out of a total of 160 scored while Cowdrey was at the wicket in roughly four and a half hours. Cricketers will realize how accurately he calculated the Australian attack ball by ball when it is known that he hit no fewer than fifteen boundaries. Nearly half a century ago, also at Melbourne, K. L. Hutchings, another Kent cricketer, scored 120 against Australia and batted only two hours, and he hit one sixer and twenty-five fours. Critics writing today of Cowdrey are agreed that he reminds them in style and appearance of W. R. Hammond; there is certainly a resemblance of shoulders, movement between wickets, a thick-set dark cast of countenance, and of brilliance of cover drive. But I like to think that something of the swift feline spring and blood of Hutchings will descend to Cowdrey biologically and by virtue of Kentish birth.

He was only a month or two beyond his twenty-second birthday when at Melbourne on the last day of 1954 he wrote his name on the roll of cricket's immortals. He reached his hundred while the vast crowd roared admiration at him with a persistence, resonance and fervour not exceeded even when Bradman completed his 100th century. Cowdrey began his masterpiece in the teeth of the best new ball bowling seen at Melbourne since S. F. Barnes, in 1911, bowled at Melbourne an hour and a half before lunch, taking 5 wickets for 9. Miller, on the occasion of the conception and advent of Cowdrey's 102 at Melbourne, bowled an hour and a half before lunch and took 3 wickets for 5 runs. Cowdrey stood firm to Miller's fast-medium in-swingers. He observed first principles and did not stretch for the ball; he played from where he could reach it and, when he couldn't reach it, he let it go harmlessly by. At Melbourne, as at Sydney on his debut there, his cricket had an 'older' look about it, so to say, than that of senior players such as Edrich, Compton, Simpson. He seldom was seen moving about uselessly; he remained still during change of overs, or he would inspect the pitch, not concernedly but rather as though for purposes of abstract botanical study. Sometimes he practised a straight bat along the line of the popping crease.

As I watched May and Cowdrey retrieving the half-lost Test match at Sydney in December, I enjoyed a private pleasure of a kind much to be treasured these days. I was looking, I thought, at a revival of amateur influence in English cricket, a restoration (as I hoped) of the amateur influence and example. For too long we have watched the increase of professional control. Frankly it has not all been to the good. The average professional cricketer is a fine sportsman and as good a fellow as the next; I have been a professional cricketer myself, so I know. But, such is nature, some of them have abused the power put their way by egalitarian tendencies recently current. They have used the game for personal if far-sighted commercial ends. They have neglected the fair hazards of a game, and have over-much studied personal achievement. Some of them have found in cricket a means to financial success in activities remote from cricket. Not a few of them have turned to advertisement and to authorship, employing 'ghost' writers who more or less are the same critics that in the Press day-by-day are supposed to deal faithfully with their 'principal's' prowess and performance.

When Lord Hawke uttered his famous cry from the heart he did not intend to disparage the character of the professional cricketer as he knew him in the period of Hirst, Tyldesley, Hobbs, J. T. Hearne, and Richardson. All he intended to suggest was that cricket would most likely lose much and suffer in spirit, style and flavour, if it ever became heavily dependent on the services of men bound to it as a means of livelihood. In the so-called 'Golden Age', the greatest batsmen were amateurs; the pace was set by the Graces,

MacLarens, Jacksons, 'Ranjis', Frys, Warners, Spooners. The professionals had to play at the same pace and in the same mood.

The resurgence of amateur cricket, signified by the batting in Australia of May and Cowdrey during Hutton's campaign, has already been worth any victory in any rubber. At Sydney in the second Test match, while May and Cowdrey grappled with an enveloping movement from the Australian attack and field, an atmosphere came into an England innings not at all familiar these last few years. The situation was dire in the extreme: England 74 behind had lost three wickets for 55 in their second innings, Hutton Bailey and Graveney out. The advance of Australia was resisted and eventually thrown back by means of batsmanship so skilful and nicely-poised that it could be appreciated without constant reference to the scoreboard. May and Cowdrey themselves obviously were relishing the way they were playing. There can be no art and no æsthetic pleasure conveyed if the art and the æsthetic pleasure do not begin at home; in other words if the executants are not the first to feel the throb of delight. For years has English cricket in Test matches suffered anxiety and looked unbeautiful; rarely indeed has the spirit of delight entered an England innings, whether it has been played against Australia, South Africa, New Zealand, India, the West Indies or Pakistan. Our leading batsmen have been put on the rack now by Lindwall and Miller, now by Ramadhin and Valentine, now by Tayfield, Goddard, Heine, Rowan and Mann, now by Mankad and now by Fazal.

The responsibilities of dual office have furrowed Hutton's cricket with lines of care. He is not by character a cricketer swift to the responses of rapturous visitation; and as England's most admired batsman he had been too frequently obliged to pilot an England innings in seasons of non-vintage batting. Hobbs, the Master, had with him the support and collaboration of such as Sutcliffe, Hendren, Hearne, Woolley, Hammond. Seldom during the Hutton régime has an England innings contributed to the gaiety of the nation; more often than not it has carried a heavy cross, and given no happiness, and provided little interest, except to the scorers and those folk for whom cricket is entirely a competitive game played wholly to obtain victory and inflict defeat. May and Cowdrey brought graciousness back to an England innings, and brought also the sting and confidence of youth, with youth's lovable and unself-conscious dignity. Each batsman drove beautifully in front of the wicket, so that agile and not convalescent fieldsmen were needed at cover-point and mid-on. This stand by Cowdrey and May at Sydney added 116; Cowdrey scored 54 and May went on almost eagerly to his first hundred against Australia. By proper cricket with strokes good to see, the stand put England in a position from which next day Tyson and Statham were able to storm a way to victory. Yet in spite of Tyson and Statham and Sydney's frisky turf, England would have lost this second Test match and the rubber, but for the superb batsmanship of May and Cowdrey in England's second innings. When Hutton got out in England's second innings, caught from a stroke to the slips from a slash at the swing of the ball —a stroke which would have made Emmott Robinson cross himself —the Australians leaped into the air as though the match were now over. And most of us shared their feelings of anticipation, though in certain cases it was rather the emotions of apprehension. May was faced now not only with impending disaster for England; also he had to fight his own uncertainty of mind based on a Test match experience not too assuring against Australia. Though I have watched much cricket in a lifetime, and have now withdrawn beyond the battle and can look at a match for long only if it transcends competitive interests and achieves personal touch of art, I confess that my heart thrilled with pride to see these two young cricketers taking charge at Sydney of a ravenous Australian attack; what is more, they played with art enough. As soon as the edge was gone from the attack, both May and Cowdrey performed drives as handsome as any seen in Australia for a decade. A moment of vision— two English players, almost unrazored, playing the game beautifully for England at Sydney, watched by eyes that long ago looked on MacLaren and R. E. Foster.

The tendency of first-class cricket since the decline in amateur influence has more and more been towards the development of protective skill and tactics justifiable by competitive results. I have never been interested in games as games, at least not since I grew out of adolescence. I have no time left to waste at my age watching batsmen supposedly first class who are afraid to display the game's great range of hits; and I have certainly no time for bowlers who out of fear of facing a fine batsman's range of strokes resort to this or that negative theory.

May and Cowdrey in Australia caused hope to awaken again in a heart that loved cricket the day a boy's eyes first looked at Hutchings and Spooner. The innings of May in the third Test match at Melbourne on 2nd January, a few days after May had celebrated his 25th birthday, was handsome with straight drives or drives to the off-side and the on. The swift power of his strokes reduced even Australian fieldsmen to open-eyed immobility. Lindwall was compelled to protect positions which nowadays are not always covered when a slow bowler is at work. And May's innings, like Cowdrey's first innings in the same match, began in an oppressive encircling gloom generated by the long-faced Old Brigade of English cricket. The game is for young men to play and inspire. Cricket was at its best when amateurs of May's present age had charge of it. MacLaren, Foster, Spooner, Jackson, 'Ranji', Fry were all in their heyday round about the mid-twenties of each!

FROM CRICKET ALL THE YEAR

MELBOURNE 1960

THE second Test match was exciting and incalculable throughout, and the end of it was for an Englishman so disappointing that even now, as I write of it long after the event, I still feel a certain sickness at heart. Merely a game?—maybe; but the spirit of irony can get at us not only in austere guise in this our life. On the losing morning the match was England's; only 151 needed for victory on a pitch that responded to spin but not at all viciously, eight wickets standing, Hutton unbeaten. Just before lunch, with but another batsman lost and Hutton still unbeaten and at his most masterful, 99 would have served. Dewes got out then, and Parkhouse, who was in next, rose superior to self-doubt and several horrible glimpses into the pit beyond the edge of the crease. He actually survived one hundred and two minutes, a crowning irony; for Hutton faltered a few overs after Parkhouse had, unsupported, walked out to face the music. England's score was 92 for four, 77 wanted. Hutton in charge 40, when W. Johnston bowled a quick ball a shade short on or near Hutton's leg-stump. Hutton, as anxious as the rest of us for the runs that would change agony to rejoicing, shaped to hit a four to the unprotected on-side boundary. (He had already driven Johnston in that direction once or twice and Hassett left the bait of an open field temptingly there while Johnston was bowling.) At the last split-second, Hutton apparently checked the swing of his bat across the line of the ball—and to begin with it was a very commanding swing, a vehement one for Hutton. The mistimed hit soared high and close to the square-leg umpire, and Lindwall ran a few yards but with an assurance and leisure dreadful to see. The suspense was all the more unbearable because we knew he wouldn't drop the catch; Hutton watched him like the rest of us; he was now no more an active and potent factor in the game but suddenly transformed into a helpless spectator. I shall remember this for many a long year; I couldn't believe my eyes. I saw the aggressive sweeping motion of Hutton's bat, an intended pulled-drive, his shoulders finely concentrated. Then I saw the hideous 'skier'. Naturally I said 'No-ball' to myself. Hutton simply doesn't

153

'sky' near the wicket; such a crudity does not come within the normal margin of error of his superb but mortal and therefore not infallible technique. The stroke could not be counted amongst his repertory of possible mistakes; you would have sworn in fact that Hutton could not have committed a stroke so primitive even if he had tried. If ever there was a great cricket match, this was it, of which we could safely say that one stroke and one ball settled the issue irrevocably, yet contrary to all logic and probability. As a last acid-tinctured barb, Bedser at the death was left standing high and dry, batting with the middle of his bat, playing forward as though guaranteed to be there for an hour at least, untroubled but lonely, for want of Hutton—victory only twenty-nine runs distant.

AUSTRALIA
First Innings

K. Archer, c Bedser, b Bailey	26
A. R. Morris, c Hutton, b Bedser	2
R. N. Harvey, c Evans, b Bedser	42
K. R. Miller, lbw, b Brown	18
A. L. Hassett, b Bailey	52
S. J. E. Loxton, c Evans, b Close	32
R. R. Lindwall, lbw, b Bailey	8
D. Tallon, not out	7
I. W. Johnson, c Parkhouse, b Bedser	0
W. A. Johnston, c Hutton, b Bedser	0
J. Iverson, b Bailey	1
Extras (b 4, lb 2)	6
Total	194

FALL OF WICKETS

1	2	3	4	5	6	7	8	9	10
6	67	89	93	177	177	192	193	193	194

BOWLING ANALYSIS

	O.	M.	R.	W.		O.	M.	R.	W.
Bailey	17·1	5	40	4	Brown	9	0	28	1
Bedser	19	3	37	4	Close	6	1	20	1
Wright	8	0	63	0					

ENGLAND

F. R. Brown, Hutton, Washbrook, R. T. Simpson, Wright, Close, Evans, T. E. Bailey, Bedser, Parkhouse and J. G. Dewes.

154

The struggle began three days before Christmas. Shortly before noon on Friday, 22nd December, as I walked to the ground through the rich foliage of the Fitzroy Gardens, a slight drizzle of rain sweetened the air but didn't discourage the hurrying throng which swept over the roadways and made for the entrances grim as an invading army. Though F. R. Brown lost the toss I couldn't feel entirely sorry; the atmosphere of the morning and the slight hint of an English 'greenness' in the wicket might again stimulate Bedser to uncommon energy and confidence. I ascended to the Long Room of the Pavilion up several flights of steps, past serried ranks of members suitably garbed for all the weathers that Melbourne can show in one and the same day. It really is a 'Long Room' at Melbourne, fit to be named with that of Lord's; dignified, polished, quiet, as high and as directly behind the wicket as the topmost gallery at Lord's, over the roof of which an Australian batsman, A. E. Trott, drove a ball from an Australian bowler, M. A. Noble.

From this point of vantage the connoisseur was privileged to enjoy bowling by Bedser of a rare kind. A perfect length, with late swings usually inward for the right-handed batsmen (but with one that abruptly went 'the other way'), and outward for Morris and Harvey, the left-handers; vitality from the pitch and almost unerring accuracy of direction. Seldom was it safe to leave a ball alone; this was an attack which challenged the highest skill possessed by contemporary batsmanship; also it was a joy to watch, and surely a pleasure to play and counter.

The first ball of Bedser's second over veered away from the off-stump, even as Morris found himself lured forward, against his inclinations, I suspect. A catch in the slips was so unavoidable that even a David Hume might well have been persuaded of a causal nexus. Morris himself no doubt appreciated, in the abstract, absolute perfection and rhythm of length and swerve as he went to his doom, much as a man being hanged might (if he were an artist) appreciate the delicate touch and timing of his executioner's technique and apparatus.

Harvey, in next, seemed charmed of life during his first overs from Bedser. A late outswinger left him with no answer except reflex-action; then Bedser sent him a ball that, instead of 'leaving' Harvey's bat, turned rapidly back, missing the leg-stump by an inch. A four over the slips' heads off Bedser was the consequence of the instinct of self-preservation, as if Harvey's bat had become suddenly electrified. Bedser was still 'on the spot'; after an hour of unrelieved effort and after the ball had lost its 'newness', he was straining batsmen's nerves and eyesight. He hit Archer's pads with a genuine breakback; and the collision made a noise like a boxer's glove knocking a man out in the stomach. In a world ruled more by justice than this one, Bedser would have been rewarded by four wickets before lunch, scarcely fewer. But at lunch Australia's score was 67 for one Archer and Harvey not out. At the end of an hour's play Brown asked Wright to bowl instead of Bailey, whose support for Bedser was always extremely determined, ready to break his back in two, if necessary. Wright unfortunately was at his most unreliable; he pitched short, and following the severe tightness of the English attack so far, his long-hops must have entered the Australian innings like refreshing air into a lethal chamber. Wright's third over was plundered for fifteen, three fours for Harvey, who in a subsequent over from Wright helped himself to two more boundaries. In Australia's first innings of 194 all out, Wright bowled eight overs for 63 runs and no wickets, in a Test match where no team's innings reached 200 and not since 1896, at Kennington Oval, had either England or Australia failed to get 200 in any of four completed innings.

Harvey threatened ignition; one or two of his rapid cuts and drives, made on quick feet, struck sparks out of the slow fire of the Australian batting; but after lunch it was quickly put out, quenched, 'dowsed'—and the entire Australian innings with it—as though hose-pipes had been brought lavishly to play on a sudden and spirited but necessarily short-lived outbreak of fire on the part of a handful of shavings.

Archer hung almost by visible suction to the wicket for more than two hours, scoring 26. He worked hard, watched the ball, submitted his nose to the grindstone with a willing and martyred concentration not, I am afraid, often to be found amongst the young aspirants in Brown's command. Archer looked vulnerable all the time and persisted rather like those obstinate invalids who live on for years, contrary to reasonable medical expectations and to the natural annoyance of relations. Still, in a responsible position, one of Australia's opening batsmen, he won his spurs by adding tenacity of character to a not yet confident technique.

It was a superb catch that accounted for Harvey. After lunch Bailey bowled from the pavilion end, Bedser crossing over. Harvey glanced an inswinger from Bedser to leg, a quite controlled stroke worth four even in Ranjitsinhji's currency. Evans leapt across to the left, and though his physical view of the ball was momentarily blotted out by Harvey's body, the eye of imagination sufficed to see 'before the event'; it was almost a catch *a priori*. Another brilliant catch finished Archer's innings. Bailey was attacking most strenuously now, not as spear-pointed maybe as Bedser's bowling, but it was a good and stunning bludgeon. Archer slashed at a quick bouncing off-side ball from Bailey, released with grunt and expletive proportionately mingled. The mishit sped swift as a bird on the wing in the direction of second-slip, and Bedser, his massive person swaying, held the catch almost indolently, much as the man hanging on a strap-hanger in a bus turns over a page of a newspaper with his unoccupied hand. Yet again we were gazing upon a rejuvenated England XI fighting hard and cleverly, not at all down-hearted by the loss of Compton, out of the action because of a swollen knee. The Melbourne crowd applauded almost every movement of an English player: Brown was applauded on principle, so to say, whether doing something clever or active or nothing at all. The cool day, now fresh and healthy, was another factor likely to make Englishmen feel at home—that and the fresh green grass of the outfield. Miller, like Harvey, suggested war in the open, out of the trenches, colours flying; Bedser needed some rest and Wright couldn't be trusted. This surely was a moment for us to fear Miller, for he had played himself in for fifty minutes, scoring only 18. Brown bowled in the responsible place of Bedser, and in his second over deceived Miller, who first shaped to push to the off-side, changed his mind, stood still rather at a loss, while his left heel was struck by the ball. Miller departed l.b.w. This was the beginning of a new lease of life and achievement for Brown which rose to a crescendo without parallel in his career so far; second-youth came to him, and apparently not only lightened the burden of forty years but, more important, the heavier burden of physical weight and girth. He was not much less quick with a pick-up and a return than anybody else in the English field. Nothing could be done to restore the broken Australian innings after Loxton got out. He defended for eighty-five minutes, while Hassett took charge and pulled four fours from four of Wright's long-hops with a remarkable majesty for a cricketer of his few inches. Loxton endured to compile 32, four runs more than England lost by! But none of us thought of Loxton or of an English defeat at the close of this enthralling first day at Melbourne; were not Australia all out for 194, on a wicket good enough for any good batsman? I doubt if W. G. Grace saw a better in all his life. As I walked through the Fitzroy Gardens, back to Menzies Hotel—and I walked all the way—I was brimming over with the spirit of Christmas, and ready to wish goodwill to everybody. It was inconceivable that, with the weather set fair, England would not leave Australia's 194 far behind. And yet—some spirit of denial at the back of my mind whispered: 'Wait.' Remember. The crease. The abyss. Will, this time, the English batsmen see beyond it, and realize it is mainly a figment of their own fearful fancying?'

SECOND DAY

AUSTRALIA
First Innings

K. Archer, c Bedser, b Bailey	26
A. R. Morris, c Hutton, b Bedser	2
R. N. Harvey, c Evans, b Bedser	42
K. R. Miller, lbw, b Brown	18
A. L. Hassett, b Bailey	52
S. J. E. Loxton, c Evans, b Close	32
R. R. Lindwall, lbw, b Bailey	8
D. Tallon, not out	7
I. W. Johnson, c Parkhouse, b Bedser	0
W. A. Johnston, c Hutton, b Bedser	0
J. Iverson, b Bailey	1
Extras (b 4, lb 2)	6
	—
Total	194

FALL OF WICKETS
First Innings

1	2	3	4	5	6	7	8	9	10
6	67	89	93	177	177	192	193	193	194

BOWLING ANALYSIS
First Innings

	O.	M.	R.	W.		O.	M.	R.	W.
Bailey	17·1	5	40	4	Brown	9	0	28	1
Bedser	19	3	37	4	Close	6	1	20	1
Wright	8	0	63	0					

ENGLAND
First Innings

R. T. Simpson, c Johnson, b Miller	4
Washbrook, lbw, b Lindwall	21
J. G. Dewes, c Miller, b Johnston	8
Hutton, c Tallon, b Iverson	12
Parkhouse, c Hassett, b Miller	9
Close, c Loxton, b Iverson	0
F. R. Brown, c Johnson, b Iverson	62
T. L. Bailey, b Lindwall	12
Evans, c Johnson, b Iverson	49
Bedser, not out	4
Wright, lbw, b Johnston	2
Extras (b 8, lb 6)	14
	—
Total	197

FALL OF WICKETS
First Innings

1	2	3	4	5	6	7	8	9	10
11	33	37	54	54	61	126	153	194	197

BOWLING ANALYSIS
First Innings

	O.	M.	R.	W.		O.	M.	R.	W.
Lindwall	12	2	46	2	Iverson	18	3	37	4
Miller	13	0	39	2	Johnson	5	1	19	0
Johnston	9	1	28	2	Loxton	4	1	14	0

On the second day before lunch a reaction set in that was rather more than 'equal and opposite'. How we English tasted the first of many of the rubber's dishes of humiliation served us! On an excellent wicket, with little of the 'greenness' which had favoured Bedser the day before, England's major batsmen broke down deplorably and six wickets fell for 61. The innings was retrieved by a brave and determined innings by F. R. Brown, who, from this moment onwards, interrupted only by the accident that removed him from the team and the scene five weeks afterwards at Adelaide, played and worked and led his broken forces day after day with an energy so tireless, a spirit so firm, and a wholesale expenditure of nature so infectious, that before long a street hawker in Sydney was shouting from the pavement to the crowd: ' 'Ere y'are; lovely lettuces— all got the 'eart of Freddie Brown.' On this second day of the Melbourne Test match, 23rd December, Brown, with a John

Bullish and Johnsonian girth, blood and authority, put the advancing Australian attack temporarily in its place. He had so far not scored fifty in an innings during the tour; today he batted with a hope that was a triumph over experience. Six out for 61, he lumbered to the crease, reminding me curiously of Warwick Armstrong in middle age; and he wasted no time or breath before he lambasted Miller for 3 to leg. In two hours he scored 62 out of 99, with a sixer and four boundaries.

The morning's first over was bowled by Lindwall, and it was as amiable and harmless as a Christmas cracker. Miller was quickly provoked into sending a 'bumper', always a sign that he isn't in the mood to bowl or doesn't like the pace of the wicket. But he caused the beginning of England's rot; as he was destined not once but thrice to do, subsequently, whether with malice prepense on his part or not. Simpson held out a bat almost sightless with speculation and was caught by first-slip. The ball which was his undoing swung to the off, the sort of ball which Sutcliffe scarcely deigned to recognize, let alone play, as he watched it go by, his bat withdrawn, as though the Sutcliffes declined to touch such stuff with their fingertips.

Dewes, in next, England 11 for one, walked to the wicket slowly. Batsmen go in to bat differently. Bradman took his time, but he was surveying the land, 'prospecting' it, so to say, staking his claim. Miller saunters forth to begin an innings, toes straight but the rest of him inclined to wander and look around, as though for familiar faces in the crowd or on the field of play. Dewes went to the crease on the present occasion apparently absorbed in himself, maybe reviewing his technique in the abstract and running over in his mind the different ways a cricketer can get out, from clean-bowled to handled-the-ball. He contrived to avoid a fatal pitfall for half an hour and actually was gathering confidence from the middle of his bat when he slashed at an off-side ball from Johnston, sent it to the slips, where Miller made a catch with his favourite flourish, diving low, swiftly and beautifully. With another fieldsman I could name the stroke would have gone for three runs, if not four. Then Washbrook, not for the first time, frustrated ours and his own hopes; his innings of promise was cut down in the blossom. Lindwall, obviously about to take a rest, pitched a not at all vivid ball well up to Washbrook, who sought to turn it to leg instead of forcing it, as easily he could have done to the on. He missed aim and the umpire deemed him lbw. For fifty-three minutes he had comfortably, we thought, played himself in. Hutton, in fourth, two wickets down for

33, seemed not as depressed as the rest of us at the downfall of Washbrook.

When Iverson bowled instead of Lindwall, Hutton drove him through the covers with his left leg forward, his balanced body and the beautiful swing and follow-through of the bat indivisible in rhythm—a stroke of grandeur and noble lineage. He coped almost condescendingly with Iverson's off-spin and three short-leg fieldsmen; and he 'took' leisurely singles at will to protect Parkhouse from Iverson. But to the second ball of Iverson's fourth over of the morning Hutton shaped for a sweep square to the on from a well-lighted length, then as though thinking better of it, he raised his bat above and away from the off-break, and the ball struck him near the knee, bouncing upwards. Iverson impulsively called out 'Catch it!' and Tallon swooped forward, made a catch, and he and Iverson appealed. The umpire's finger went up. A mistake of judgment; but nothing could be done about it. The umpire's decision is final on the cricket field, whatever may be the case when he is in his own house.

Good God, we said, whoever heard of Hutton hitting a ball up over his head in a Test match, or anywhere else; he couldn't make such a stroke if he tried. We couldn't guess that next innings Hutton would get out from as 'unlikely' a stroke, one not remotely connected with him, yet caught near the umpire, victory within reach. This unjust blow to England should have inspired Close, another Yorkshireman, to most grim obduracy, but it didn't. On the contrary, Close 'swiped' horribly across another nicely-flighted ball from Iverson; and it is fervently to be hoped he was suitably chastened to see himself caught not far behind his back on the leg-side. In an Eton v. Harrow match, in a situation as serious for his side as his, any boy who lost his wicket through such weakness, such lack of sense and effort, would not be forgotten or forgiven for it all his life, wherever he might isolate himself in the world, Tanganyika, the Melbourne Club or Montreal. Close was out—five for 54—in the last over before lunch, Parkhouse not out, 7, after much labour.

At a quarter-past two the game proceeded, watched by a great concourse tier on tier, thousands in the shade in the great enclosures, thousands packed side by side in the sun, everybody quiet as a mouse as the bowler began his run. In Miller's second over following the adjournment, Parkhouse received a short rising ball that whistled past his left ear, probably making the sound of a tuning-fork. He struck at the next ball without conviction as it went past

F
161

the off-stump; Hassett, at short 'gully' moved quickly sideways and caught him. Parkhouse for three-quarters of an hour had hinted at a liking for strokes of taste; but his general aspect recalled the old hymn: 'Brief life is here our portion.'

With Bailey his companion at the wicket, Brown began his onslaught, not at first with as much accuracy as belligerence. A perfect drive to the off from Iverson got his eye in focus; he hit his six, beyond long-on, from Ian Johnson; and he will hear the generous roar of Melbourne's fifty thousand to his life's end. It was a Rubicon stroke. While Bailey stuck to the crease as though by some physical act of clinging to it, Brown put red corpuscles into England's innings; he usually looks as if he knows what red corpuscles are, also phagocytes well stimulated. When he reached 50 with a drive that changed his bat (to the eye of imagination) to a hammer in a smithy, the multitude roared louder, affection in the sound and the tumult. The seventh wicket added 65 in seventy-one minutes. Bailey, who scored 12 of them, was too late against a grand inswinger from Lindwall, goaded to his fastest. As he heard the rattle of the stumps Bailey bowed a sorrowful head; but he had done his side some service.

As we watched Brown and Bailey—not England's two most skilful batsmen—lift the score from 61 for six to 126 for seven, we could realize how many opportunities had gone abegging. Brown, aiming red as a lobster at another six, was caught soon after tea, eight out at 153; then Evans demonstrated what quick feet and impertinence could do with bowlers now desperately keen to get England out for less than Australia's first innings score of 194. The fight for first innings lead, indeed, aroused the crowd to hysteria. Evans batted like a cheeky Cockney, yet there was skill as well as character in his cricket. A drive though the covers, off a fast ball from Miller, was faultless and timed so well that it raced over the grass and hit the fence with a resounding crack. Sixty thousand Australians were with Evans to a man, even to a small boy—and it is not easy for a small boy to rise above patriotism. The acclamation which announced that England had passed Australia's 194, and the greeting to Evans as he came home, caught at square-leg from another pugnacious stroke, was like the myriad-throated applause to Brown, of the warmth that fills the heart and makes the lover of cricket love the game more than ever. But at the day's end, the eve of Christmas, something of the season's cheerfulness was shaded by the thought of how England had missed a rare chance to leave Australia's 194 so far behind that now we might have been in a position to toast victory in the champagne (Australian) at the parties and celebrations imminent and about to engulf us. We couldn't believe in another breakdown of Australia's batting—and this Melbourne wicket wasn't likely to be an easy one on which to play a long innings if England should be set 300 to win; and none of us dreamed there would be fewer needed.

THIRD DAY

AUSTRALIA

First Innings		Second Innings	
K. Archer, c Bedser, b Bailey	26	c Bailey, b Bedser	46
A. R. Morris, c Hutton, b Bedser	2	lbw, b Wright	18
R. N. Harvey, c Evans, b Bedser	42	run out	31
K. R. Miller, lbw, b Brown	18	b Bailey	14
A. L. Hassett, b Bailey	52	c Bailey, b Brown	19
S. J. E. Loxton, c Evans, b Close	32	c Evans, b Brown	2
R. R. Lindwall, lbw, b Bailey	8	c Evans, b Brown	7
D. Tallon, not out	7	lbw, b Brown	0
I. W. Johnson, c Parkhouse, b. Bedser	0	c. Close, b Bedser	23
W. A. Johnston, c Hutton, b Bedser	0	b Bailey	6
J. Iverson, b Bailey	1	not out	0
Extras (b 4, lb 2)	6	Extras (b 10, lb 5)	15
Total	194	Total	181

FALL OF WICKETS

First Innings

1	2	3	4	5	6	7	8	9	10
6	67	89	93	177	177	192	193	193	194

Second Innings

1	2	3	4	5	6	7	8	9	10
43	99	100	126	131	151	151	156	181	181

ROWLING ANALYSIS

First Innings

	O.	M.	R.	W.		O.	M.	R.	W.
Bailey	17·1	5	40	4	Brown	9	0	28	1
Bedser	19	3	37	4	Close	6	1	20	1
Wright	8	0	63	0					

Second Innings

	O.	M.	R.	W.		O.	M.	R.	W.
Bailey	15	3	47	2	Brown	12	2	26	4
Bedser	16·3	2	43	2	Close	1	0	8	0
Wright	9	0	42	1					

ENGLAND

First Innings		Second Innings	
R. T. Simpson, c Johnson, b Miller	4	not out	10
Washbrook, lbw, b Lindwall	21	b Iverson	8
J. G. Dewes, c Miller, b Johnston	8		
Hutton, c Tallon, b Iverson	12	not out	2
Parkhouse, c Hassett, b Miller	9		
Close, c Loxton, b Iverson	0		
F. R. Brown, c Johnson, b Iverson	62		
T. E. Bailey, b Lindwall	12	b Johnson	0
Evans, c Johnson, b Iverson	49		
Bedser, not out	4		
Wright, lbw, b Johnson	2		
Extras (b 8, lb 6)	14	Extras (b 8)	8
Total	197	Total (2 wkts)	28

FALL OF WICKETS

First Innings

1	2	3	4	5	6	7	8	9	10
11	33	77	54	54	61	126	153	194	197

Second Innings

1	2
21	22

BOWLING ANALYSIS

First Innings

	O.	M.	R.	W.		O.	M.	R.	W.
Lindwall	12	2	46	2	Iverson	18	3	37	4
Miller	13	0	39	2	Johnson	5	1	19	0
Johnston	9	1	28	2	Loxton	4	1	14	0

Second Innings (to date)

	O.	M.	R.	W.		O.	M.	R.	W.
Lindwall	3	0	6	0	Johnson	4	1	6	1
Miller	2	1	4	0	Iverson	4	1	4	1

This was one of the most astonishing and thrilling days in the annals of cricket, and it ended with the balance so precarious that the merest wisp of a straw from luck would sway it decisively, England's or Australia's way. Yet again Australian batsmanship was rendered poverty-stricken; the second innings was all over at five minutes to five for 181. England counter-attacked grandly from the position to which they were thrown back on Saturday; the wicket, though not altogether after a contemporary batsman's heart, was on the whole true—in spite of a ball that kept low now and again—and easy for run-making. Keener bowling than Bedser's, Bailey's and Brown's, and keener fielding, couldn't be imagined; and the raging battle was infused by a spirit of sportsmanship that honoured the finest and oldest traditions of cricket, the Melbourne crowd contributing a generous if ear-shattering part.

After a two-days' pause the match began again in hot weather, the sun streaming from a sky of blue satin stretched without a crease in it. From the heights of the members' pavilion, looking straight down and behind the line of the ball's flight, the wicket resembled a light-brown oblong coffin in which, you might have said, reposed the hopes of all bowlers. But it was a deceptive wicket really—good enough for a good batsman, but, as I say, a ball occasionally kept low; and there was always enough hardness in the rolled baked earth to create that illusion in cricket of increase of speed after the ball has pitched. A Test match wicket in Australia, let alone Christmas Day and Boxing Day, could scarcely be expected to remain sober all the time. So once again we were privileged to enjoy a fair fight between bat and ball, fortune never distributing her favours unequally among the opponents. At first I resigned myself to hours of slow attrition while Morris and Archer set themselves to reduce Bedser, Bailey and Wright to limp, moist, ineffectual bodies. Only one wicket fell before lunch, and in ninety minutes not more than 57 runs were scored; and now Australia were 79 ahead, nine batsmen to come. Morris played back to a well-flighted length from Wright, got into position for a glance to leg, changed his mind, and allowed his pads to stop a 'googly', and to his unconcealed surprise was given out lbw. Still, nobody foresaw the wrath to come. Archer suggested obduracy if not a technical control that has been taught by experience to work at leisure and by instinct.

The fun began at half-past two when the great ground was packed and inflammable. Archer was caught a few yards from the bat by Bailey, off Bedser in the 'gully', and five minutes afterwards Harvey backed-up impulsively as Miller stabbed defensively forward at a surprisingly quick one from Wright. Washbrook, at mid-off, fielded swiftly, threw at one wicket and struck it with Harvey yards out. I was obliged to ask the brilliant fielder's name; he was so thoroughly disguised in a white hat that he might have been wearing the Tarnhelm. Miller also protected himself from the sun by use of a cap; and Miller with his hair invisible is as though W. G. Grace had appeared without his whiskers. Indeed, Miller was not happy; his aggression hinted of some mental unease. Clearly the occasion

165

was not going to be a sort of extra Christmas dinner for Australian batsmen. He made two great strokes off Wright, a voracious sweep to leg, the whole man coming full circle, and a leap of a drive to the off. Then Bailey clean-bowled him with dramatic abruptness. Miller tried to change from offence to defence, but the ball's speed was even quicker than Miller's eyesight; the middle stump was hit before the bat could intervene.

Now Brown came into action again, rolling to the crease like a man-of-war. A rasping ball removed Loxton, caught at the wicket: Australia five for 131, and what with the boiling temperature of the afternoon and the roars and the zoological screams of the women in the crowd, the wonder is that typewriters in the Press Box were not dislocated and infinitives split asunder. The frenzy of it all was intensified by the impersonal tranquillity of the stainless blue sky. Brown next go rid of Lindwall, also caught at the wicket; and in the same over Brown, insatiable and very warm, defeated Tallon, who played back to succumb lbw.

After tea Bailey held a catch worth going miles to see, even by transport in Melbourne. Hassett, who was batting belligerently, edged a ball from Brown low to the grass and Bailey grasped it one-handed, flinging the heart and soul of him at the chance. Brown's antagonistic bowling, which had disposed in rapid sequence Loxton, Lindwall and Hassett and changed the day's course, was all done with an old ball and less by the arts of length and variation of pace (which were excellent) than by vehemence of will and power of a good right arm. With every run invaluable and every ball a nail in somebody's coffin for certain—England or Australia's—a stand by Johnson and Johnston (only Iverson to come) came as more and more fuel to the flames of a game which burned and singed us as though all of us, crowd, cricketers, bats and balls and surrounding nature, were being caught up in the conflagration of an Australian midsummer. The ninth wicket added 25; Ian Johnson's portion was 23; and England tomorrow, so it was written, but mercifully we couldn't know it, would lose by 28. A day of irony, a day of cricket long to be remembered.

Brown again sent Simpson in first with Washbrook to begin England's task (if it couldn't be called a duty); a mere 179 to win a victory. It was a risky move surely, for if ever an England innings needed a masterful lead it was now. But Washbrook was the first to fall, well beaten by Iverson with a ball that kept low. Hassett lost no time before he brought his spin-bowlers into action, but I fancy he was as hopeful of collaboration from the batsmen's fears or imaginings as from the wicket itself, which if it didn't reject spin, scarcely imparted the pace or 'snap' that kills. Bailey, sent in twenty minutes before close of play, was bowled by Ian Johnson for nothing, stretching forward to an off-break. Why was Bailey asked to bat in a position so responsible at the end of an afternoon on which he had not spared himself in the field? Hutton, who was possibly becoming accustomed to arriving at the crease not with a clean, confident sheet behind him but in the midst of falling wickets, dallied calmly with the last long agonizing minutes, as the sun cast the shadows of the great stand over the grass in stark black blocks.

FOURTH DAY

AUSTRALIA

First Innings		Second Innings	
K. Archer, c Bedser, b Bailey	26	c Bailey, b Bedser	46
A. R. Morris, c Hutton, b Bedser	2	lbw, b Wright	18
R. N. Harvey, c Evans, b Bedser	42	run out	31
K. R. Miller, lbw, b Brown	18	b Bailey	14
A. L. Hassett, b Bailey	52	c Bailey, b Brown	19
S. J. E. Loxton, c Evans, b Close	32	c Evans, b Brown	2
R. R. Lindwall, lbw, b Bailey	8	c Evans, b Brown	7
D. Tallon, not out	7	lbw, b Brown	0
I. W. Johnson, c Parkhouse, b Bedser	0	c Close, b Bedser	23
W. A. Johnson, c Hutton, b Bedser	0	b Bailey	6
J. Iverson, b Bailey	1	not out	0
Extras (b 4, lb 2)	6	Extras (b 10, lb 5)	15
Total	194	Total	181

FALL OF WICKETS

First Innings									
1	2	3	4	5	4	7	8	9	10
6	67	89	93	177	177	192	193	193	194

Second Innings									
1	2	3	4	5	6	7	8	9	10
43	91	100	126	131	151	151	156	181	181

BOWLING ANALYSIS

First Innings

	O.	M.	R.	W.		O.	M.	R.	W.
Bailey	17·1	5	40	4	Brown	9	0	28	1
Bedser	19	3	37	4	Close	6	1	20	1
Wright	8	0	63	0					

Second Innings

	O.	M.	R.	W.		O.	M.	R.	W.
Bailey	15	3	47	2	Brown	12	2	26	4
Bedser	16·3	2	43	2	Close	1	1	8	0
Wright	9	0	42	1					

ENGLAND

First Innings		Second Innings	
R. T. Simpson, c Johnson, b Miller	4	b Lindwall	23
Washbrook, lbw, b Lindwall	21	b Iverson	8
J. G. Dewes, c Miller, b Johnston	8	c Harvey, b Iverson	5
Hutton, c Tallon, b Iverson	12	c Lindwall, b Johnston	40
Parkhouse, c Hassett, b Miller	9	lbw, b Johnston	28
Close, c Loxton, b Iverson	0	lbw, b Johnston	1
F. R. Brown, c Johnson, b Iverson	62	b Lindwall	8
T. E. Bailey, b Lindwall	12	b Johnson	0
Evans, c Johnson, b Iverson	49	b Lindwall	2
Bedser, not out	4	not out	14
Wright, lbw, b Johnston	2	lbw, b Johnston	2
Extras (b 8, lb 6)	14	Extras (b 17, lb 2)	19
	—		—
Total	197	Total	150

FALL OF WICKETS

First Innings

1	2	3	4	5	4	7	8	9	10
11	33	37	54	54	61	126	153	194	197

Second Innings

1	2	3	4	5	6	7	8	9	10
21	22	52	82	92	95	122	124	134	150

BOWLING ANALYSIS

First Innings

	O.	M.	R.	W.		O.	M.	R.	W.
Lindwall	12	2	46	2	Iverson	18	3	37	4
Miller	13	0	39	2	Johnson	5	1	19	0
Johnston	9	1	28	2	Loxton	4	1	14	0

Second Innings

	O.	M.	R.	W.		O.	M.	R.	W.
Lindwall	12	1	29	3	Iverson	20	4	36	2
Miller	5	2	16	0	Johnston	13·7	1	26	4
Johnson	13	3	24	1					

As we have seen, England stumbled on the doorstep of victory. The first ball of the morning, almost a 'shooter', from Ian Johnson, nearly sped under Hutton's bat. Moreover, such a ball, so early in the day, sounded an alarm. Simpson was as a man encased in heavy armour of suspicion and self-distrust; yet he rendered his side staunch service for forty minutes. Hutton soon settled down to a chess-player's scrutiny of every gambit of the bowlers. With time to spare he played any dangerous off-spinner, especially from Iverson, down to the earth with the break, thus frustrating the leg-side fields-men clustered round his legs. Iverson bowled with no slips, not a single one, a sign that he wasn't spinning away from the batsman. I cannot agree that he is yet a great, as distinct from a good, bowler if he doesn't command that trick.

At half-past twelve Iverson was 'rested' for Lindwall. I breathed relief; this change of bowling was a testimony to the defensive play of Hutton and Simpson in the crucial opening period. England would prevail if a good stand occurred now. But I chafed for signs of strokes calculated to put the bowlers out of conceit with them-selves. It was not a fast bowler's commission to win the match on this wicket. Lindwall, though, is not one of those whom George Lohmann counted amongst the 'brute force' school of fast bowlers; Lindwall has brains—so many, apparently, that it is a wonder he went in for fast bowling at all. His fourth ball, indeed, which clean-bowled Simpson, was a shade less than fast, with a curved flight; and it swung in. Simpson, before he left the crease for the pavilion, picked up one of the fallen bails and gave it to the wicket-keeper, a sad but courtly action.

Dewes, straight from a sickbed (he had caught a chill on a chilly Christmas Eve following a sweltering day), brought his bat down in the nick of time to a 'yorker' which Lindwall sent him as soon as he could get at him. For nearly two hours Dewes stuck to his wicket; it was pure adhesiveness. When at last Dewes scored a single he ran like a sparrow that has quickly and apprehensively picked up a crumb, after long inspection of it from a distance. A cover-drive by Hutton, off Ian Johnson, announced and made plain to everybody present that we were looking at the greatest contemporary batsman, the most thoroughly organized in technique, the most soundly schooled in first and last principles; never an improviser, always an architect of an innings.

When Iverson bowled again in place of Lindwall, an off-spinner bounced abruptly, but Hutton dealt with it one-handed, so that the

ball came into contact with a 'dead' or passive bat and fell harmlessly to the earth, all venom spent. In the same over Hutton drove
to the off for four, a perfectly poised hit, bat swinging on high; so,
in a few balls, we were shown models of acts of self-preservation
and of confident self-expression.

Five minutes before lunch Dewes pushed his bat too forcibly and
fatally at a spinner he couldn't reach because he would or could
not 'go to the ball'; and twenty minutes after lunch, the disaster
and the ironic sport with Hutton occurred. He left the field, leaving
behind him a mortal wound; not a lover of cricket in the crowd saw
this dethronement without sorrow. . . . The rest should be silence.
Close was miserably lbw to Ian Johnson, bereft of ideas, synthetic
or analytical. Six for 95, and now Brown joined Parkhouse, whose
occasional strokes of bright decision were as flickering fireflies in
the night of doubt that mainly covered him.

England's only chance at this point was dependent on assault
and battery; but even Brown groped shortsightedly out at Iverson.
The Australian attack was too accurate to encourage any belief
that eighty runs could be obtained by waiting for them. I still dared
to hope that Parkhouse might prevail; for his cricket improved in
touch when speed was employed by Hassett instead of spin. But
again we were mocked: Lindwall rediscovered in his rusting
armoury a magnificent ball, vintage or arsenal of 1948, and he
wrecked Brown's stumps entirely; then Miller, on for Johnson,
trapped Parkhouse leg-before. Wright prolonged the agony by
putting a quite affable blade to an attack which was now as ravening
as triumphant; and Bedser was not out at the end, standing like a
solitary column left erect, on the bare plain of England's defeat.

FROM SECOND INNINGS

LAST MAN IN

To be the official number eleven in the order of going in is not always irresponsibility and easy nerves and conscience. There are times when this batsman has to support an unreasonable burden, times when the weakest link in the chain is expected to withstand the severest strain. He may have to go to the wicket with a crucial question at stake of saving a 'follow on'; worse still, he may have to face that most searching of mortal ordeals—eight to win and the last man in. Such a situation was my portion once on a calm day in Worcestershire, aeons ago, during the golden age of country cricket reported every week in *The Field*; columns of scores and lovely names, 'Somerset Stragglers', 'Sussex Martlets'. 'Devonshire Dumplings', 'Derbyshire Friars', or 'Shropshire Gentlemen, with Thompson'—Thompson being the paid professional. On this calm day in June, I had bowled tolerably, and our eleven had been given not too many runs to score for victory. The wicket was good and we began well, so that when the tinkle of teacups sounded on the drowsy afternoon air, a tranquil end to the encounter was only a matter of time. After refreshment we all settled in our deck-chairs once more: I mean those of us occupying a place low down in the batting order. Pipes were lighted, and some dalliance with lady spectators was feasible, when suddenly a collapse began in the field before us, only a moment ago a field of formal procedure and rural decoration. A man of immense physical substance—I think he was Burrows the Worcestershire fast bowler—had returned to the attack with a new ferocity; stumps flew about like splinters. I was obliged to haul myself from a deckchair, go into the dark dressing-room, and put on pads with my fingers fumbling, making a mess of straps and holes and buckles. All the time I secretly prayed that the batsmen now facing the music would endure and conquer. But no; I heard another sickening noise of a dismantled wicket in the failing light.

I walked down the wooden steps when we wanted exactly eight runs. Everything depended on me; the other batsman was our 'crack'; he was seventy not out and well in charge of the bowling, even the bowling of the resurrected Burrows. A ripple of handclaps supposedly to encourage me came to my ear, but it was as noise from a far removed and very external universe; the world was now nothing but mine own fears and prayers. The long, lonely walk to the scene of crisis was ageing, and oh! the unfriendliness of everybody when I got there—most cricketers know of this sensation of bereft isolation. I began to take guard by force of habit, only to be told that the next ball would begin a new over from this end. Confusion and humiliation, and a public revelation of one's so far hidden poltroonery.

I must be ready to run, to collaborate with my masterful partner, to see that he obtained the bowling, and if possible always a single from the sixth ball. I might run him out. But these dread apprehensions were as naught to the actual happening; the master could not score a run at all in this first over, bowled to him as I backed up with my every nerve a pin-point of suspense. I was delivered unto Burrows, at the other end. I saw the ghostly fieldsmen changing position. I heard the remote umpire say, 'Two leg, sir.' I felt somebody patting my block-hole; I felt a hand tightening the grip on my trousers above the left hip. A ventriloquial voice said, 'A little closer, Harry.' Then I saw Burrows looming and growing as he charged at me, larger and larger, a figure on the cinema that comes at you, widening and widening circles until the screen is overwhelmed and your vision is ready to burst into explosions of blinding nearness.

What to do? Play back or forward or not move an inch from the block-hole, or take courage and go for glory and swing the bat and to hell with it? Thought quicker than light shot through the brain. What in God's name to do?—but here is the ball, hot from muscle and temper, a ball of fire, a ball of—— Merciful heaven, it is nothing of the kind; it is a straight half-volley to the off. But dare I? If I mishit I shall be outcast, mocked at, the vainest of earthworms; but if I hit truly—— I did indeed hit truly. From the middle of the good blade, running up my arms, came sensations of joy beyond compare, music and tympani of nerves, vibrant to the brain and the heart; a four smack from the middle of the bat. A ball was thrown back from the distance, then I had a terrible momentary feeling of having looked over the rim of terror into the void. Applause and shouts hailed me hero; and I experienced the illusion of a growth in actual stature.

Next, anti-climax; for there were more balls to face alone from

Burrows, now outraged and silent. Four to win, remember. Again he strides and again the mighty arm swings. Gloria in Excelsis, if it isn't a long-hop this time, to leg! I couldn't believe my eyes. And nobody placed deep on that side of the field. I must not falter; Burrows already is cursing his folly, vowing revenge next ball, if I miss this chance worth a soul's ransom. I do not understand why I did not excitedly cleave the air 'too soon', but I didn't. I waited until the ball was 'leaving me'; then I struck it almost from behind. No more certain boundary hit has been executed; the ball went there quicker than from the bat. I had 'won the match' in two blows myself. And I did not wake up; it was not a dream. Thirty-five years ago, and true and real this present minute. I can see it all, the formal chase of a fieldsman after my decisive stroke; he ran only a few yards. The cheering and the intense relief to mind and nerve. Then at once the feeling that it is over, and will never come back, the actual ecstatic doing of it, never . . .

FROM MANCHESTER GUARDIAN

ENGLAND v. AUSTRALIA 1930 TEST SERIES

FIRST TEST 1930
1st Day Trent Bridge

ENGLAND

First Innings

Hobbs, c Richardson, b McCabe	78
Sutcliffe, c Hornibrook, b Fairfax	29
Hammond, lbw, b Grimmett	8
Woolley, st Oldfield, b Grimmett	0
Hendren, b Grimmett	5
A. P. F. Chapman, c Ponsford, b Hornibrook	52
Larwood, b Grimmett	18
R. W. V. Robins, not out	28
Tate, b Grimmett	13
B 4 lb 5, nb 1	10

Total (for 8)   241

Tyldesley (R.) and Duckworth to bat

FALL OF WICKETS

1	2	3	4	5	6	7	8
53	63	63	71	153	188	215	241

AUSTRALIA

W. M. Woodfull, V. Y. Richardson, A. F. Kippax, W. H. Ponsford, D. G. Bradman, S. McCabe, A. Fairfax, W. A. Oldfield, C. V. Grimmett, T. Wall, and P. M. Hornibrook.

O N a beautiful Trent Bridge wicket the first Test match began this morning, and England had the felicity of taking first innings—an important advantage in a four-day match. It was the sort of wicket on which Arthur Shrewsbury seldom began an innings without taking the precaution of ordering a cup of tea to be brought out to him at a quarter to four exactly. Wall attacked Hobbs with a long run and every other outward show of a bowler of much velocity save that his captain thought fit to place the field with only two slips in it. A gap between backward point and second slip was quickly found out by Hobbs, whose strokes from the outset robbed Walls fast medium deliveries of a yard of speed which they could not afford to yield. When Grimmett joined issue neither Hobbs nor Sutcliffe gave the field substantial encouragement. True, Sutcliffe sent a sharp slip catch to Hornibrook from a spinning-away ball by Grimmett when England were 22, but the unexpectedness of this mishap—Hornibrook was clearly an astonished man—may be taken as the measure of the general ease and certainty of touch whereby both Sutcliffe and Hobbs had batted so far. Few strokes were made behind the wicket from Grimmett—a certain sign that the bat was meeting the break in the blade's true middle. When a leg-spin bowler is causing batsmen to come forward to him he inspires himself further by the knowledge that a cricket bat possesses an edge. Hobbs and Sutcliffe contrived for an hour to keep that knowledge entirely abstract and academic.

DISASTERS FOLLOW CONTENTMENT

Sutcliffe once or twice drove Hornibrook through the covers with a freedom and grace which in a Lancashire and Yorkshire match might have savoured of bad taste and wantonness. Wall struck Sutcliffe on the hand twice in one over, but little other encouragement came Australia's way. The situation of England after an hour's cricket was apparently lapped round by calm and prosperous waters. Hobbs and Sutcliffe quite set, Grimmett face to face with his masters—why, at this period I imagined that Woodfull was wondering to himself at what time of day the new ball would be available. The Trent Bridge crowd sat round the field in ample contentment. Thus did the sporting gods cunningly prepare for us a nice opiate of complacence.

At a quarter to one, with England 53, Fairfax, who so far had worked with a quite moral ardour and never looked likely to get anybody out until Richard Tyldesley came in, sent to Sutcliffe a ball which whipped off the turf at a very deceitful pace, leaving Sutcliffe no alternative but a reflex action. A catch high up in the slips was the inevitable consequence of bat's edge touching an outswinger. When Hammond's innings opened we were straightway put back into the fool's paradise by two strokes which could modestly be described as fine fruit of cricket's long culture. One of them was a quick-footed drive past cover-point off Grimmett: the movements were done so much in advance of the stroke itself that when

176

we saw the drive the effect was statuesque—a thrilling instance of energy transfixed and rendered more durable than the life of any event because of the art that had gone into it. But Hammond was out leg before wicket to a surreptitious top-spinner from Grimmett when England were 63. The very next ball, exquisitely flighted, drew all of Woolley's elegance forward, and, though his toe was over the crease for only the twinkling of an eye, Oldfield found time both to stump him and also to perform a flourish which I can only call callous.

Grimmett, who is a curiously furtive bowler and as quick to jump to a chance as Catastrophe in the old comedy, seemed to spin the ball quicker from the earth and to curve it more and more two-facedly through the air as he realized that the game's wind was blowing luck in Australia's tracks for the while. His bowling gave me the impression of fixing Hendren in an eternal attitude of what somebody in Dickens would have called nonplussedness. The second ball to him and the one after that hung in the air, and then, while Hendren jumped speculatively out of his ground with a bat sweeping across desperately, it dropped and spun away. Oldfield nearly stumped Hendren, and apparently he thought he had done so. Hendren never looked durable: Grimmett held him in thrall—he put on him what the music-halls used to call the 'fluence'. Hendren was fourth out at 71, and if he played the ball into his wicket he was fortunate to find any point of contact with the ball at all.

LEG–BREAKS OF LENGTH

In quick sequence England lost Sutcliffe, Hammond, Woolley, and Hendren while the score was moving from 53 to 71. Grimmett's bowling was as clever as slow spin possible could be on a Trent Bridge wicket. Seldom has the leg-break been given Grimmett's accuracy of length in all of cricket's history. It is a real finger spin, quick to seek out the bat's edge—not a mere fractional turn done by the wrist and arm. At lunch England were 91 for four, and few of us were in the mood to eat. For two hours Hobbs had defended, scoring only 37, though, to say the truth, a severe portion of that time had seen him damnably isolated at the wicket's other end, helpless to move a finger to stop a collapse that threatened to shake the England eleven to the foundations. The game's change of fortune made new men of the Australians: when Hendren departed from the scene they were to be observed throwing one another jubilant catches. On the popular side I heard a man inquiring whether Larwood would bowl from the pavilion or from the end opposite.

After the lunch interval the weather was appropriately funeral colour; clouds of sable came over the sky. The declining light stopped cricket, and then rain fell. Australia had reason to deplore their luck hereabout, for when the game went on at three o'clock Grimmett's fingers had to grip a slippery ball. On the other hand Hobbs and Chapman had to tackle in a dubious light keen bowling and a perilous situation. Chapman gambled superbly, and this time he won. He flung his bat at the off-side ball, and sheer heart and a good eye enabled him to get on very well without observance of first principles. According to the proved science of batsmanship Chapman's hits through the covers or past the old-fashioned place called point ought on several crucial occasions to have gone into the air. Chapman's hits were frequently dangerous while he was about to make them—and safe as the holy writ of William Gunn himself after they actually left the bat. Chapman achieved ten fours in an innings most likeable because of its determined and responsible irresponsibility. Here was a clear and invigorating instance of a cricketer overwhelming a trying corner by giving no heed whatever to the danger signals. It was a headlong innings, and Chapman himself probably knew or cared little of the end waiting sooner or later for his escapade. At the right moment he gave us the right gesture.

82 FOR FIFTH WICKET

In little more than an hour Chapman and Hobbs scored 82 for England's fifth wicket. Then Chapman gave the catch which long off had been expecting, and no doubt expecting bitterly, almost from the moment Chapman came in. The suspense of Chapman's innings was indeed terrible to all of us: that in itself rendered it heart and soul of the game.

At half-past three, while Larwood was doing his very best to look like a number seven batsman for All England, rain came again inopportunely for both sides, for Hobbs was thoroughly set and the wicket was drying to the condition suitable to Grimmett and Horni-brook.

During the afternoon news was given circulation that the wicket contained an amount of moisture which prevented the bowlers' labours from falling into moods of hopelessness. Everybody agreed that the turf was definitely a batsman's, but at the same time it was thought that the slight dampness in it made the difference between

178

a good and an uncommonly good ball. For my part I would have paid a more serious attention to this diagnosis of a Trent Bridge wicket had I heard of it before the collapse of England's second, third, and fourth wickets. The explanation of that collapse was Grimmett's spin—simply that and nothing more.

The rainy afternoon cut a two hours' gap in the game between half-past three and half-past five. Then Larwood made strokes to the off which were so handsome that I was reminded of an old saying of my own to the effect that time would prove Larwood to be the best batsman since Lockwood who has ever played for England as a fast bowler. When he was stumped at 188 Hobbs's score stood at 66. He fell to a catch in the slips at 218, and then he had made 78 in three hours and forty minutes. It was a kindly innings because of its quiet authority, its observance of constitutional principle, its devoted service to the cause. His strokes never protested too much: they were ripe as true loyalty. Now and again a pull of great sweep and power lifted the innings into the realms of the heroic. On the whole, though, it was the batsman's high content to place rare skill and judgment, with a quiet modesty and patience, at the service of a side much harassed by a tenacious enemy.

In the day's last over England lost the wicket of Tate—he played on—and so the end was not good for England and held promise to this Australian eleven, whose talents so far this summer have been the source of controversy. The bowling was usually steady apart from Grimmett's, which was always good and sometimes achieved the remarkable, and an alert and agile field worked its hardest. Grimmett's five wickets have been taken at a cost of 106 runs.

After this day's cricket the Australians are bound to be a better side than they were when this morning they took the field, not, I believe, too confidently.

The number of people who paid for admission was 15,763, and the receipts amounted to £1,523 7s. 6d.

FIRST TEST
2nd Day Trent Bridge

ENGLAND
First Innings

Hobbs, c Richardson, b McCabe	78
Sutcliffe, c Hornibrook, b Fairfax	29
Hammond, lbw, b Grimmett	8
Woolley, st Oldfield, b Grimmett	0
Hendren, b Grimmett	5
A. P. F. Chapman, c Ponsford, b Hornibrook	52
Larwood, b Grimmett	18
R. W. V. Robins, not out	50
Tate, b Grimmett	13
Tyldesley (R.), c Fairfax, b Wall	1
Duckworth, lbw, b Fairfax	4
B 4, lb 7, nb 1	12
Total	270

FALL OF WICKETS

1	2	3	4	5	6	7	8	9	10
53	63	63	71	153	188	218	241	242	270

AUSTRALIA
First Innings

W. M. Woodfull, c Chapman, b Tate	2
W. H. Ponsford, b Tate	3
A. Fairfax, c Hobbs, b Robins	14
D. G. Bradman, b Tate	8
A. F. Kippax, not out	60
S. McCabe, c Hammond, b Robins	4
V. Y. Richardson, b Tyldesley, (R.)	37
W. A. Oldfield, c Duckworth, b Robins	4
C. V. Grimmett, st Duckworth, b Robins	0
P. M. Hornibrook, not out	0
B 4, lb 4	8
Total (for 8)	140

T. Wall to bat

FALL OF WICKETS

1	2	3	4	5	6	7	8
4	6	16	57	61	105	134	140

BOWLING ANALYSIS

ENGLAND—First Innings

	O.	M.	R.	W.		O.	M.	R.	W.
Wall	17	4	47	1	Hornibrook	12	3	70	1
Fairfax	21·4	5	51	2	McCabe	7	3	23	1
Grimmett	32	6	107	5					

Fairfax bowled one no-ball

NOTTINGHAM, SATURDAY

Today's play had been hard to understand because cause and effect have made rather a tangled mesh of circumstances. Rain in torrents came on Friday evening to spoil the beautiful wicket which England had wasted. This afternoon's glorious sunshine must have shone an inimical light in Australian eyes, but the question for realistic criticism to settle is whether the cricket and all its changes and vicissitudes can be discussed and accounted for in terms of a difficult pitch.

To the onlooker at the field's edge there is one trustworthy sign of a bowler's wicket—the sight of a ball jumping or popping after it has dropped a good length. This afternoon very few balls jumped or popped once the Australian innings had lasted half an hour. Moreover, these balls were sent not by the spin bowlers but by Larwood and Tate. If a cricketer is told of a batting collapse on a bad pitch he immediately thinks of spin and flight: he does not expect to learn that a fast-medium bowler has been part of the attack at all. It was Tate and none other who broke the back of the Australian innings—Tate, who revels in a ground which is dry enough to give scope to his pace from the wicket. Now, in my view, Tate was indirectly helped this afternoon by a tactical move of Woodfull—a move which though theoretically justifiable, did not work out well in practice. Woodfull declined to use the heavy roller, but instead asked for a lightish one before Australia batted. His plan was to keep as much moisture as possible under the surface of the grass out of reach of the sunshine. Apparently his plan was formed on some such logic as this: 'It is true that if I employ the heavy roller moisture will be brought up out of the earth and will leave the pitch tolerably easy for an hour. But at the end of that time dampness will turn to stickiness, and then I shall lose any advantage gained while the turf was easy. Therefore I will try by use of a light roller to keep moisture underground in the hope that a June day will dry up the earth's horrid humours slowly, secretly, and more or less harmlessly.' As I say,

181

here was good political thinking in the abstract: it was strategy designed to defeat England's spin bowlers.

TATE'S CHOICE

Unfortunately for Woodfull, it played into the hands of Tate who from the first ball he aimed down at Australia today was free to feel, no doubt to his great relief, that his pace from the earth was after all not going to be put under the anaesthetic of a slow turf. Thus did he find his opportunity behind Woodfull's back while Woodfull was fixing policy's eyes on the peril that might come to Australia from spin pure and simple. It is dangerous for a spectator to argue strategy based on the state of the wicket: only the players in the game can really know how a pitch is behaving or is likely to behave. But I fancy I am not mistaken in supposing that had Woodfull put the heavy roller on Trent Bridge's turf this afternoon the attack of Tate would, as a consequence of the moisture brought up, have been considerably less dangerous than it was.

Tate attacked magnificently; in the absence of a left-handed bowler Woodfull, after the rain, had really no greater danger to look to than Tate at his best. Tate overwhelmed Ponsford, Woodfull, and Bradman in seven overs and four balls, and only six runs were got from this mettlesome attack. When Tate makes a red and glossy cricket ball move down a pitch like a curving spear—why, what is the use of mechanical talk about a sticky pitch?

The wicket was troublesome now and again; I can discover no proof either out of my own observations of the play or from those of cricketers engaged in the action to support the opinion that Australia were trapped on a definitely sticky wicket. It was the bad luck of Woodfull and his ten colleagues to run into a night of rain and to fall victims thereby to the suggestions of conditions material and unfriendly. If a cricketer gets merely the notion of a bad pitch into his head, very well, then, the wicket might as well be unplayable: 'I think, therefore I am,' argued Descartes, who may or may not be a favourite writer of Australia's very thoughtful captain.

The time of day was a quarter-past two when the match went on with June opening the pride of summer all around us. The vast crowd made the buzzing noises of expectancy when Robins lifted up his bat and all the heart of an English boy. Richard Tyldesley lost his wicket with alacrity; a fast ball from Wall rose up at the back of him. Tyldesley, with no room to swing his bat, so swiftly

182

was the ball on him, tried to drive with a congested action and a very red face. He was caught from a mis-hit to Fairfax on the off side behind the wicket: the stroke was not so much a hit as a collision. With Duckworth in last and a very urchin of confidence and nimbleness, Robins cracked the ball through the covers with a bat that was stylish, strong, and free as youth ought ever to be. He reached 50, to the joy of thousands to whom only the other day he was but a name—a Middlesex name. Now did the Trent Bridge crowd take Robins to its heart: tongues of strangers spoke of him with pride and affection. Such is cricket and the humanity thereof. Robins scored his 50 in five minutes less than an hour—bless us, and it was a Test match in this year of nineteen hundred and thirty. What is more, it was his first Test match. Let him go his ways, this boy Robins; let nobody sophisticate cricket out of him. The Australian fielding was again admirable. Fairfax and Wall, who bowled the English innings to its end, made the ball rear nastily—a hint of the wrath to come from Tate, only Woodfull did not seem to see it that way.

THE AUSTRALIAN INNINGS

At three o'clock Larwood bowled at Woodfull: he ran over the earth like a young horse. Several times did he compel Woodfull to play at off-side balls which Woodfull did not want to play—tried not to play, yet had to play simply because reflex action is not rational. The unease of Woodfull spread over the field: I felt that it was communicated to the Australians waiting in the pavilion for their moment. The English bowling was from the outset allowed to get on top: a sense of Australian dubiety was in the air, and the crowd gloated that they could see it growing like a storm-cloud. Here was revenge coming for the torments and humiliations England suffered at Trent Bridge nine years ago. Every time a ball beat the bat of Woodfull ten thousand eyes were glad.

Only four runs were scored from Tate and Larwood in twenty minutes: then Ponsford was totally bowled by Tate. He padded up overmuch to the off side, played back instead of forward to a ball which swung across and hit the leg stump. By reaching out down the line of a ball Ponsford might have glanced a comfortable two or three to leg. The crowd sent up a shout of welcome as Australia's next batsman was seen to be coming down the pavilion steps. But the ovation was mistakenly directed at Fairfax, who had been sent out in place of Bradman. Thus did Fairfax find reposing on his brow a laurel wreath not intended for him. I was reminded of the laurel wreath which was aimed at Miss Snevellicci at her benefit performance: it missed her and reposed upon the brow of a gentleman in the pit. Woodfull sent Fairfax out to bat first wicket down in the hope that two solid cricketers would play the wicket easy— more excellent theory turned awry by practice. Fairfax held onto the crease tenaciously, but he could not attack bowlers who must have felt themselves growing in stature at the thought that Australia was seeing so much trouble about them that even the celebrated Bradman must needs be withheld from harm's way for as long as may be. Fairfax was nearly caught in the slips straight away, playing speculatively at the spin of Richard Tyldesley. Tate changed ends, and immediately got the wicket of Woodfull: the ball was beautiful. It swung away late, a very scimitar of a ball, too sinister in its curve for our image of the spear. The ball found the edge of Woodfull's bat as he tried to push to the off side. The inevitable mis hit was caught by Chapman behind backward point: it was a clever catch, and Chapman spectacularly made what was possible seem incredible. When Woodfull's wicket went my imagination heard noises of catastrophic happenings, for Woodfull is the great foundation of an Australian innings in a Test match.

A DIFFERENT BRADMAN

Bradman came forth now, but not the Bradman of the popular legend. He looked no older than his actual years; he wore the earnest aspect of the apprentice. We could understand now that recently he has but been masquerading for us with clever boyish apishness in the habilaments of mastership. Tyldesley bothered him. Tate tormented him until mercifully bowling him with a breakback to which Bradman held out a bat as limp as it was crooked.

With the gulf open to Australia like bankruptcy itself, Fairfax and Kippax came together; three wickets were down for sixteen. Kippax played like a cricketer of quality; his bat had both refinement and substance. He played forward to Richard Tyldesley, and quickly Richard's length wavered. Thrice in quick sequence Kippax hit Tyldesley for fours, the only boundaries in the Australian innings for a long stretch of time. Fairfax was stiff but persistent until Australia were 57 and the tea interval had been taken. His wicket was the fourth to fall, and an indiscreet hit at Robins's going away-spin was the canny man's ruin. Hobbs at cover held a pretty catch.

Spin quite waspish overcame McCabe, whose catch to Hammond from a leg-spinner of Robins was elementary.

Five Australian batsmen had been settled at five o'clock for 61 runs. Robins hereabout was spinning from the pitch quite passionately. But Richardson, goaded by the sorry hour, looked for the bad-length ball voraciously, and three times in one over he drove Robins for fours, then hit two boundaries from consecutive balls by Tyldesley. There was the cavalier poise and temper in Richardson's play; meanwhile Kippax went along his reliant and handsome way, borrowing as much from style as from science. Another mistake of judgment, distinct from an advantage gained by a ball obviously unplayable, broke the Richardson–Kippax stand just as it was looking unpleasant in English eyes and heroic in the eyes of Australians. Richardson changed his mind to a well-pitched ball from Tyldesley, played back instead of forward, and was bowled. While scoring 37 out of 44 in half an hour he hit seven boundaries. Robins snatched at the chance left open to him by Richardson's passing; he spun Oldfield and Grimmett almost out of their senses. While stumping Oldfield, Duckworth let the Australian wicket-keeper hear how an appeal can be, if it ought not to be, made in a Test match.

At the ripe day's fall, when sunshine touched Trent Bridge's antiquity to agelessness, Kippax was still unbeaten. For nearly two hours his cricket had kept the Australian innings within the category of skill, personal and representative. When he had hit seven boundaries they were all from Richard Tyldesley, who pitched too short a length.

Larwood, who did not take a wicket, bowled with a fine mingling of pace and length and direction. But the afternoon was Tate's and Robins's, with Tate the first cause of Australia's breakdown—that is, the first cause technically, for essentially Australia's troubles were the consequence of rain and sunshine and too much thought and speculation about either. When Mr Winkle collapsed on the ice he complained to Sam Weller, 'These are very awkward skates.' And Sam replied, 'It's a werry orkard gen'lman wearing 'em, sir.' The bearing of that observation, as it affects the Australians and their collapse today, lies in the application of it, to borrow further still from Charles Dickens.

FIRST TEST
3rd Day Trent Bridge

ENGLAND

First Innings		Second Innings	
Hobbs, c Richardson, b McCabe	78	Hobbs, st Oldfield, b Grimmett	74
Sutcliffe, c Hornibrook, b Fairfax	29	Sutcliffe, retired hurt	58
Hammond, lbw, b Grimmett	8	Hammond, lbw, b Grimmett	4
Woolley, st Oldfield, b Grimmett	0	Woolley, b Wall	5
Hendren, b Grimmett	5	Hendren, c Richardson, b Wall	72
A. P. F. Chapman, c Ponsford, b Hornbrook	52	A. P. F. Chapman, b Wall	29
Larwood, b Grimmett	18	Tate, c Kippax, b Grimmett	24
R. W. V. Robins, not out	50	R. W. V. Robins, b McCabe	7
Tate, b Grimmett	13	Larwood, b Grimmett	4
Tyldesley (R.), c Fairfax, b Wall	1	Tyldesley, b Grimmett	5
Duckworth, lbw, b Fairfax	4	Duckworth, not out	14
B 4, lb 7, nb 1	12	B 5, lb 1	6
Total	**270**	**Total**	**302**

FALL OF WICKETS

1	2	3	4	5	6	7	8	9	10
53	63	63	71	153	188	218	241	243	270

Second Innings

1	2	3	4	5	6	7	8	9
125	137	147	211	250	260	283	292	302

AUSTRALIA
First Innings

W. M. Woodfull, c Chapman, b Tate	2
W. H. Ponsford, b Tate	3
A. Fairfax, c Hobbs, b Robins	14
D. G. Bradman b Tate	8
A. F. Kippax, not out	60
S. McCabe, c Hammond, b Robins	4
V. Y. Richardson, b Tyldesley (R.)	37
W. A. Oldfield, c Duckworth, b Robins	4
G. V. Grimmett, st Duckworth, b Robins	0
P. M. Hornibrook, lbw, b Larwood	0
T. Wall, b Tyldesley (R.)	4
B 4, lb 4	8
Total	**144**

FALL OF WICKETS

1	2	3	4	5	6	7	8	9	10
4	6	16	57	61	105	134	140	141	144

Second Innings

W. M. Woodfull, c Chapman, b Larwood	4
W. H. Ponsford, not out	21
D. G. Bradman, not out	31
lb 4	4
	—
Total (for 1 wicket)	60

FALL OF WICKETS

$$\frac{1}{12}$$

BOWLING ANALYSIS
ENGLAND
First Innings

	O.	M.	R.	W.		O.	M.	R.	W.
Wall	17	4	47	1	Hornibrook	12	3	30	1
Fairfax	21·4	5	51	2	McCabe	7	3	23	1
Grimmett	32	6	107	5					

Fairfax bowled one no-ball

Second Innings

	O.	M.	R.	W.		O.	M.	R.	W.
Wall	23	4	67	3	Hornibrook	11	4	35	0
Fairfax	15	4	58	0	McCabe	14	3	42	1
Grimmett	30	4	94	5					

AUSTRALIA
First Innings

	O.	M.	R.	W.		O.	M.	R.	W.
Larwood	15	8	12	1	Tyldesley	21	8	53	2
Tate	19	8	20	3	Robins	17	4	51	4

TRENT BRIDGE, MONDAY

The Australian first innings went to a sudden and wan end. On a cool, sunless morning Larwood bowled at a pace that seemed to find more and more inspiration in the knowledge that Hornibrook looked very definitely a cricketer played for his bowling and fielding. In a quarter of an hour England made certain of an advantage of 144.

With a lack of cricket sense surely unprecedented in Australian cricket Kippax allowed Wall to take Tyldesley's bowling by running a three for a leg-glance from an over's first ball; the batsmen, indeed, ran as though Australia needed two runs to tie and three to win. Tyldesley saw to it that Kippax had no further opportunity to score: Wall is as mortal a No. 11 batsman as the old Trent Bridge bowler of legendary humour who caused the old horse to back instinctively into the shafts of the heavy roller whenever he walked down the pavilion steps with a bat in his hands. Kippax ought to have moved heaven and earth to keep English bowling in his control, and by hitting a few challenging fours, perform a gesture calculated to lift up the hearts of his companions. The feeble collapse of Australia's last two wickets must have damaged still further a confidence thin-skinned compared with the hardened old brass of Armstrong's men.

THE REAL HOBBS

At half-past eleven a vast multitude shouted Hobbs and Sutcliffe to the wicket. Straight away Hobbs plunged the English innings into the key of the dominant colour. His bat had for a while no half-lights about it. He struck forth something of his ancient fire when he cut Fairfax square with a hammer blow. Grimmett spun his fingers vainly at Hobbs hereabout; the master moved forward and found the ball with his bat's middle so inevitably that I was made to think of the magnetism that attracts bodies together. The moment he was played in Hobbs found his youth again in a sudden moment which came to us and passed like thunder from the old years. He leaped out of his ground and from three consecutive balls drove Hornibrook for fours, each of them eager, with the bat swinging through splendidly on high.

Fairfax and Wall had to pitch short of a length to curb the voracity of the old lion: Hobbs cannot any longer exploit the swift short-armed strokes which are wanted for the making of runs against the sort of ball a cricketer can get into his control only at the last minute. Hobbs has to see the ball quickly now—which means his forcing strokes are very much dependent on balls in the air for a longish time or those that pitch conveniently short. Yet for all his middle years he remains our greatest Test match batsman: how eloquently that truth came home to us this afternoon immediately after Hobbs got out through walking forward to the leg spin of Grimmett rather casually. Hobbs made 74 out of 125 in just under two hours, and he hit ten fours, all of them definitely aggressive, full-blooded drives or cuts.

WOOLLEY'S FAREWELL?

After lunch Sutcliffe was hurt on the hand by Wall, who enjoyed a period of authentic pace, though Woodfull still provided him with two slips only and a backward point. With their old bugbear out of the way—which is Hobbs and Sutcliffe—the Australian attack suddenly seemed to discover new life, good and evil. Grimmett's spin disconcerted Hammond and Woolley abominably: we actually were compelled to ask whether the Trent Bridge wicket was about to crumble. At 137 Hammond was leg before wicket to Grimmett; we had been watching the process of this doom for too long a time. At 147 Woolley played back at a fast ball well up to him; his bat was aslant terribly. Woolley departed sadly, perhaps out of Test cricket for ever. Well, a lovely star has set; felicity has been born under it. I shall see him until I die, a cricketer unparalleled, touched by the sunshine of Kent cricket fields.

Hendren was nearly stumped, and apparently his heart came into his mouth while he escaped, as he reached the wicket and stretched his bat out at a leg spinner as though sightless as speculation. He is a batsman who will not be put down, though: he drove Grimmett to the straight on boundary, and cut him for four with a stroke quick as a shaft of light. His cricket thrived the longer it lasted: when Grimmett was taken off he gave us once more to understand that he is one of the busiest and best of batsmen against quick bowling that comes through unambiguously after pitching.

Chapman again placed his off-side strokes under a science of his own. He and Hendren had to face the imminence of another English breakdown, and they did not merely evade it but answered or threat, bat for ball. In three-quarters of an hour Chapman and Hendren scored 64 for England's fourth wicket; then Chapman, trying a drive, played on to Wall, who returned with the new ball and a gallant energy and more speed than I have before known him to send down an English wicket. Perhaps it is as well for England that Wall when he bowls does not show his left side to the batsman; his action denotes the fast bowler's breakback. Wall's action is full-fronted, and his weight tends to fall backwards as his arm comes over. Yet today he has by determination and the virility of young manhood given the English batsman no time at all to waste in the making of strokes from him.

CHAPMAN'S PLANS GO AMISS

The cricket between lunch and tea gave us cause to realize how greatly dependent the English team is upon Hobbs and Sutcliffe for reliant batsmanship. Chapman must have hoped, after the fine attack of Hobbs on the bowling, to be able to declare his innings closed at the tea interval, especially as there were signs of another break in the weather. The truth is that the moment Hobbs got out the Australian attack was able to revive technically and spiritually England could score no faster than a run a minute; always had we to work by sweat of the brow to push home a strong advantage got not only by skill but by the help of Friday night's rain. We could not knock the enemy sideways in the hearty fashion of the Australian victors of nine years ago. Leading as England were by two hundred and fifty runs with nine wickets in hand, there ought not to have been any need for an English batsman laboriously to play himself in as though retrieving a doubtful situation.

For three-quarters of an hour after lunch a stranger coming to the field would have picked out England as the side struggling and unhappy. Had Hendren failed England might have had reason for tears—and for a period Hendren's life hung on a very frail thread. The Australians pulled themselves together admirably after the passing of Hobbs and Sutcliffe. It would seem that Hobbs in all his middle years must still shoulder the two main jobs of Test match batsmanship: he must save the dangerous day and speed the victorious one. Hendren's innings of seventy-two lasted one hour and three-quarters, and when he came to the wicket England were two hundred and sixty-three ahead with six wickets in hand, assuming Sutcliffe would not bat again. The English innings finished at a quarter past five, and despite an innings of Tate boisterous as Beachy Head the speed at the end did not work out at much more than sixty runs an hour. After lunch Hornibrook bowled only one or two overs.

AUSTRALIA'S SECOND INNINGS

By the course of the afternoon's events Chapman was able to attack the Australians again in that closing three-quarters of an hour which no batsman likes to face after a period in the field, especially when he is on the losing side. But the outward show of sovereignty would have been served better had Chapman been at liberty to ask the Australians to face the music at his own sweet pleasure. Larwood bowled at a great and thrilling pace, and well might he have done at the sight of Ponsford's transparent mortality. Even Woodful played hopelessly late at off-side balls with strokes against which the voice of reason in him must have cried out beseechingly.

How alive was the atmosphere at Trent Bridge this evening and how thin-spun seemed the life of Australia's innings will be realized when I saw that we were expecting a wicket to fall every ball, even Woodfull's wicket. Not once last summer did the South Africans look a team so down and out as these Australians looked tonight. The torments we suffered nine years ago may now be forgotten; desire for revenge may even give way to magnanimity. Bless us, that we should have lived to feel sorry for Australia at cricket!

Woodfull made a stroke at an off-side ball from Larwood as instinctive, as far removed from the control of a seat of judgment and intellect, as the quick, apprehensive movement the hand of man makes at a wasp buzzing about his ears. Chapman caught the edged stroke, leaping sideways in glee and yet again turning a good catch into an act spectacular and phenomenal. Woodfull departed a sad captain with Australia's score not more than twelve.

Ponsford, after appearing to sway and ready to topple like a man dizzy with vertigo at the sight of immense depths below him, tightened his nerve and technique. And this time Bradman's bat was determined; even though his first hit was an intended drive which flew over the head of the slips, none the less this was a sign of temper, a snap of the fingers at damnable consequences. At a quarter past six Ponsford drove Robins straight for four as though enjoying hitting practice at the nets. He was a cricketer just raised from the dead; this was a very Lazarus of an innings. When it began it was not long for this world. In forty minutes Ponsford and Bradman sent up the 50; the batting had won through to confidence if not to assurance. Twice in one over Bradman drove Tyldesley to the on boundary, and there was then only a few minutes to go. I loved the opportunism of this young player, who though on the verge of close of play saw a bad ball as a bad ball and clouted the life out of it. If Larwood and Tate can be stopped for half an hour in the morning there may be fresh history for Trent Bridge before the match is won and lost.

FIRST TEST
4th Day Trent Bridge

ENGLAND

First Innings		Second Innings	
Hobbs, c Richardson, b McCabe	78	Hobbs, st Oldfield, b Grimmett	74
Sutcliffe, c Hornibrook, b Fairfax	29	Sutcliffe, retired hurt	58
Hammond, lbw, b Grimmett	8	Hammond, lbw, b Grimmett	4
Woolley, st Oldfield, b Grimmett	0	Woolley, b Wall	5
Hendren, b Grimmett	5	Hendren, c Richardson, b Wall	72
A. P. F. Chapman, c Ponsford, b Hornibrook	52	A. P. F. Chapman, b Wall	29
Larwood, b Grimmett	18	Tate, c Kippax, b Grimmett	24
R. W. V. Robins, not out	50	R. W. V. Robins, b McCabe	4
Tate, b Grimmett	13	Larwood, b Grimmett	7
Tyldesley, (R.), c Fairfax, b Wall	1	Tyldesley, b Grimmett	5
Duckworth, lbw, b Fairfax	4	Duckworth, not out	14
B 4, lb 7, nb 1	12	B 5, lb 1	6
Total	270	Total	302

FALL OF WICKETS
First Innings

1	2	3	4	5	6	7	8	9	10
53	63	63	71	153	188	218	241	242	270

Second Innings

1	2	3	4	5	6	7	8	9
125	137	147	211	250	260	283	283	302

AUSTRALIA

First Innings		Second Innings	
W. M. Woodfull, c Chapman, b Tate	2	W. M. Woodfull, c Chapman, b Larwood	4
W. H. Ponsford, b, Tate	3	W. H. Ponsford, b Tate	39
A. Fairfax, c Hobbs, b Robins	14	D. G. Bradman, b Robins	131
D. G. Bradman, b Tate	8	A. F. Kippax, c Hammond, b Robins	23
A. F. Kippax, not out	60	S. McCabe, c sub, b Tate	49
S. McCabe, c Hammond, b Robins	4	V. Y. Richardson, lbw, b Tyldesley	29
V. Y. Richardson, b Tyldesley (R.)	37	A. Fairfax, c Robins, b Tate	14
W. A. Oldfield, c, Duckworth, b, Robins	4	W. A. Oldfield, c Hammond, b Tyldesley	11
C. V. Grimmett, st Duckworth, b Robins	0	C. V. Grimmett, c Hammond, b Tyldesley	0
P. M. Hornibrook, lbw, b Larwood	0	P. M. Hornibrook, c Duckworth, b Robins	5
T. Wall, b Tyldesley	4	T. Wall, not out	8
B 4, lb 4	8	B 17, lb 5	22
Total	144	Total	335

FALL OF WICKETS

First Innings

1	2	3	4	5	6	7	8	9	10
4	6	16	57	61	105	134	140	141	144

Second Innings

1	2	3	4	5	6	7	8	9	10
12	93	152	229	267	296	312	322	324	335

BOWLING ANALYSIS

ENGLAND—First Innings

	O.	M.	R.	W.		O.	M.	R.	W.
Wall	17	4	47	1	Hornibrook	12	3	30	1
Fairfax	21·4	5	51	2	McCabe	7	3	23	1
Grimmett	32	6	107	5					

Fairfax bowled one no-ball

Second Innings

	O.	M.	R.	W.		O.	M.	R.	W.
Wall	26	4	67	3	Hornibrook	11	4	35	0
Fairfax	15	4	58	0	McCabe	14	3	42	1
Grimmett	70	4	94	5					

AUSTRALIA—First Innings

	O.	M.	R.	W.		O.	M.	R.	W.
Larwood	15	8	12	1	Tyldesley	21	8	53	2
Tate	19	8	20	3	Robins	17	4	51	4

Second Innings

	O.	M.	R.	W.		O.	M.	R.	W.
Larwood	5	1		1	Tyldesley	35	10	77	3
Tate	50	90	69	3	Hammond	29	5	74	0
Robins	17·2	1	81	3	Woolley	3	1	3	0

TRENT BRIDGE, TUESDAY

At twenty-five minutes to six on a June evening of sunshine England won the first Test match by 93 runs, and Australia lost it with honours. In an uphill fight Woodfull's men were not put out until they had made the highest score ever achieved in a fourth innings of a Test match played in this country.

England had to bowl without aid from Larwood, who fell ill last night, and, indeed, suffered a headache even while on Monday evening his speed rendered Ponsford like a man in the presence of forked lightning. The casualties to Sutcliffe and Larwood were, of course, scurvy tricks for England to bear, but Australia deserved a share of the game's luck after the shabby turn served them on

Friday and Saturday by rain. All day long England have needed to work severely; time after time we could feel the tide in the secret deeps of the match turning in Australia's direction. As the hurly-burly proceeded, now favouring the one side, now the other, I had a vision of Woodfull sitting aloft somewhere, anxious, yet willing his warriors with all his heart, sitting with arms uplifted in the hope that by endurance and supplication he could keep the battle in Australia's keeping.

MOMENTS OF ANXIETY

Twice during the afternoon there occurred moments of trial to our faith—when Bradman and McCabe seemed set, and when Bradman had passed his hundred and was forging ahead. These two sinister stands were broken by an exceptional catch in the one instance and an exceptional ball in the other. McCabe seemed ready to hit hard an attack not exactly hopeful when he drove to mid-on, where a substitute fielding for Sutcliffe ran quickly after starting late and held his prize despite toppling forward perilously. The ball whereby Robins bowled Bradman was one which the most skilful man might not be able to achieve even on his luckiest day. A 'googly' of perfect length is a gift from well-disposed gods; Bradman could not get his pads in front of the wicket quickly enough to frustrate spin which had evil in it. Another hour of McCabe and Bradman might have—but what is the use of might-haves? poor Woodfull will ask now.

Hammond was England's opening bowler with Tate; he kept a length and gave to the ball pace from the pitch. Tate worked with all his heart to be Tate and Larwood as well—he dropped noble sweat, and for an hour almost his attack was stopped only by bats laden with heavy labour. Neither Bradman nor Ponsford exactly looked to be great batsmen, yet both of them are beaters of Mac-Laren's highest score. From this morning I concluded their superiority with MacLaren is strictly statistical.

TYLDESLEY'S BOWLING

Tyldesley was a good bowler today; his length was often of the kind which makes a batsman's fallible reason say 'Go forward' when his instincts cry out 'Keep back.' Only one four was hit in an hour and a quarter, and that was from the edge of Ponsford's bat. Even with Larwood out of his sight he did not seem happy, and when he was bowled playing back at Tate the English scorer was able to put down on paper what he had probably been itching to write all morning.

At 93 for two Kippax came in, and immediately the contrast he made with Bradman was that of accomplishment and dexterity. Kippax's bat had a flavour; he enjoyed his cricket, while obviously Bradman was a cricketer working well by scorning delights and living a laborious day. Several times Bradman played back with a bent right knee, causing a crooked bat. But his eye was keen and his nerve steady—and he persisted. Kippax, who is, while Jackson is out of form, easily Australia's most cultivated batsman, drove Robins through the covers with a grace of a day that is gone; I was reminded of a forgotten summer when at Trent Bridge Reginald Spooner's cover drives seemed to clothe the grass with gold.

At one end of the wicket today there was a spot which the spin bowlers rooted out from time to time. Robins pitched his leg break on this flake of mischief, and Kippax, who seemed expectant of the 'googly', held out an indeterminate bat and edged a catch to the slips. Now came forward McCabe, who hit the first ball he received to leg with the temper of one blowing a trumpet call. He laid into Robins lustily and at lunch Australia were 199 for three. The crowd ate while talking all manner of speculation.

A BETTER BRADMAN

After the interval Bradman hit his first four of the day; he opened out his stroke technique, and the game's thrilling kettle began to boil. Before lunch Bradman's cricket had been of the suspicious order which gives hope to bowlers; his body was bent like a note of doubtful interrogation. McCabe's swift bat struck the match-winning note, and Bradman emerged from the minor to the major key of batsmanship—an honest, natural C major bold as brass. He reached his hundred amidst generous cheers; his strokes, nearly all to leg and to the on, were vigorous, with a plebeian energy.

In seventy-five minutes McCabe and Bradman carried Australia from 152 to 229; then occurred the catch by the mute but not inglorious substitute already described. His name is Copley, and tonight it is being pronounced in Nottingham in noble numbers. Just after Bradman acquired his hundred a ball from Tyldesley spun away gigantically—another sign of a wicket not free of that original sin which no modern groundsman can purify. Australia were within 162 of victory with time to get the runs when Robins bowled the exemplary ball mentioned above. Bradman batted four and a quarter hours; this will be by no means his highest score, against England this summer. His style may be open to criticism but it is his own and he knows his own limitations—at least until he has been keeping the bowlers at work for an hour or two.

RICHARDSON'S GAMBLE

The downfall of Bradman gave the England eleven a sure sight of the game's prize; as he passed, the fieldsmen engaged in flippant conversation and Tate relaxed his body into the lassitude of relief. Richardson lost no time launching an attack; it was the only game now for Australia, for they could hardly hope to play out three hours for a draw with only five wickets, containing those of Hornibrook, Grimmett, and Wall. Richardson hit six boundaries, each of them a smack in the face to the perspiring bowlers—and Richard Tyldesley, by his Lancashire sweat, made Tate seem a man just come from some shady arbour. Tyldesley lumbered up to the wicket doggedly and kept his length.

Richardson tried to sweep a well-pitched ball from him over the square-leg boundary; he missed and was leg before. The stroke was injudicious, but this was no moment for an Australian batsman to observe the niceties. Richardson gambled, and only a gambler's throw could save his side now. All was over the moment Richardson threw his dice. Fairfax resisted grimly, and while he batted I got the impression of the Australians being pushed back only step by step. At the end Wall hit the one and only six of the game—a hearty way of dying and the true cricketer's way.

Australia will be a harder side to beat at Lord's—and perhaps England may have to try to beat them with a team lacking Sutcliffe. Larwood and Sutcliffe were severe casualties, but, after all, Chapman won the toss and then—it rained.

SECOND TEST MATCH 1930
1st Day Lords

ENGLAND
First Innings

Hobbs, c Oldfield, b Fairfax	1
Woolley, c Wall, b Fairfax	41
Hammond, b Grimmett	38
K. S. Duleepsinhji, c Bradman, b Grimmett	173
Hendren, c McCabe, b Fairfax	48
A. P. F. Chapman, c Oldfield, b Wall	11
G. O. Allen, b Fairfax	3
Tate, c McCabe, b Wall	54
R. W. V. Robins, c Oldfield, b Hornibrook	5
J. C. White, not out	10
Duckworth, not out	7
B 2, lb 7, nb 1	10
	—
Total (for nine wickets)	401

FALL OF WICKETS
ENGLAND—First Innings

1	2	3	4	5	6	7	8	9
13	53	105	209	236	239	337	363	387

Umpires—Chester and Oates

AUSTRALIA: W. M. Woodfull, W. M. Ponsford, D. G. Bradman, A. Fairfax, A. F. Kippax, S. McCabe, V. Y. Richardson, W. A. Oldfield, C. V. Grimmett, P. M. Hornibrook, and T. Wall.

LORD'S, FRIDAY

A warm June sun cast a resplendent light on Lord's this morning. The old place was magnificent; we could get the sense of pomp and circumstance as we walked over the field before the first ball was bowled in the second Test match. In the crowd great cricketers of the past were to be seen; we could also feel the invisible presence of the ancient ghosts whose immortality is housed at Lord's.

History was beating her wings when, at half-past eleven, the action began. Chapman's luck stayed with him, for again did he win the toss—a very important advantage at Lord's, where the turf is not only always sensitive to rain and sunshine, but even in fine weather tends to be a batsman's enemy, while it shows signs of disintegration on a third, let alone a fourth afternoon. There were things to talk about immediately. I got the impression from the multitudinous voices that sensation was smacking voracious chops, for the news went round that Sandham and Larwood were not playing, and that Woolley was going to be sent in with Hobbs to open England's innings. Nine years ago Woolley batted first with Hardinge for England at Leeds. I can see the scene now—the fall of a hot day on which Australia had made 400, and in a fading light Gregory sent Woolley's wicket flying Catherine wheels for none. There was no thunderous Gregory for any English batsman to tackle today, and no silently running Macdonald. Wall tried hard to bowl fast, but his endeavour was always far ahead of his achievement. Woolley lost no time making the match seem a midsummer holiday. His bat, all sweet shapes and movements, sent the ball here, there, and everywhere, swift as light. The ease and grace of his poise denied his power. Yet the force of his strokes left the fieldsmen helpless—reduced them to white pillars of immobility.

WOOLLEY'S FINE DRIVING

The second ball of Wall's second over was driven straight for four, and Woolley merely seemed to lean on it. Then in Fairfax's second over he drove past cover, handsome as a prince. The stroke was a bright ribbon of a boundary unfurled in a flash. But while one end of the wicket was white with lustre the other end saw Hobbs in cold grey durance; the master was not at ease, so little so that we were shocked rather than surprised when, with England's score only 13, Hobbs's bat grazed an outswinger from Fairfax into the gloves of Oldfield. Hammond came in now, but frankly nobody observed his advent. When we have looked at the sun our eyes are not able to see illumination in much else. Woolley's batting was radiant with felicity. As he drove in front of the wicket his bat swung down so effortlessly, yet with all of that great energy which we can be sure forces up the loveliest gush of water in a garden's spraying fountain. At twelve o'clock—high noon on a summer's day—England were 25 for 1 and Woolley 22, including four boundaries. Then, in swift and enchanting sequence, he drove three fours, two from Fairfax one from Wall. The drives off Fairfax were remarkable because the balls pitched just short of the length which to other batsmen invites a full-armed hit. Woolley has a heavenly length to his reach; like every other great batsman he makes his own bad bowling. For three-quarters of an hour Woolley turned this solemn occasion of a Test match into a Canterbury pleasance; his play conjured up sights and sounds of Kent's own delectable fields—white tents and bunting in the breeze. He hit—nay, let's have a tenderer word, Samivel,—he stroked, caressed, and cajoled seven boundaries in 45 minutes. Then—a thousand pities in the sight of the angels—a matchless innings was damnably ended. Fairfax went on at the pavilion end. His first ball rose to cutting height and Woolley lay back, lifted up all his tallness, and cut gorgeously. The ball sped straight down at a thrilling pace. And Wall, at point, scooped up an incredible catch, even though the force of the hit sent him staggering backwards. Woolley's innings deserved this swift end—your bright bird, if die he must, ought to be brought down while full on the wing. When Woolley departed—giving the sun of summer a chance to show itself at last—England were 53 for 2. Only one mistake did Woolley make, and that happened when he played forward, with his score 28, to the second ball bowled by Grimmett, missed his aim, and was nearly stumped.

TOIL FOR HAMMOND

The wicket was good enough for good batsmen, but its smoothness was part and parcel of English turf honestly prepared. No anaesthetics had been used in the preparation of it. Therefore a bowler could hope always that now and again his pace and spin would have full scope. Hammond had to toil for his runs; he was always servant to the attack. In an hour and a quarter he could score not more than seven runs from Grimmett. Hammond's range of strokes does not widen as time goes on, he has, indeed, lost much of his old strength with the drive. Duleepsinhji sized up the bowling shrewdly before he got to work. Truth to tell, it was very moderate bowling. Grimmett's spin did not contain the waspishness which made it deadly at Nottingham; Wall was just a hard-working plodder, while Fairfax and Hornibrook bowled like everyday county men. The fielding was admirable, Bradman on the boundary speeding a youthful track and picking up and throwing in with all of life's energy when its years are not heaped up.

Hammond and Duleepsinhji scored 52 for England's third wicket in 85 minutes. Hammond was then bowled playing forward to a ball too short for him to reach, even though he went quite a way after it. It was a spinning ball that kept scandalously low. At lunch the match was even—England 129 for the loss of Hobbs, Woolley, and Hammond.

DULEEPSINHJI AND HENDREN

After lunch Duleepsinhji and Hendren saw the Australian attack as in itself it really was—persevering but not enigmatical. Grimmett alone required a second scrutiny, and even he was not today at his most dangerous. His spin could be watched so late that errors of judgment committed while the ball was in the air were remediable after it had pitched. An on drive by Duleepsinhji was in the grand manner. MacLaren, sitting in the pavilion, had the privilege of admiring this stroke with more appreciation than that of the rest of us, for it mirrored MacLaren's own majesty when he was wearing his purple against Australia at Lord's. Duleepsinhji's cricket had the polish of wristwork. His late cuts were sweet as fruit. Hendren's vigour contrasted well with Duleepsinhji's suppleness. The difference between the two was that of the Orient and the Occident, between the slightly ambiguous and the utterly tangible. Hendren gave us fair craftsmanship; he forced the ball off his pads to the on with certain aim and power, and he raced his first run carrying his bat like a jolly urchin. For an hour and a half Duleepsinhji and Hendren delighted the crowd with true cricket, cricket loud with the game's cracking noises. Applause was endless. This indeed was Lord's in high summer—over head the blue sky, round the field a happy throng, the cricketer's white flannels catching the soft bloom of the day.

The batsmen were so thoroughly set that they were making their strokes while the ball was in the air, coming to them. The Australians stuck to their work, but they found little encouragement. In ninety minutes Duleepsinhji and Hendren added 104, fifty of them in thirty-five minutes. Then, at 209, Hendren tried to hit a long hop for four, and fell to a catch at long leg. The ball was technically bad, but pragmatically excellent. Hendren seldom if ever looked like losing his wicket, his innings was good blood and brawn, with animal spirits rendering it very human. I can never get the conviction, though, that he belongs to the elect amongst batsmen of Test match history. The Duleepsinhji–Hendren partnership ought to have come to an end when England were 185 and when Duleepsinhji was 65. Duleepsinhji sent a catch to Woodfull at square leg: it was dropped, and Woodfull looked sad; he even exculpated himself in dumb show, to use the charming language of the Reverend Pycroft.

A USEFUL SEVENTH WICKET

Chapman was rather inept and Allen definitely so. Both were outclassed and dismissed by the time England's score stood at 239. Six wickets were down now—not good enough. The wicket enlivened the attack of Fairfax, who often caused the ball to jump even after it had pitched a good length. Winning the toss ought to mean victory sure and certain in this match. Tate played with customary gawkiness of bat and body, and also with customary straightness of eye. He was even discreet at times, actually keeping his head down. Duleepsinhji moved back on his wicket and cut the leg-spin of Grimmett deliciously late and intimately. When he was 98 he horrified everybody by giving a chance to third slip, who changed dismay to thanksgiving by promptly dropping the ball. Grimmett made the mistake of bowling short to Duleepsinhji; a half-volley is more likely than a short ball to trouble a batsman who can cut—if bad balls are to be sent to him at all. Duleepsinhji does not drive through the covers after the manner born. I fancy M. A. Noble would have instructed his bowlers to keep a length well up, but not too far up, to Duleepsinhji, and of course Noble would have had his field deeply placed on the off side. The Australians repeatedly favoured Duleepsinhji this afternoon with his favourite length, a shade short.

Tate has his moments of humour. He clouted against Grimmett's spin and beat the air. Next ball he missed with a riotously crooked bat and was nearly bowled. And the next ball he punched straight for four. His cricket was himself—rustic and likeable. A dazzling leg glance by Duleepsinhji let us understand who is his uncle. Ranjitsinhji, by the way, was present as his nephews scored a century in his first match against Australia. Now and again Duleepsinhji would commit a strange solecism—some wild beat, primitive and unscholarly. He is a beautiful player, but here and there he suggests that he has not yet altogether made culture second nature. He sometimes drops an aitch in the drawing-room of civilized cricketers.

By means of an on drive, mighty and tangible as Beachy Head, Tate reached 50 in 65 minutes. At 25 minutes past five Duleepsinhji and Tate had scored a priceless 98 runs for England's seventh wicket in 70 minutes. Tate then was caught at mid-off from a blow which saw the whole of his weight falling backwards on his wrong foot. It was a gallant stand in a challenging hour, and it made all the difference between the Australians having a reasonable and only an outside chance of winning the match. I did not feel, while Tate batted, that the Australians were thoughtfully led; there was too little concentration on Tate's weakness for an off-side 'bang'. The ball ought to be kept so far from Tate's bat that he has to stretch his arms to find it; he is not likely to thrust his left leg across swiftly. It would have grieved the heart of M. A. Noble to see the Australian bowlers aiming at Tate's wickets so that he was able to trust to his eye and had not to worry about the problem of quick adjustments of footwork. When Grimmett is out of form this Australian team's attack is not better than that of the South Africans of last year—if it is as good.

Duleepsinhji reached his 150 at 20 minutes to six, after an innings of four hours and 20 minutes' length. At six o'clock White came in, when England were 367 for eight, and defended with bat and pads, giving us the impression that he was doing his best to save the game by playing out time. His behaviour in the presence of Grimmett's spin was quaint. Fortunately England's position was by now as sound as any cricket team of sportsmen could wish. Duleepsinhji's innings finished at 387. He was roared home by the crowd at every step, and at the end he ran up the steps of a pavilion standing as one man in acclamation. A superb on drive by White brought England's total to 401, and this consummation sent home countless happy men and women, all of them brown from a good day in the sun.

SECOND TEST MATCH
2nd Day Lords

ENGLAND
First Innings

Hobbs, c Oldfield, b Fairfax	1
Woolley, c Wall, b Fairfax	41
Hammond, b Grimmett	38
K. S. Duleepsinhji, c Bradman, b Grimmett	173
Hendren, c McCabe, b Fairfax	48
A. P. F. Chapman, c Oldfield, b Wall	11
G. O. Allen, b Fairfax	3
Tate, c McCabe, b Wall	54
R. W. V. Robins, c Oldfield, b Hornibrook	5
J. C. White, not out	23
Duckworth, c Oldfield, b Wall	18
B 2, lb 7, nb 1	10
Total	425

FALL OF WICKETS
ENGLAND
First Innings

1	2	3	4	5	6	7	8	9	10
13	53	105	209	236	239	337	363	387	425

BOWLING ANALYSIS

ENGLAND
First Innings

	O.	M.	R.	W.		O.	M.	R.	W.
Wall	29·4	2	118	3	Hornibrook	26	6	62	1
Grimmett	33	4	105	2	McCabe	9	1	29	0
Fairfax	31	6	101	4					

Fairfax bowled a no-ball

AUSTRALIA
First Innings

Woodfull, st Duckworth, b Robins	155
Ponsford, c Hammond, b White	81
Bradman, not out	155
Kippax, not out	7
B 1, lb 5	6
Total (for two wickets)	404

FALL OF WICKETS
AUSTRALIA—First Innings

1	2	3	4	5	6	7	8	9	10
162	393								

Umpires—Chester and Oates

AUSTRALIA: W. M. Woodfall, W. H. Ponsford, D. G. Bradman, A. Fairfax, A. F. Kippax, S. McCabe, V. Y. Richardson, W. A. Oldfield, C. V. Grimmett, P. M. Hornibrook, and T. Wall.

LONDON, SATURDAY

There was historical cricket at Lord's today. The Australians had to bat against 425 and an England eleven which was feeling high and mighty and superior. And in a single afternoon on an English turf the Australians scored 404 for two wickets—both of them lost not to good bowling but to those accidents which sooner or later trip up the best batsmen. This superb act of retaliation will go down with the finest of all the many fine uphill fights achieved by Australians in the past. The traditions were honoured. Even Clem Hill, Trumper, and Noble never pulled a game round with more skill and courage than the skill and courage displayed by Woodfull, Ponsford, and Bradman in this engagement.

The rare virtue of the rally of Woodfull's team is that it was not ceaselessly grim; though a stiff hill had to be climbed we were not deprived of those delights which are life and soul of cricket. After a dour enough beginning by Woodfull and Ponsford defence was changed to offence. The old Australia opportunism inspired the batting. First of all a sound foundation was established, then came an onslaught which laid the bowling waste. Woodfull and Ponsford scored 30 in the opening hour of their stand; at the end of three hours and five minutes Australia were 162 and Ponsford was out. Whatever of edge the English attack had ever possessed was now blunted totally. Bradman, from the first ball he got, let his feet jump about the wicket and the bat swing right and left. In two hours and a half Bradman and Woodfull made 231 for the second wicket—and Bradman reached his 100 in 105 minutes.

DISSOLUTE RAMPAGING

The facts need no adornment, they tell their own tale of batsmanship reliant and imaginative, circumspect and aggressive at the right moments. The annals of Test matches contain no better example of cricket played uphill with true sportsmanship. Would the England eleven, face to face with 425, have given the crowd occasion to shout home brilliant boundaries? We expect as a matter of course to sit in silence watching any cricket team that is batting against a heavy first innings' score, we look then as a rule for moral excellences such as fortitude and patience. The Australians for three hours were models of most virtuous parsimony, but none of us looked for the dissolute rampaging in the afternoon's closing hours, when young Bradman knocked solemnity to smithereens and attacked with a bat which might well have appeared excessively care-free even on the smooth lawn of a country house cricket match. It was good at last to see again batsmen in a crucial match belabouring weak bowling in the closing hours of a summer's day.

At the drawing of stumps Australia had not only attained the summit of an adverse hill, they had caught the first glimpse of a prospect of one of the most wonderful victories ever won in a Test match. England's position is dangerous. Woodfull's men now require nothing so much as the imagination to see their chance of bringing about something of a miracle. The match is at the moment magnificent with possibilities.

During the week-end the impression has gone round that the Australian batsmen won through only after hours of severe resistance against an attack which, for long, was keen and skilful. Without in the least disparaging the Australians' play, the plain truth must be recorded that England's bowling was merely moderate from the very outset. At lunch, when Australia were 96 for none, the nakedness of the attack of Tate, Allen, White, and Robins had been quiet indecently revealed. The man in the crowd, even while he was eating his lunch, was resigning himself to a huge Australian score. When Allen bowled his fifth over I got myself ready for the wrath to come. Ponsford hit a ball in this over straight past mid-off for three, a smack in the face for Allen which resounded all over the field. The stroke was proof positive that Larwood was not playing. I doubt if Ponsford has ever in his life driven or had time to contemplate driving Larwood in front of the wicket. Allen was hard-working but never fast; his four slips were, I gathered, intimidatory rather than accessory. True, Allen hit Ponsford on the body twice in his first over, but that was because Ponsford was walking into the ball, hoping to place it to leg. When Ponsford has batted against Larwood it has not usually been his intention to place the ball to leg, but rather to place himself to leg—as close to the umpire as time will allow.

FIELDSMEN WITHOUT HOPE

Allen hardly once gave his slips reason to throw up expectant hands, and before the afternoon was over Allen was bowling to one slip only, with Chapman busy at backward point stopping cuts which were being made by the free face of the bat. Ponsford's first four, a snick from Allen's third over, was the one and only edged stroke made from Allen all day. Not another dangerous stroke was to be seen until Australia were 113. Then Woodfull played forward to Robins and sliced a ball over Hammond's head. No other hope was given to England's bowlers or fieldsmen; not a ball did I see miss the bat unless the batsman preferred not to play a stroke—which was so very seldom as scarcely to be worth mentioning.

Tate hit the bat's middle with sad accuracy even while the ball was new. England's severe lack was spin that went away from the bat. Richard Tyldesley would not have been as harmless as White. Robins could not consistently find the length which draws the batsman farther than he wants to go. It was discouraging to see how safely Ponsford and Woodfull could play the forward push to Robins and send the ball cleanly to the off side. More discouraging still was it to see both Woodfull and Ponsford playing Robins as though their pads were merely being worn at the dictation of fashion. Hardly ever were they compelled to use pads to stop the spin.

The slow rate of scoring for the first hour of the Woodfull–Ponsford stand was very menacing to those of us who understood how weak was England's bowling. Neither batsman had to sweat blood for the quiet runs that trickled over the grass. There was sinister reserve power to be felt in every calculated stroke. The Australians were obviously aware that, at last, the enemy had been delivered into their hands. They were making assurance double sure. Woodfull you could see, was not going to get out: his very life seemed set on every ball as he watched it to his bat's broad base. After lunch the rate of scoring increased as though to a policy cold-blooded and unsparing. At half-past two Australia were 100 for none—Ponsford 60, Woodfull 37. At a quarter past three 150 was reached, and Ponsford was 77, Woodfull 70. While Ponsford slowed down Woodfull went ahead, using his feet beautifully.

THE KING'S ARRIVAL

The King arrived on the field at half-past three when Australia were 162 for none. After he had shaken hands with the players and the game had been resumed, Ponsford lost his wicket from the third ball bowled to him. He followed a wide ball from White and inexplicably put into Hammond's hands at first slip. Ponsford could easily have left the ball alone or hit it hard to the ground. His lapse was the sheerest good fortune for England; he seemed thoroughly set and happy. He is a good batsman whenever he has time to give play to a technique that is not too swift in its adjustments. His on-strokes are dapper and he is very good at forcing strokes from his pads or body. In some ways he reminds me of Hendren; perhaps he is even cleverer— if Mr Croyme will allow for a moment that Providence could possibly make a better batsman than Hendren.

At half-past three Bradman came forth when his captain's score was 78. White bowled the first ball to Bradman, who hit it to long-off from a position which found him close enough to White to enjoy any expression of consternation which may have come into the face of a bowler who is not accustomed to seeing any batsman meeting his slow bowling so indecorously. Bradman then hooked Hammond to the square leg boundary—a short armed stroke of power and voracity. The advent of Bradman was like combustible stuff thrown on fires of batsmanship that had been slumbering potentially. The bat sent out cracking noises; they were noises quite contemptuous. Nearly every ball was scored from: maiden overs seemed beyond the reach of possibility. Bradman ran out to White and drove two fours to the on in one over. He actually compelled White to bowl short—then he cut him triumphantly.

WHITE'S BOWLING EXPOSED

Frankly, Bradman let us see the bowling of White in a rather exposing brilliance. Some of us have argued for years that White's slow and almost spinless bowling has thrived on the tight-footed batsman of post-war years: we have maintained that the old quick-footed drive in J. T. Tyldesley's manner would have put White in his place as a good but not distinguished toiler under the sun. White's very direction—which goes with his arm into the bat— favoured Bradman's on drive. But the sight which ravished eyes tired of strokeless cricket was the way Bradman, by jumping out and hitting White on the half-volley, compelled him to bowl short. White, supposed to be an honest brake for any giddy wheel of batsmanship, could not find a length for Bradman. He even served up a full toss, which was at the square-leg boundary quick as lightning.

Bradman reached fifty in forty-five minutes. The tea interval did not stay his cheeky course. He cut Tate for four, then in one over he hit three fours from Robins, one to fine leg, the others to square-leg. When he raced to his hundred in one hour and three-quarters he had hit thirteen fours. At twenty-five minutes past five Australia's score rounded 300: half an hour later it was 350, and in that brief and gaudy space Bradman made 35. Woodfull 13. Every ball was dry fuel to the fire. An ovation was given to Tate when he bowled a maiden—the first for more than an hour. Chapman fielded gorgeously, stopping all manner of dazzling hits, but some of the other Englishmen seemed hot and bothered wanderers in a wide-open country. Outfielders were wanted of pace; only Robins could beat the speed of Bradman's hits. Hendren panted and toiled after the ball, often in vain. Woolley fielded at long-leg one over, then marched a vast distance to deep third man. For Bradman Chapman had to put more men deep than he could spare. At times he seemed to be waving Woolley to some far-off horizon. Later, when Woolley was asked to bowl, he had the satisfaction of directing his captain to an outpost of similar remoteness.

MODERN THEORIES SMASHED

As I saw the infield put to rout, and saw also the harried scouts on the field's edge, I asked myself, 'Goodness, where are all our modern theories gone? Where the hypnotic leg trap, where the clutching hands of "silly" mid-off? Where the inner and outer ring? Why, all of a sudden, is the new ball robbed of all its celebrated terrors? Where are all the latest snares to tie batsmen down to the confined space bounded by the popping crease? Where and why, forsooth?' Bradman batted as though Duckworth did not exist, as though there were no wickets behind him. He sent the 'leg traps'- and the 'booby-traps' flying for their lives because he gave a cricket bat freedom of power and action. There is nothing so potent as thoughts of a recumbent position on a shutter to render the 'leg-trap' of these days temporarily obsolete.

Bradman's cricket justified the ever-lasting canon of batsmanship—'Find where the ball pitches and go after it.' A bat is wider than a ball, when you come to think of it. Bradman brought the fact home once again to us today. His innings was different altogether from that which he played at Nottingham. This Bradman was a great player fit to be mentioned with the best of them; despite the headlong pace of his cricket it was cool and precise. He never hit the ball into the air, and seldom did he send it to the field. When he batted eleven men were not enough. Lord's was too big to cover; holes were to be seen in the English field everywhere. Chapman tried his best to fill them up, but in vain. None of us, least of all the English bowlers, hoped to get another wicket by the close of play.

WOODFULL'S FALL

Woodfull's end came like the falling of a stout tree that had seemed rooted for ages. At twenty minutes past six Woodfull played out at a ball from Robins to push to the off with the spin. He missed his stroke, and was stumped. For five and a half hours he wore the aspect of infallibility, save for that one glimpse into his human stock of error when, at 47, Robins baffled him. The quick play of his feet denied the stiffness of his strokes. Few English batsmen cover Woodfull's floorspace in and out of the crease.

Bradman so far has batted for two hours and forty minutes, and has given not the shadow of a chance. Only once, when he was 129, did his bat seem to have about it anything but lusty willow. Then he snicked Hammond behind the wicket. One of the notable points of Bradman's innings was the way he drove the full-toss along the grass powerfully and accurately. Not every batsman can hit a full-toss and not look vulgar. Bradman today established himself amongst the authentic batsmen of England and Australia of all time. Quality does not need to argue itself; we feel it intuitively the moment we see it. Until today I had looked at Bradman's batting as a thing of promise: I have now seen signs of a glorious fulfilment.

We may understand how precarious is England's position if we realize that the state of the game is exactly as though in a three-day match Australia had dismissed England for 151 and then gone in and scored 130 for two wickets. Readers who saw the Australians at Old Trafford last week will be wondering whether I am writing in this article about the same team. I am not.

SECOND TEST MATCH
3rd Day Lords

ENGLAND
First Innings

Hobbs, c Oldfield, b Fairfax	1
Woolley, c Wall, b Fairfax	41
Hammond, b Grimmett	38
K. S. Duleepsinhji, c Bradman, b Grimmett	173
Hendren, c McCabe, b Fairfax	48
A. P. F. Chapman, c Oldfield, b Wall	11
G. O. Allen, b Fairfax	3
Tate, c McCabe, b Wall	54
R. W. V. Robins, c Oldfield, b Hornibrook	5
J. C. White, not out	23
Duckworth, c Oldfield, b Wall	18
B 2, lb 7, nb 1	10
	—
Total	425

FALL OF WICKETS
ENGLAND—First Innings

1	2	3	4	5	6	7	8	9	10
13	53	105	209	236	239	337	363	387	425

BOWLING ANALYSIS

ENGLAND—First Innings

	O.	M.	R.	W.		O.	M.	R.	W.
Wall	29·4	2	118	3	Hornibrook	26	6	62	1
Grimmett	33	4	105	2	McCabe	9	1	29	0
Fairfax	31	6	101	4					

Fairfax bowled a no-ball

AUSTRALIA

First Innings

Woodfull, st Duckworth, b Robins	155
Ponsford, c Hammond, b White	81
Bradman, c Chapman, b White	254
Kippax, b White	83
McCabe, c Woolley, b Hammond	44
Richardson, c Hobbs, b Tate	30
Oldfield, not out	43
Fairfax, not out	20
B 6, lb 8, w 5	19
	—
Total (for six wickets)	729

Grimmett, Hornibrook and Wall did not bat.

FALL OF WICKETS

AUSTRALIA—First Innings

1	2	3	4	5	6	7	8	9	10
162	393	585	588	643	672				

BOWLING ANALYSIS

AUSTRALIA—First Innings

	O.	M.	R.	W.		O.	M.	R.	W.
Allen	34	7	115	0	Robins	42	1	172	1
Tate	64	16	148	1	Hammond	36	8	82	1
White	51	7	158	3	Woolley	6	0	35	0

Allen bowled four wides and Robins one

ENGLAND

Second Innings

Hobbs, b Grimmett	19
Woolley, hit wkt, b Grimmett	28
Hammond, not out	20
Duleepsinhji, not out	27
B 4	4
	—
Total (for two wickets)	98

FALL OF WICKETS

Second Innings

1	2	3	4	5	6	7	8	9	10
45	58								

Umpires—Chester and Oates

LORD'S, MONDAY

The fires of midsummer were burning hot and bright when the second Test match went on this morning under a blue sky. A great crowd sat round the field, everybody saying that the first hour's play might easily mean defeat for England. If Bradman and Kippax were able to survive Tate's fresh onrush armed with a new ball— why then Australia would forge ahead to score legions of runs and leave England to struggle on a wicket none the better for three days' wear. Opportunity could be heard at the Australians' door. The heat and the golden light were as allies to them.

Allen and Tate attacked with an air of desperation, and Allen's third ball actually flew past Kippax's bat in a way that suggested Kippax must have been mightily thankful he had not snicked the ball, but Allen provided no other justification for his use of three slips. He quickly faded away and Tate came on at the pavilion end, leaving the nursery end for Robins to exploit spin. Robins this time temporarily bowled well, and once or twice Bradman was compelled to cover up with his pads, though never did he withhold a true stroke. Neither batsman looked likely to get out save by some error gross and unaccountable. Tate worked hard. On one occasion he sent Bradman a clever slow ball, but the shrewd young–old cricketer was ready for it. Bradman is not only a brilliant player; also he possesses not less patience and judgment than Woodfull.

BRADMAN'S 200

Kippax batted elegantly, sending exquisite strokes straight to the field, but Bradman seldom let his bat go hard without finding a gap somewhere. Woolley stopped a terrific hook by Bradman at mid–on. Again did we feel that the Australian innings was moving as safely and prosperously as a great ship in comfortable waters. A voice in the press box was heard to ask whether the King was coming this morning. At a quarter past twelve Bradman drove Robins to long on for two and reached 200 in five minutes less than four hours. Multitudinous applause roared over the field and triumphant whoops from the Australian stand. Bradman had joined W. L. Murdoch—

the only batsmen to score 200 in a Test match innings in this country. His young heart must have swelled with pride as he stood at the wicket on this glorious summer's day and heard in his ears the acclamation of thousands of generous voices. Chapman in vain tried to find qualities in the bowling at his command, but, though it was steadier than on Saturday, there seemed little resourcefulness anywhere, no problems for the batsmen to consider, no untamable power. One felt the absence of a plan in the English side. Each ball was apparently bowled piecemeal on the off chance of something turning up. And the batsman was at liberty to play each ball without having at the back of his mind the thought that also he had to be careful not to get trapped by some deep-laid scheme.

The batsmen did not hurry. Bradman was not the quicksilver Bradman of Saturday. Today he played Australian cricket according to the revised testament. That is to say, he waited for the loose ball. At lunch, after two hours and a half's play, the Australians' score had been taken from 404 to 544. Bradman and Kippax were still unbeaten, and to all appearances unbeatable. Their plain policy was to pile up a vast total—and to keep the English batsmen in the field until dead tired and until perhaps the wicket had developed a few worn spaces and spots.

After the interval Bradman and Kippax began again exactly where they had left off. They looked easy of heart immediately, so much so that there seemed little point in another question asked in the press box—whether the King was coming again and this time bringing the whole Court with him. The English bowlers plugged away, waiting for the mistake which Bradman or Kippax was bound to make sooner or later, being men born into a mortal vale. When Australia's score passed 551 the highest of all totals in English Test matches was left behind.

BRADMAN'S DISMISSAL

At ten minutes past three Bradman, after a dazzling drive from White, hit a ball into the air—the only one he lifted as far as I was able to notice in all his innings. Chapman ran yards and dexterously caught out Bradman one-handed—Australia 585 for 3, every wicket the consequence of a batsman's momentary lapse. Bradman batted five hours and a half. A hundred of his runs came from boundary hits. He gave no chance, and only once or twice did the ball find anywhere but the middle of his blade. Today he scored 99 in three hours, and played so well within himself, and had so little effort in any of his strokes, offensive or defensive, that I can only conclude he did not move along more impetuously because of some policy of attrition.

A few minutes following the downfall of Bradman England got another wicket, and again it was palpably, a case of temporary absence of mind in a batsman, not an effect of a ball good in itself. Kippax tried to cut a slow ball from White as it bounced up to the bails. Seemingly he struck under it and played on. Kippax was obstinacy in the dress of elegance for three hours. Bradman and Kippax in three hours made 192.

A FEROCIOUS ONSLAUGHT

Now came the ferocious Australian onslaught which all day had been in grim preparation. Richardson and McCabe treated the attack sardonically. Nearly every ball was hit with a bat that made the sweep and flourish of disdain. In 25 minutes 56 runs were flogged: it was not a partnership but a race. Richardson drove a ball from White over the screen for six. The highest of all Test match totals, 636, was beaten before Richardson mishit gorgeously and fell to a delicious catch on the off side by Hobbs. McCabe drove and cut handsomely. Once when he shaped for a forward stroke from Tate he found at the last second that the ball was too short. Quick as a thought he changed his action and glanced through the slips along the grass. When Australia was 661 for five refreshments were taken into the field and were immediately absorbed. So far the innings had lasted nine hours, and Duckworth had allowed only two byes, though, truth to say, he was not at his most accurate in holding the ball and anticipating the leg glance. Richardson played the right happy-hearted game for his side, and the stroke which got him caught was a very high-spirited mishit. Now onwards until the tea interval every boundary hit was merely another adorning ribbon for England's wreath.

The innings was declared at the gigantic aggregate of 729, and one of the scoring boards patriotically broke down and refused to register the seven. Australia batted ten hours and ten minutes. The bowling analysis tells the truth and nothing but the truth about the labour spent in that time by the English attack. Allen was a total failure, Tate was a willing slave. Robins now and again achieved a ball that put a definite problem before the batsmen, White could not be trusted to keep runs down, and Hammond was as good as anybody else in a bowling team which never once, from the first over sent down on Saturday by Allen, really looked capable of beating the bat, technique for technique. If there exists a cricketer in the land who can flight a ball and spin it away toward the slips, let him appear. And also let there be forthcoming an outfielder or two who can run fast. An England eleven must never again go into action with only one swift scout on the boundary. And Chapman might bear in mind for future guidance that, though a Bradman is capable of rendering a second slip unnecessary for Robins, any other batsman of inferior footwork is always likely to send a catch to second slip from the leg spinner, especially at the outset of his innings.

ENGLAND'S INSECURE START

England, 704 behind, made an insecure start. Woolley hit a characteristic off drive, and then, in Wall's third over, flashed at a rising ball and sent a swift chance to Oldfield. The ball bounced from his gloves amongst the slips, but nobody could hold it, despite somebody's quite ghoulist howl of appeal to the umpire. This mishap occurred when England were eleven and Woolley five. Wall caused a ball to rise high as the shoulders of Hobbs, who then came out of his ground to look at the pitch and prod it with a solicitous bat. Hobbs drove Wall imperially to the on for four, and Woolley smote a full toss from Grimmett to square leg. The next ball, a 'googly', beat him and went for four byes. Again did Hobbs walk out of his ground to look at the wicket. No Australian batsman gave the English attack moral support of this kind. When Bradman came out of his crease it was to put his bat to the ball, not to the hard wicket. Grimmett spun a ball a foot to Hobbs, one leg bye was run, and now Woolley patted the turf. All was done that possibly could be done to help the Australians to thrive psychologically. The pitch, no doubt, contained a spot or two, though only an hour previously none of the English bowlers had been keen-sighted enough to search out the rough places at all.

Hobbs and Woolley made 45 in little more than thirty minutes before Hobbs tried to push to the on a leg-break well up to him. He played across the flight, and the ball turned enough to hit the wicket. Hobbs looked a consternated man, and he departed in silence. It was not the spin that beat Hobbs; he missed the ball while it was in the air well within reach of a straight stroke. Hammond as soon as he came in missed Grimmett's spin and escaped bowling by a few inches. At this moment I noticed the reappearance in modern cricket of 'silly' point. This fieldsman has been away for his health over the week-end. England were only 58 when Woolley hit a ball from Grimmett to the leg boundary, and in doing so trod on his wicket. This was the only instance I have ever seen where you could not entirely ascribe to bad luck a wicket lost by a mischance of this description. There was a 'silly' mid-on to Woolley a few yards from him. But for the presence of this fieldsman Woolley probably would have driven to the on the ball that got him out. It was pitched far enough up for the stroke, but, apparently fearing 'silly' mid-on, Woolley decided to pull the ball square, and in order to shorten the length for this stroke he had to move back on his stumps. Woolley did not play his natural game this time, for reasons best known to himself.

Hammond and Duleepsinhji played out the day, which has seen English cricket in a very low state. Neither batsman inspired confidence, for, though fine strokes occurred from time to time, there were hints of minds and bats perplexed in the extreme. Duleepsinhji once tried to drive Grimmett to the on, but it was third man who returned the ball to the wicket after the stroke had been made. Only rain or the batting of Titans can now deprive the Australians of a victory as grand and as remarkable as any in the history of Test cricket.

SECOND TEST MATCH
4th Day Lords

ENGLAND
First Innings

Hobbs, c Oldfield, b Fairfax	1
Woolley, c Wall, b Fairfax	41
Hammond, b Grimmett	38
K. S. Duleepsinhji, c Bradman, b Grimmett	173
Hendren, c McCabe, b Fairfax	48
A. P. F. Chapman, c Oldfield, b Wall	11
G. O. Allen, b Fairfax	3
Tate, c McCabe, b Wall	54
R. W. V. Robins, c Oldfield, b Hornibrook	5
J. C. White, not out	23
Duckworth, c Oldfield, b Wall	18
B 2, lb 7, nb 1	10
	—
Total	425

215

FALL OF WICKETS

ENGLAND—First Innings

1	2	3	4	5	6	7	8	9	10
13	53	105	209	236	239	337	363	387	425

BOWLING ANALYSIS

ENGLAND—First Innings

	O.	M.	R.	W.		O.	M.	R.	W.
Wall	29·4	2	118	3	Hornibrook	26	6	62	1
Grimmett	33	4	105	2	McCabe	9	1	29	0
Fairfax	31	6	101	4					

Fairfax bowled a no-ball

AUSTRALIA

First Innings

Woodfull, st Duckworth, b Robins	155
Ponsford, c Hammond, b White	81
Bradman, c Chapman, b White	254
Kippax, b White	83
McCabe, c Woolley, b Hammond	44
Richardson, c Hobbs, b Tate	30
Oldfield, not out	43
Fairfax, not out	20
B 6, lb 8, w 5	19
	—
Total (for six wickets)	729

Grimmett, Hornibrook and Wall did not bat.

FALL OF WICKETS

AUSTRALIA—First Innings

1	2	3	4	5	6	7	8	9	10
162	393	585	588	643	672				

BOWLING ANALYSIS

AUSTRALIA—First Innings

	O.	M.	R.	W.		O.	M.	R.	W.
Allen	34	7	115	0	Robins	42	1	172	1
Tate	64	16	148	1	Hammond	36	8	82	1
White	51	7	158	3	Woolley	6	0	35	0

Allen bowled four wides and Robins one

ENGLAND

Second Innings

Hobbs, b Grimmett	19
Woolley, hit wkt, b Grimmett	28
Hammond, c Fairfax, b Grimmett	32
Duleepsinhji, c Oldfield, b Hornibrook	48
Hendren, c Richardson, b Grimmett	9
Chapman, c Oldfield, b Fairfax	121
Allen, lbw, b Grimmett	57
Tate, c Ponsford, b Grimmett	10
Robins, not out	11
White, run out	10
Duckworth, lbw, b Fairfax	0
B 16, lb 13, w 1	30
Total	375

FALL OF WICKETS

Second Innings

1	2	3	4	5	6	7	8	9	10
45	58	129	141	147	272	329	354	372	375

BOWLING ANALYSIS

ENGLAND—Second Innings

	O.	M.	R.	W.		O.	M.	R.	W.
Wall	25	2	80	0	Hornibrook	22	6	49	1
Fairfax	12·4	2	37	2	Bradman	1	0	1	0
Grimmett	53	13	167	6	McCabe	3	1	11	0

Wall bowled one wide.

AUSTRALIA

Second Innings

Woodfull, not out	26
Ponsford, b Robins	14
Bradman, c Chapman, b Tate	1
Kippax, c Duckworth, b Robins	3
McCabe, not out	25
B 1, lb 2	3
Total (for three wickets)	72

FALL OF WICKETS

Second Innings

1	2	3
16	17	22

BOWLING ANALYSIS

AUSTRALIA—Second Innings

	O.	M.	R.	W.		O.	M.	R.	W.
Tate	13	6	21	1	Robins	9	1	34	2
Hammond	4·2	1	6	0	White	2	0	8	0

LORD'S, TUESDAY

There is a passage in *Tom Jones*, greatest of English novels, where Henry Fielding, having got his plot terribly complicated, calls on all the high Muses, in person and severally, for aid, because, as he tells us, without their guidance 'I do not know how I am going to bring my story to a successful conclusion.' As I write these lines, after a day of wonderful cricket, I feel also the need of inspired and kindly forces. The day's play, in the old term, simply beggars description. England lost the match at noon, nearly won it again at the last hour, and lowered the flag only when forced down by sheer odds.

When twelve o'clock struck in the clock covered with ivy near the nursery, England were 147 for five, with Hobbs, Woolley, Hammond, Duleepsinhji, and Hendren all gone and 157 still needed to save themselves from defeat by an innings. Grimmett was master. Against his spin Hammond, Duleepsinhji, and Hendren had been batsmen sorely troubled and helpless. Now Chapman came in, and before making a run he mis-hit Grimmett's spin and sent the easiest of catches conceivable in a Test match. Victor Richardson seemed to lose sight of the ball, which fell to the grass. Chapman's lucky star has never shone with today's brightness: he lived to play one of the most astonishing innings I have ever seen. Allen helped him in a stand which, coming as it did after the impotence of Hammond and Hendren, was incredibly secure once Chapman had found that he could kick Grimmett's breakaway with legs and pads which were quite indecently unconcerned with any academic relationship between a batsman's footwork and his bat. Chapman and Allen were undefeated at lunch, by which time they had taken England's score from 147 for 5 to 262 for 5. After the interval Grimmett's straight ball baffled Allen at 272. The sixth English wicket scored 125 in 25 minutes.

Allen's courage and his trustfulness in the forward stroke, defensively and offensively, put rather to shame the aimlessness and shiftlessness which we had witnessed (very painfully) when some of his superiors in technique were at the wicket. The day indeed was

218

a triumph for courage and optimism—and an exposure of that professionalism which is too often content to work according to its own routined machinery and has too little use for the influences of imagination. Chapman's innings was no doubt technically very bad at parts, but probably the hardened county expert was inclined to look indulgently upon Chapman's many and fortunate mis-hits. But if Chapman's innings could not be called batsmanship in the strict technical sense, it was something better than that in the eyes of Providence—it was an act of faith and cheerfulness. Before Chapman arrived at the wicket technique (of a sort) had proved useless for England in a dark hour—useless because it was technique and nothing else, lacking as it did the beard of men determined not to look at difficulties save to see them as hills that could be scaled granted the effort and the risk.

While Hammond and Hendren tried to tackle Grimmett you would have sworn the wicket was sticky; each batsman thrust out a bat protectively and groped for the ball. Hendren, true, hit a beautiful four through the covers and a desperate on-drive against the spin, but the stroke which got him caught at 'silly' mid-off was a purely speculative stab in the dark. Hendren's innings was distressingly touched with mortality and not worthy of a Test match player.

CHAPMAN AND GRIMMETT

After Allen's wicket fell, Chapman's innings went gloriously insane, yet retained some method in its madness. No cricketer, no matter how blessed by the gods, can hope to hit Grimmett simply by flinging his bat at the air. As a fact, Chapman, by a curious compound of push work with his pads and a delayed forward stroke, quite upset Grimmett's tactics at the beginning of his innings, even while England's position was at its worst. Grimmett packed the off-side field to Chapman, and pitched his leg break wide of the off stump. As soon as Chapman had got sight of the ball, he pulled Grimmett round to the on, often in the grand manner, and sometimes sending the ball to fine leg with a very likeable lack of intent. Three times he achieved colossal on drives from Grimmett for six. When his score was in the nineties and everybody on the ground save Chapman in a state of proud and affectionate anxiety, Chapman gorgeously mishit a ball over the slips for four, and he seemed to enjoy the escapade even more than he enjoyed those of his hits which observed the unities.

In an hour after lunch Chapman plundered 69 runs from the Australian attack, and his most remunerative if not his most violent strokes were square-leg hits from Grimmett, a straight drive from Grimmett, a clout into the people on the mound stand from Grimmett, a pull toward leg from Hornibrook, another clout into the mound stand, a drive to long-on from Hornibrook, a thoroughly characteristic snick from Hornibrook, and then another six, all the more delightful because four of the runs were given away for nothing by overthrows which sent the crowd into fits of laughter and applause. Seldom can an innings in a Test match have caused more jubilation and hubbub amongst a crowd. Probably we should have to go as far back as Jessop's great routing of the Australians in 1902 to find an equal to this innings by Chapman that is, an equal as far as animal spirits are concerned, for of course Jessop's greatest innings was not only energy, strong and fearless, but energy concentrated and made whole by a masterful range of strokes all over the field. Nearly all of Chapman's major strokes today were drives theoretically or in practice. He came to the wicket when most of us were looking up trains for home. By the time he had been batting two hours we were as busy ringing up our hotels asking for a room for one night longer. Chapman fell to a clever catch by Oldfield at 351. In two hours and a half he made 121 out of a total of 207 scored while he was at the wicket.

THE MYSTERIOUS SPOT

The less said of the remainder of the English innings the better. There was a spot on the pitch at the pavilion end. I am told on excellent authority that it was there all Monday. The English bowlers were very remiss not finding it out with Grimmett's alacrity. It must be recorded as a curiosity that when Chapman batted the imp of evil in the turf seemed temporarily to become exorcized, or, if it remained there at all, had no intent more malicious than to provide that impetus which always makes a snick behind the stumps a certain four. Grimmett apart, none of the Australian bowlers were troublesome. Chapman played himself in to the fast bowling of Wall. Fairfax was for a while curiously neglected.

The day so far had been hectic enough and thousands of throats must have hurt from the shouts that had punctuated every hit by Chapman. But sensation had not finished with us yet. She had yet another shriek to set our hearts beating. At ten minutes to four Woodfull and Ponsford walked confidently into the sunshine to score the mere 72 needed for an Australian victory. Against Hammond and Tate Ponsford batted as though eager to hit off the score himself, and two fours from Tate set his innings into excellent motion. Woodfull when only one hit a ball hard to Duleepsinhji at mid-on. To Chapman the chance would have been easy, but Duleepsinhji could not hold the catch. Scarcely had the crowd subsided from this alarum than Ponsford was bowled by Robins. The first Australian wicket—it was not to be the last—fell in Robins's first over; indeed Ponsford was out the very next ball. Robins found the spot at the pavilion end, and his spin was excellent and, for a while, his length of the sort that keeps the batsman tortuously in two minds.

A WONDERFUL CATCH

It was not good bowling but marvellous fielding that captured the second Australian wicket at 17. Bradman cut Tate magnificently; it was one of the best strokes of the match. The ball flashed hard toward the ground quicker than sight could follow. The crack of the bat was triumphant. Chapman took the ball at his feet with both hands and threw it in the air almost before we knew what had happened. I have never seen a finer catch or a more beautiful one for that matter, and I have never seen a finer or more beautiful fieldsman than Chapman. Bradman could scarcely believe his eyes, and he walked slowly back to the pavilion. The ovation to Chapman was probably heard a mile away.

Then came another of those dramatic silences which fall on a cricket field after a moment of tumult. Robins bowled at Kippax, the ball spun, and Kippax tried a cut. Duckworth's clamant crow split the skies, and another roar from the crowd went up as the finger of the umpire was seen pointing on high. The appeal of Duckworth was worthy of the word great: the occasion demanded it. His catch was a masterpiece of clean alacrity. And now Australia were 22 for 3 and the whole of Lord's was a bedlam, the heat of the afternoon was as though thrown out from the action. Voices everywhere were asking could England, after all, win? Was it possible? 'You never know,' said a man in white spats non-committally. And he added, as though discovering an entirely new and original thought, 'It's a funny game is cricket.' When McCabe came in Woodfull went towards him to meet him. Words were spoken. The scene and the occasion were obviously trying to Woodfull himself let alone to a young cricketer with his spurs still to win. Woodfull again was Australia's good anchor. He watched Robins's spin to his bat, yet had one or two narrow escapes from edged strokes through the slips. McCabe, reliant as Woodfull, played finely, meeting the ball cleanly and confidently. Here is another great batsman in the making. Sad to say the end was anticlimax. Robins raised our hopes by a spell of bowling clever and as waspish of spin as anything achieved in the match by Grimmett. Then, with a quite sickening suddenness, his length went to pieces. Thirteen were hit from one over—and once again the Australians' crowd on the stand lifted up heart and voice. The winning hit was made at five o'clock, and a memorable day was at an end.

CHAPMAN'S MATCH

As the cricketers came from the field sunshine fell on them, touching them with a lovely light. It might well have been a light cast by immortality, for this match will certainly never be forgotten. Australia won against a first-innings score of 425; England, though compelled to bat needing 304 to avoid defeat in an innings, made 375 on the fourth day of a match played at Lord's in dry weather— a gallant performance. Victors and vanquished emerge from the game the better and the more historical for it. The finish when Australia were sweating by the brow to score 72 for victory was ironical. Only the day before they had waxed fat to the strength of 729 for six. The game of cricket played by men of true sport is incomparable.

Perhaps in years to come this match will be known as Chapman's match. Though for the first time he is a defeated English captain, his renown has been increased thereby, and not only because of a lion-hearted century. The match's greatest cricket was Chapman's fielding; it was fielding unparalleled. The catch that dismissed Bradman was a good crown for work which, by its swiftness, its accuracy, and for its beauty, will assuredly go down for good and all in the most precious annals of the game.

THIRD TEST 1930
1st Day Headingley

AUSTRALIA
First Innings

W. M. Woodfull, b Hammond	50
A. Jackson, c Larwood, b Tate	1
D. G. Bradman, not out	309
A. F. Kippax, c Chapman, b Tate	77
S. McCabe, not out	12
B 1, lb 8	9
	—
Total (for three wickets)	458

To bat: V. Y. Richardson, E. L. a'Beckett, C. V. Grimmett, T. Wall, W. A. Oldfield, and P. M. Hornibrook.

FALL OF WICKETS

1	2	3	4	5	6	7	8	9	10
2	194	423							

ENGLAND: A. P. F. Chapman, K. S. Duleepsinhji, Hobbs, Sutcliffe, Tate, Larwood, Duckworth, Hammond, Leyland, Tyldesley (R.), and Geary (G.).

Umpires: Bestwick and Oates.

LEEDS, FRIDAY

Nature, they say, breaks the mould when she has made a master-piece. It is not true: nor is it true that history repeats only her hum-drum pages. Beauty changes her modes and aspects, but the sub-stance, the ultimate vision, is the same. Nature is never tired of her good things: every year she repeats the miracle of the spring-time's rapture and the summer's fulfilment. Today in a game of cricket Nature has lived again in a bygone experience, lived it as though with greater intensity because the genius of it all had once before thrilled her sensibilities.

Four years ago on this very same field of Headingley the Austra-lians began an innings disastrously: they lost the wicket of Bardsley for none, then Macartney came forth and scored a hundred before lunch. Today Australia lost Jackson with only one run made: then Bradman before lunch made a hundred also. Woodfull, who was Macartney's good companion and audience, was Bradman's. But whereas Macartney gave a chance when he was only two, Bradman sent no catch at all before lunch and was guilty of but a solitary mis-hit, when he was 35 and a high cut flashed yards wide of Chapman at backward point. But this great innings will best be appreciated if I let an account of it emerge from a plain narrative of the match and thus gain the significance of dramatic context.

The wicket was dead easy at the outset it contained enough moisture to prevent Larwood from getting the ball to rise higher than half of the stumps. His first few balls satisfied me that with reasonable luck Australia would bat all day. But Jackson was out in Tate's first over: he played too soon at an inswinger, the stroke of a cricketer who is out of form and terribly anxious to get going again. The ball was played straight into Larwood's hands at forward square-leg.

THE MUSIC STARTS

Woodfull then drove Larwood straight for two—and whenever a fast bowler allows himself to be forced in front of the wicket during his first overs, and by a scrupulous batsman, then can we conclude as a matter of logic pure and simple that a cricketer so pugnacious as Bradman will most certainly take the hint and jump at the opportunity of scoring quick runs on a perfectly tame stretch of turf. Bradman immediately hit Tate hard and forward for four—an aggressive back shot. He knocked Larwood out of action almost contemptuously by plundering eleven runs in one over—an off-drive, a square hit in front of the umpire, a leg hit, and a single. Bradman seemed a disappointed man when he scored only singles: it was as though he was saying to himself, 'Only a one—that means I've lost the bowling for a while, and I do so like it.' Geary as soon as he came on saw Bradman achieve a violent on-drive of that very same length which in country cricket is always most tenderly and solicitously caressed and regarded.

In three-quarters of an hour Bradman reached 51 of 62: he hit fours nearly every over and let us enjoy every stroke of the game save the leg glance. He cut Tate dazzlingly for four: as soon as Tyldesley went on Bradman jumped out of his ground and crashed two straight drives. Yet despite the rare pace of Bradman's batting it was eminently secure and sound. He has a marvellously quick eye for the ball that is at all short or overpitched: but, better still, he is as wonderfully quick to see a good ball. I have never before seen a batsman play at Bradman's pace and take so few risks. Shall I describe him as a forcing defensive batsman? The paradox is more apparent than real. Bradman treated all the bowlers alike—as grist to his busy mill. The speed of his strokes rendered even the out fields futile and immobile. Larwood, after bowling five overs at the day's beginning, did not attack again until ten minutes past one. It would be interesting to have the opinion of Walter Brearley on fast bowling so intermittent as this. Bradman immediately hit Larwood to the square leg boundary off his legs: this is his most brilliant and drastic stroke: he makes it with his bat cracking sweet in the middle, and the velocity of it cannot be followed by many eyes, naked or bespectacled.

BRADMAN'S CENTURY

At ten minutes to one Bradman attained his hundred, and so joined the immortal company of Victor Trumper and Macartney, the only cricketers who have yet scored centuries in Test matches before lunch. Bradman's bat hammered perpetually: when he ever did stop scoring for a few balls it was as though he had merely run out of nails momentarily. Richard Tyldesley at one o'clock actually bowled a maiden over to Bradman: from internal and external evidence, I concluded that it was one of the cleverest bits of bowling he has achieved in his hard-working career. At lunch Australia were 136 for one, and Bradman's innings was arbitrarily compelled for a while to stay its course.

Woodfull had by this time made 29 in two hours. He was as much a man to be noticed in conjunction with Bradman as Kreisler's conscientious accompanist. It can make no better compliment to Bradman—and give no clearer idea of his cricket—than to say that Woodfull of the two men seemed the more vulnerable and fallible. Yet Woodfull was at his stoutest and most watchful. I imagine the English bowlers were trying to get Woodfull out—leaving Bradman to Providence. Not often is an attack reduced to trying to get the stonewaller out while washing its hands of the brilliant player as a problem insoluble, and apparently everlastingly so. Think of it—a brilliant batsman with no edge to his bat and who never takes a risk In this respect he is different from any other cricketer I have ever known; Macartney, Trumper, and Johnny Tyldesley were always living dangerously on the verge of their resources; Bradman races along on firm feet, with shrewd eyes where he is going. Not once today, in spite of all his crashing thunder and brilliance, did he ever pay anything but respect to the really good ball. The difference between Bradman and the ordinarily good county batsman is that it takes a really good ball to keep Bradman's bat steady. This genius

H   225 consists of quick feet, a sure eye, colossal confidence, and strokes all round the wicket.

AUSTRALIA 268: BRADMAN 200

At four o'clock Bradman reached 200, after three hours and a half of cricket which for mingled rapidity and security is unparalleled in my experience. But when Bradman achieved his 200 the scoreboard read: Australia 268 for two. Has ever before a Test match batsman made a proportion of runs so handsome as this? At 194 Woodfull was suddenly bowled, and a Yorkshireman near me said volumes when he cried out, 'Who'd a thowt it?' Woodfull tried to push a stroke to the on. He defended for two hours and fifty minutes; with Bradman he helped to make 192 in two hours and forty minutes; Bradman's share was 142.

Kippax did not look unconquerable when first he came in; Larwood beat him twice in an over. For a while Larwood seemed almost fast—that is, when Bradman was not playing him. In half an hour Kippax got two runs: then he drove Larwood straight for four, which was another taste of that encouragement which must always come to batsmen at the sight of a hard, forward hit from alleged bowling of speed. Richard Tyldesley did not bowl after lunch until a quarter to four: he had meanwhile been trying to perform the duties of an outfield manfully and perspiringly. Larwood also was to be observed during the day in the long field. Chapman did not appear to have any positive plan in mind: Bradman governed the situation entirely. His forcing shots from the back foot became more and more brilliant.

Kippax at last settled down, though with his score 24 he hit a ball perilously into the air near Tate at mid-on. The English fieldsmen wore hereabout a depressed and drooping air; they were men without hope, and Chapman's head hung low. Adversity measures a man and his leadership. It is true that the wicket gave the English bowlers absolutely no help; the trouble was that apart from Tyldesley nobody could present to the Australians problems of flight. The best bowling of Tate, Geary, Larwood, and Hammond was as an open book to Bradman; he revels in unambiguous speed and the attack direct. England had no 'googly' bowler they could look to for the ball of unexpected venom.

SELECTORS' BLUNDER REVEALED

All summer it has been agreed by cricketers of judgment that slow spin was the answer to Bradman. Robins won the Test match at Trent Bridge with the ball that bowled Bradman. Yet, in this game the Selection Committee have sent an England eleven into the field with less spin bowling in its ranks than we possessed at Lord's and Nottingham. Perhaps now, at long last, the Selection Committee will come to see the stark fact that Australian batsmen, Bradman especially, revel in the vastly over-rated fast medium new-ball bowlers of our credulous epoch. Bradman did not this afternoon pause to consider whether or not a new ball was being used; his only concern about the seam was apparently to flatten it at once.

The notable contribution of Bradman to English cricket this year is an exposure of mediocrity: he has done it by sound but fearless use of orthodox methods. The exposure is all the more complete because Bradman is not a magical Macartney: you can argue nothing from the arts of the inexplicable masters. It has been maintained by some of us for years that the contemporary fraud of the spineless medium-paced bowler would be shown up the first day there was a finely tempered return to batsmanship which played the good ball shrewdly and smote the bad ones with a bat free and with the feet active.

At six o'clock, after slightly under five and a half hours' play, Australia, for the second match in succession, reached the aggregate of 400 for two wickets. Amidst multitudinous cheers Bradman beat the record for the highest innings by any Test-match batsman: it was good that Foster's score had been passed not by a stonewaller hoarding up runs covetously, but by a true son of the game. Bradman arrived at 288 in five hours and a half out of a grand Australian total of 414: no chance to hand had he given and not more than three strokes had he shown which told us that it is human to err. At 423 Kippax's suave innings was ended by a catch of Chapman from a slash cut: the third wicket made 229 in two and three-quarter hours. Just before the close of play and after McCabe had twice cracked strokes to the deep field Bradman's score rounded 300: he had now hit no fewer than forty fours. His stamina is as remarkable as his skill and imperturbability.

It has been a day calculated to cause acute cerebration in the minds of the least introspective Selective Committee. The bowling has probably been steadier than at Lord's, but the fielding has been ordinary, merely an accessory and not a factor in the attack. From the last ball of the day Bradman, by a superb drive through the covers, a stroke handsome enough for any batsman who has ever done honour to cricket, hit his forty-second boundary. That was the royal way to finish a day which Australia will not forget as long as the game is played and loved there.

THIRD TEST
2nd Day Headingley

AUSTRALIA
First Innings

W. M. Woodfull, b Hammond	50
A. Jackson, c Larwood, b Tate	1
D. G. Bradman, c Duckworth, b Tate	334
A. F. Kippax, c Chapman, b Tate	77
S. McCabe, b Larwood	30
V. Y. Richardson, c Larwood, b Tate	1
E. L. a'Beckett, c Chapman, b Geary	29
W. A. Oldfield, c Hobbs, b Tate	2
C. V. Grimmett, c Duckworth, b Tyldesley	24
T. Wall, b Tyldesley	3
P. M. Hornibrook, not out	1
B 5, lb 8, w 1	14
	—
Total	566

FALL OF WICKETS
AUSTRALIA—First Innings

1	2	3	4	5	6	7	8	9	10
2	194	423	486	491	508	519	544	565	566

BOWLING ANALYSIS
AUSTRALIA—First Innings

	O.	M.	R.	W.		O.	M.	R.	W.
Larwood	33	3	139	1	Tyldesley	33	5	104	2
Tate	39	9	124	5	Hammond	17	3	46	1
Geary	35	10	95	1	Leyland	11	0	44	0

Geary bowled a wide.

ENGLAND

First Innings

Hobbs, c a'Beckett, b Grimmett	29
Sutcliffe, c Hornibrook, b Grimmett	32
Hammond, not out	61
K. S. Duleepsinhji, b Hornibrook	35
Leyland, c Kippax, b Wall	44
Geary, run out	0
Duckworth, not out	0
B 5, lb 5, nb 1	11
	—
Total (for five wickets)	212

FALL OF WICKETS

ENGLAND—First Innings

1	2	3	4	5	6	7	8	9	10
53	64	123	206	206					

To bat: A. P. F. Chapman, Tate, Larwood, and Tyldesley (R.)

Umpires: Bestwick and Oates.

LEEDS, SATURDAY

The wicket was faster this morning, but for a while Bradman and McCabe played their strokes with time to spare. McCabe pulled two short balls from Larwood for fours, yet from the evidence that they were made with the batsman's body erect the fact of the turf's pace and hardness as compared with yesterday's became plain. McCabe is a beautiful forward batsman, powerful and fluent. He will before long make a handsome hundred for Australia. McCabe was bowled at 486: Larwood sent him a superb breakback which McCabe played with a stroke directed to the off-side; the leg stump was felled.

Richardson again disappointed: he pushed a short ball from Tate to Larwood's hands at forward square leg. I am afraid Richardson is a club cricketer in excelsis: he throws his head back overmuch and seems to lose sight of the ball after it is half-way in the air. He is at the extreme to Bradman, who never takes his eye from the attack. Those curious persons who imagine that the alternative to the stonewalling of average English batsmen is an indiscreet beating of the air ought to study Bradman's technique and then compare it with Richardson's.

BRADMAN'S DISMISSAL

At 506 Bradman's innings came to an end: the swifter speed of the pitch beat him when he seemed set for another day. Tate sent him a good-length ball to which Bradman exploited a characteristic back stroke. The ball came from the pitch with a velocity never possible on yesterday's wicket: the additional speed rendered the outswing difficult, making all the difference between an edged stroke and a stroke in the bat's middle. Bradman snicked a catch to Duckworth, who for the first time in the match had cause to appeal as though he really meant it. Bradman batted for six hours and a half, made his 334 out of 506, and gave only one reasonable chance to the field. That happened when at 202 he lofted the ball towards mid-on, where Tate did not move quickly enough, no doubt not expecting Bradman to fall into any manner of mortal insecurity.

Bradman's innings was the most remarkable I have ever seen for mingled solidity and brilliance. He hardly ever gives hope to the fieldsmen, for he never takes a chance against a really trying ball. When he does put a stroke even a shade wide of his intended direction we are as astonished by the lapse from reason and foresight as though Arthur Shrewsbury himself were batting. Because of the unfaltering and essentially orthodox technique of his great range of strokes he seldom thrills the imagination: unlike Macartney, he never sets the heart jumping by trafficking with dangersome swift butterfly flutter of wings into the flame. Bradman is as careful as Makepeace himself: his swiftness and power are mechanical rather than of the spirit: steel, not sensibility, is the stuff of his batsmanship, which really is all substance with little of that volatility of human pulse which no power of reason can perpetually control. The animal spirits in Bradman are never likely to go mad and persuade his shell to any divinely incalculable subversions of its own laws. He is a purist in a hurry: he administers the orthodox in loud and apostolic knocks.

After Bradman got out the Australian innings became a thing of shreds and patches. What a heap of mediocrity is hidden in this Australian eleven by the broadcloth of Bradman's batsmanship! Australia's later wickets were very poor sticks; the last four fell for 68, and they were not worth half the sum. Still, the frailty of them was sufficient to cheer up and console the crowd— and, incidentally, to lead an illusion of deadliness to the England bowling. As a fact only Tate bowled well: apart from him the Selection Committee might do worse than discharge the lot. Straight stuff does not cause Bradman a minute's worry: yesterday he was free all the time to trust to the instinctive workings of his technique: he might as well have left his brains in the pavilion, so few were the strategical problems put before him by an attack without a single surprise or ambuscade. Tyldesley once or twice compelled him to look twice at a nicely flighted ball: the others were unsubtle toilers under the sun. An English bowler must be found who can serve an unexpected trick now and again. Australia's innings lasted seven hours and forty minutes: the runs were made at about 73 an hour, thanks to Bradman, whose tempo was just above 50 an hour.

ENGLAND'S INNINGS

England went in at one o'clock and scored seventeen before the interval arrived and rendered the Headingley ground noisy, congested, and unseemly with its teeming masses. The civilizing influences of sanitation have apparently not yet attained the twentieth century at Headingley. After lunch Hobbs and Sutcliffe more or less painfully extracted from the game the true strokes of cricket. 'Silly' point and 'silly' mid-on stood on the doorstep of the crease, and they were never in danger of the slightest disturbance. Hobbs, indeed, might quickly have been caught in the booby trap from Grimmett, but the stroke or push went a little too wide. The Australian attack was allowed to assert itself: no effort at punishment was attempted. Even the loose ball to leg escaped free and unhurt.

In an hour and a half fifty runs trickled over the field: the tactics of Hobbs and Sutcliffe were questionable. With two days and three-quarters to go, the clock was too formidable an enemy to beat unless runs hit from the bad balls were always safely if slowly coming as an ally to patience and circumspection. It was rather pitiful to see a ball blocked on the popping-crease and a run stolen as though by schoolboys. Bradman's hands would need to be padlocked to compel him to hit a ball no farther than the blockhole. The strokelessness of the play could have only one end: sooner or later the best batsman makes a mistake. If he has not got his runs while able to avoid fatal mistakes his innings at the end is not likely to possess any sort of value either material or psychological. Indeed, the play of a strokeless batsman is always flattering to the attack and depressing to the cricketers waiting with pads on in the pavilion.

HOBBS AND SUTCLIFFE OUT

Hobbs and Sutcliffe in 95 minutes made 53; Hobbs then pushed out an almost dead bat to Grimmett and spooned a catch to a'Beckett at 'silly' mid-on. The fieldsman flung himself to the earth, scooped up his prey, and rolled over. In dreadful suspense all eyes turned on the umpire at the bowler's end; but Oates did not promptly give a decision. He consulted Bestwick, and only then did Hobbs walk back to the pavilion.

Eleven runs after this disaster Sutcliffe edged Grimmett's leg spin to first slip; the ball went away beautifully. Thus had quick retribution fallen upon cricketers who had too readily committed the greatest of errors a batsman can make—which is to treat an attack not on its merits and not according to one's natural game but according to some abstract plan based on a philosophy neither idealistic nor realistic but merely negative.

Duleepsinhji drove his first ball to the off for four; the bowler was Grimmett, and the crack of the bat was like thunder clearing the air of an encircling gloom of dubiety. A different temper came into England's innings now: Hammond also hit the loose ball, though for a while he perpetuated a mannerism which lately has been spoiling his true game—that is to say, he stabbed his bat many times as though in the presence of vicious 'yorkers' which had to be beaten deep into the earth. Once in a time Hammond's bat was as a chivalrous sword; today it has been for too long a time a grim bludgeon. But there is at any rate temper in a bludgeon; anything was bound to be better for England than a bat flimsily made of lath. Duleepsinhji was graceful yet strong, watchful in attack and defence alike.

BALL WORTH A HUNDRED RUNS

He and Hammond scored 59 in 45 minutes, and Grimmett wanted a rest. Hornibrook came on at the pavilion end, and at the very moment when we felt the tide moving gently England's way Hornibrook found a lovely ball which drew Duleepsinhji forward full stretch and beat his bat by spinning from the leg to the off wicket. The ball probably cost England a hundred runs, for Duleepsinhji was defeated at the full bloom of his skill and culture. England were now 123 for three—precariously poised on the game's brink.

Leyland was beaten and nearly bowled first ball by Hornibrook, who, though moderate in his work as a whole, is capable at intervals of a spinner of which Blythe, most delectable of left-handed bowlers, might have been proud. The Australian attack was better than England's because with all its fluctuations in length it contained moments of unexpected difficulty simply because there were two spin bowlers in action both making the ball leave the bat. This is he deadliest ball in all cricket: you simply cannot put your pads to it. Wall, the fast bowler, laboured manfully, but seldom looked likely to take a wicket. Bradman would have hooked and cut prodigiously. A'Beckett was a Saturday afternoon bowler pure and unsophisticated: England's batsmen really had the chance of a lifetime against a side with only two bowlers.

Leyland, cool and vigilant, hit Grimmett for two sixes, both of them delightfully easy straight drives. Again did the flash of an honest cricket bat seem to brighten the day for us. Leyland played proper cricket—as many as the situation demanded, yet all of reliant strokes. There is a world of difference between strokeless and defensive cricket: obstinacy should be as highly tempered as aggression. Leyland caused a temporary retirement of Grimmett for reason other than the man's occasional need for rest and a breathing space. Moreover, Leyland caused the Australian field to spread a little: now the game looked like a Test match on the second day and not a house match with the two last men in and six runs wanted. Leyland had the advantage of his right-handed colleagues in that the spin of both Grimmett and Hornibrook turned towards and not from his bat: Grimmett's 'googly' was not acute enough to trouble Leyland—his best ball is a leg-break. But Leyland played all the bowling with a delightful mingling of manly sturdiness and boyish freedom and confidence. His off-drives made with a forward incline of the body into the stroke were pretty as well as prosperous. He glanced to leg daintily—and then, to remind us of his Yorkshire blood and honours, he swung a ponderous bat full at the ball's pitch, and thus let us know that there is in his play as much nature as art.

A CRITICAL PERIOD

As soon as Leyland settled down the Australian bowling began to assume the aspect of competent pertinacity. The afternoon taught again a venerable lesson: flatter the bowler at your peril, O batsman: often he is only as good as you think he is. Leyland not only eased the sense of dire struggle in the English innings: he attended to the airs and graces of cricket, and by doing so reminded us that the game does not find its soul until it is played with relish.

Until six o'clock Leyland and Hammond held the important fourth wicket, terribly important in view of the fallible batsmen to follow. Hammond was missed at the wicket at 203, when his own score was 52: the snick was low and swift, but Oldfield usually

233

takes such chances as a matter of course. The crowd breathed unspeakable relief at Hammond's escape: here was luck for England at a moment when we could not afford to lose another wicket during the next few moments till the close of play. But England did not hug this gift of fortune: three runs after the missing of Hammond Leyland tried to turn a ball to leg, only to see it fly upwards to where third slip waited quite ravenously—so eager were the Australians to achieve another advance before half-past six.

As a solemn fact the match's ironical wheel swung clean round in the afternoon's sunny fall, and now England is unmistakably in danger. A quick and accurate throw in ran out Geary, who against Wall was for all he knew caught in the slips or at the wicket three times—only he had not the certainty of eye or touch to get his bat near the ball. With Duckworth sent in as a stop-gap Grimmett bowled again, and Duckworth passed through an over by getting his legs, body, and lastly his bat in the way of the spin. Hammond so far has been at the wicket nearly three hours—a batsman in chains but not abashed or to be put down. On Monday responsibility will be seen sitting visibly on his shoulders: is he capable of finding his true self again in this hour? It is not too much to say that England is threatened by the loss of the rubber.

THIRD TEST
3rd Day, Headingley

LEEDS, MONDAY

No play was possible until half-past five today, and then on a dead wicket Hammond and Duckworth played easy cricket—Duckworth, indeed, was able to play back with his left elbow well up to Wall, who tried in vain to enliven a perfect corpse of a pitch. Duckworth scored 15 to Hammond's 12 before bad light stopped the game for the day at a quarter past six.

With a hot, sunny day tomorrow England may still have to struggle. But, frankly, the Australians' attack ought not to be really dangerous on anything less than an absolutely unplayable wicket.

THIRD TEST MATCH
3rd Day, Headingley

AUSTRALIA

First Innings

W. M. Woodfull, b Hammond	50
A. Jackson, c Larwood, b Tate	1
D. C. Bradman, c Duckworth, b Tate	334
A. F. Kippax, c Chapman, b Tate	77
S. McCabe, b Larwood	30
V. Y. Richardson, c Larwood, b Tate	1
E. L. a'Beckett, c Chapman, b Geary	29
W. A. Oldfield, c Hobbs, b Tate	2
C. V. Grimmett, c Duckworth, b Tyldesley	24
T. Wall, b Tyldesley	3
P. M. Hornibrook, not out	1
B 5, lb 8, w 1	14
Total	566

FALL OF WICKETS

AUSTRALIA—First Innings

1	2	3	4	5	6	7	8	9	10
2	194	423	486	491	508	519	544	565	566

BOWLING ANALYSIS

AUSTRALIA—First Innings

	O.	M.	R.	W.		O.	M.	R.	W.
Larwood	33	3	139	1	Tyldesley	33	5	104	2
Tate	39	9	124	5	Hammond	17	3	46	1
Geary	35	10	95	1	Leyland	11	0	44	0

Geary bowled a wide

ENGLAND

First Innings

Hobbs, c a'Beckett, b Grimmett	29
Sutcliffe, c Hornibrook, b Grimmett	32
Hammond, not out	73
K. S. Duleepsinhji, b Hornibrook	35
Leyland, c Kippax, b Wall	44
Geary, run out	0
Duckworth, not out	15
B 5, lb 6 nb 3	14
Total (for five wickets)	242

To bat: A. P. F. Chapman, Tate, Larwood, and Tyldesley (R.).

FALL OF WICKETS

ENGLAND First Innings

1	2	3	4	5	6	7	8	9	10
53	64	123	206	206					

Umpires: Bestwick and Oates

THIRD TEST
4th Day, Headingley

AUSTRALIA
First Innings

W. M. Woodfull, b Hammond	50
A. Jackson, c Larwood, b Tate	1
D. G. Bradman, c Duckworth, b Tate	334
A. F. Kippax, c Chapman, b Tate	77
S. McCabe, b Larwood	30
V. Y. Richardson, c Larwood, b Tate	1
E. L. a'Beckett, c Chapman, b Geary	29
W. A. Oldfield, c Hobbs, b Tate	2
C. V. Grimmett, c Duckworth, b Tyldesley	24
T. Wall, b Tyldesley	3
P. M. Hornibrook , not out	1
B 5, lb 8, w 1	14
Total	566

FALL OF WICKETS

AUSTRALIA—First Innings

1	2	3	4	5	6	7	8	9	10
3	194	423	436	491	506	519	544	565	566

BOWLING ANALYSIS

AUSTRALIA—First Innings

	O.	M.	R.	W.		O.	M	R.	W.
Larwood	33	3	139	1	Tyldesley	33	5	104	2
Tate	39	9	124	5	Hammond	17	3	46	1
Geary	33	10	95	1	Leyland	11	0	44	0

Geary bowled a wide.

ENGLAND

First Innings

Hobbs, c a'Beckett, b Grimmett	29
Sutcliffe, c Hornibrook, b Grimmett	32
Hammond, c Oldfield, b McCabe	113
K. S. Duleepsinhji, b Hornibrook	35
Leyland, c Kippax, b Wall	44
Geary, run out	0
Duckworth, c Oldfield, b a'Beckett	35
Chapman, b Grimmett	45
Tate, c Jackson, b Grimmett	22
Larwood, not out	10
Tyldesley, c Hornibrook, b Grimmett	4
B 9, lb 10, nb 3	22
Total	391

FALL OF WICKETS

ENGLAND—First Innings

1	2	3	4	5	6	7	8	9	10
53	64	123	206	206	233	319	370	375	391

BOWLING ANALYSIS

ENGLAND—First Innings

	O.	M.	R.	W.		O.	M.	R.	W.
Wall	40	12	70	1	Hornibrook	41	7	94	1
a'Beckett	23	3	47	1	McCabe	10	4	23	1
Grimmett	56·2	16	135	5					

Hornibrook bowled three no-balls.

ENGLAND

Second Innings

Hobbs, run out	13
Sutcliffe, not out	28
Hammond, c Oldfield, b Grimmett	35
K. S. Duleepsinhji, c Grimmett, b Hornibrook	10
Leyland, not out	1
lb 8	8
Total (for three wickets)	95

FALL OF WICKETS

Second Innings

1	2	3
24	74	84

237

BOWLING ANALYSIS

ENGLAND—Second Innings

	O.	M.	R.	W.		O.	M.	R.	W.
Wall	10	3	20	0	Hornibrook	11·6	5	14	1
a'Beckett	11	4	19	0	McCabe	2	1	1	0
Grimmett	17	3	33	1					

Umpires: Bestwick and Oates

THIRD TEST
4th Day, Headingley

LEEDS, TUESDAY

On a wicket that never became difficult England contrived to make a draw today, assisted by an appeal against bad light which put an end to cricket forty minutes before the legal hour of drawing stumps.

The light was not to normal eyes at all unsatisfactory; at Nottingham in 1905 Australia gave England a brave fight to a finish against odds in a light which was positively an encircling gloom. The appeal made today, at ten minutes to six, was one of the least sportsmanlike of my acquaintance Thus did a match brilliantly begun by Bradman finish very shabbily. England emerged from the game with little credit, technical or other. Still, there was perhaps some satisfaction in knowing that they had beaten Bradman's score.

Rain in the night and early morning softened and soothed still further the Leeds wicket, so much so that at eleven o'clock, when the match went on under a sunless sky, Duckworth was actually able to play a good length ball from Grimmett to leg boldly and flagrantly against the spin. On a hard turf this stroke would not have improved Duckworth's normal batting averages. Grimmett and Hornibrook quickly if temporarily gave up trying to turn the ball on a pitch that was about as sensitive as a wet hearthrug: Hornibrook once in three overs tossed the ball well up to Hammond, and the consequent stroke, tentative and insecure, ought to have persuaded Hornibrook that a short length on a moist English turf is useless. But it did not, and Hornibrook gave way to Wall, while a'Beckett went on in Grimmett's place.

Woodfull probably thought that while the pitch was lifeless he might as well give somebody a chance to see what he could do with the ball while it was going through the air. Wall's pace was medium:

he dared not trust to a full and free run on the heavy earth. Duckworth made a stylish cut, standing up on his toes and tapping the ball on top as it went tamely past on the offside.

A more comfortable wicket for batsmen would have been hard to find anywhere. It was, however, impossible to feel sorry for the Australians in their unhelpful circumstances. They bowled absurdly short: indeed, the length was much the same as that which they aim at on a fast ground. After all, we do not usually discuss Duckworth's ability to bat in terms of the wicket: we do not say at Old Trafford, 'The wicket is slow, therefore George will stay in for a long time.' There is such a thing as an unplayable length for the less than really first-class batsman: the Australians could not bowl it to Duckworth, who in its absence played really well, not at all suffering in comparison with Hammond. I hope the Southern critics were again made to think, as it seems they were made to think yesterday, that Duckworth as a batsman is quick on his feet. But I trust they will not forget this favourable opinion when next the case of Duckworth versus Ames comes before their judgment. Not until ten minutes past twelve was Duckworth's wicket taken: then he was caught at the wicket emulating most perkily the cut stroke. England were now 289 for six: Duckworth had helped Hammond to score 80 in two hours and ten minutes.

HAMMOND'S CENTURY

Just before Duckworth departed, which he did to great applause, Hammond reached his hundred after four and a half hours of more or less serene and stately batsmanship. Chapman nearly snicked a catch from a'Beckett to the slips as soon as he came in, but even Chapman was allowed to play back at ease on a wicket where the bowlers' only hope of success rested in their skill at so flighting and so tossing up the ball that the batsman was tempted to lunge forward. The Australian attack possessed steadiness: I am not saying it was at all loose. My point is that it was in the circumstances before lunch most ineptly short and wrong strategically. I could at last understand how Australian bowling lost a Test match a year or two ago on a Melbourne sticky wicket. No doubt even a Rhodes or a Peel would have been pretty mild and harmless on this morning's turf: but they would at any rate have flighted the ball and tried to draw the batsmen farther than they wanted to go.

Hammond achieved a square drive of rare brilliance from McCabe: the shortness of the length was positively offensive in the eyes of students of cricket. This is not to belittle the handsome cricket of Hammond: I am merely making a protest against the Australians' quite wrong-headed bowling methods on a dead easy pitch. Patriotism is not everything: no lover of the game likes to see a match conducted by any side in a fashion that is unintelligent, and regardless of the finer shades. The crassest blunder in the Australian attack before lunch was that when a ball was by accident or design not short it came from a quick bowler who, of course, could present no problems of flight. Hammond's innings was finished by a catch by Oldfield; for five hours and a quarter he mingled style and defence in proportion. Today he seemed admirably suited by the length that gave scope to his strong back stroke.

GRIMMETT SPINS AGAIN

The Australian slow bowlers were kept off for too long when Chapman and Tate were in: both batsmen made the most of their chances until Grimmett returned to the attack and bowled Chapman round the legs with a ball which the batsman sought to play entirely by his pads. After lunch the wicket played quicker, and at once Grimmett's spin proved too much to batsmen chosen primarily for their bowling. Larwood, however, gave an example of how quick feet can cope safely and strongly with Grimmett. Richard Tyldesley drove a six to the on from Grimmett, and next ball was caught at first slip, the ball spinning across really viciously. England thus failed to save the follow on by the 25 runs which might easily and safely have been made last night and this morning by batsmen not obsessed by the idea that the job of keeping wickets up was the only one that mattered. While the wicket was thoroughly dead Hammond scored 52 in two and a half hours.

When England batted again the threat of sunshine passed away, and the rollers' influence put to sleep the wicket again. Hobbs and Sutcliffe played as usual defensively and well. There was no value in runs now. All the more reason, then, that Sutcliffe and Hobbs should not have dashed for a run when Sutcliffe drove a ball hard and fast to Australia's most brilliant fieldsman, who is Bradman by name. Bradman picked up magnificently and hit the stumps to which Hobbs was running—hit them smashingly! Hobbs was out at twenty minutes to four, and the first wicket had played out forty minutes of the three hours and a quarter available for a decision when England's innings began.

ENGLAND *v.* AUSTRALIA 1930 TEST SERIES

A SURPRISING APPEAL

Shortly before Hobbs was run out an appeal against the light was surprisingly made and granted, but the interruption lasted a few minutes. From my seat in a distant stand I had not once lost sight of the ball, not even against the background of the crowd.

Hammond's second innings gave us consolation for many disappointments in a match that has not seen English batting at its best. The way he played Grimmett suggested that he has regained his true form against the best of contemporary leg spin bowlers. He moved on quick feet and hit hard with something of his old freedom and easefulness of swing and with his old accuracy of timing. As soon as he came in he glanced a ball from Wall dangerously behind the wicket to the leg side: Oldfield did not seem to anticipate the snick. It was the sort of difficult chance which Duckworth runs over to and holds in front of the middle of his body. Oldfield merely clutched outwards at the snick and made no ground. Hammond was eventually caught at the wicket, and then England, with eight wickets in hand, needed to bat only another ninety minutes.

Sutcliffe proceeded to hold on to his wicket, his temperament more impressive than his technique. He seems to have no strokes nowadays, but in other respects he is a Test match batsman of the best post-war stock. He and Duleepsinhji defended England's third wicket until twenty to six, though neither was masterful.

When Leyland had opened his score the decisive appeal against the light was lodged and upheld: the players left the field at ten minutes to six. The sympathies of the crowd seemed to be with the Australians: myself, I was astounded that anybody had imagined a bad light. It was not good to feel even a hint that English batsmen, with seven of them to be dismissed, were eager to clutch at an ally from the outside which would free them from the necessity of pitting technique against technique for a mere period of forty minutes. If the light really was bad I am still surprised that I could not find anybody on the ground who was a willing and dogmatic witness to the fact. England were fortunate that rain was on their side yesterday: that ought surely to have rendered them grateful and chivalrous enough to have allowed the Australians the benefit of the doubt about this evening's visibility—at the very end of the game's last round.

A man in the crowd, born in England and, what is more, born in Yorkshire, put the affair in a phrase of pungent if crude satire when he said: 'Ah'm thinkin' as there's somebody as 'ud be better wearin' glasses.' Possibly Sam Weller would have suggested his double-glass binoculars of hextra power.

FOURTH TEST
1st Day, Old Trafford

AUSTRALIA
First Innings

W. M. Woodfull, c Duckworth, b Tate	54
W. H. Ponsford, b Hammond	83
D. G. Bradman, c Duleepsinhji, b Peebles	14
A. Kippax, c Chapman, b Nichols	51
S. McCabe, lbw, b Peebles	4
V. Y. Richardson, b Hammond	1
A. Fairfax, not out	21
W. A. Oldfield, b Nichols	2
C. V. Grimmett, not out	21
B 15, lb 2, nb 7	24
	—
Total (for seven wickets)	275

To bat: T. Wall and P. M. Hornibrook.

FALL OF WICKETS
AUSTRALIA—First Innings

1	2	3	4	5	6	7	8	9	10
106	138	184	189	190	239	243			

ENGLAND: A. P. F. Chapman, K. S. Duleepsinhji, I. A. R. Peebles, Hobbs, Sutcliffe, Hammond, Tate, Leyland, Duckworth, Nichols, and Goddard.

Umpires: Chester and Hardstaff.

FOURTH TEST MATCH 1930
1st Day, Old Trafford

Yesterday the Australians made a moderately good score on an Old Trafford wicket which, very easy to begin with, gave some measure of help to the attack from three o'clock onwards. England for a while did reasonably well by keeping the batsmen quiet while the turf was useless for spin or peace; they began to take wickets at the opportune moment, but disappointed us sadly by an inability to run rapidly through the Australian innings after the back of it had been broken for only 190. A good left-handed slow bowler was needed during this period—a period which, before the match is over, may well turn out to have been crucial. In unsettled weather a total of nearly 300 is not to be despised.

The Australians were strangely negligent of runs while the wicket was in its most comfortable state. Before lunch only a matter of 70 were scored in two hours. Had Woodfull been suddenly seized with plenary inspiration at the outset of the match he might have sent Bradman in first with Ponsford. While the ball was coming through slowly and with little spin it is possible Bradman would have again been in punitive mood. When Bradman did arrive at the wicket after lunch he was put into the second class by the spin of Peebles. The wicket was taking the break now, though not lending to it any amount of venom. Bradman's innings suggested that before he is ranked with Victor Trumper or Macartney we must wait to see him achieve a great innings on a bowler's wicket.

PEEBLES THE BEST BOWLER

Peebles was the only distinguished member of the English attack. Though not exactly suited by the pitch, he demonstrated once and for all that the spin the Australian batsmen least like is spin away from the bat. Goddard requires a faster wicket than yesterday's; possibly he would prefer a wicket definitely sticky. Most bowlers would. But his off-break, turning as it does into the bat, ought not to trouble cricketers celebrated for their off-side technique. The English fielding was respectable on the whole, and altogether the team seemed more of a piece than at any other time this season. We must bear in mind though that the conditions yesterday were not favourable to Australian batting methods. Woodfull has therefore every reason to feel that his men did all that could have been expected of them when, having won the toss, he had no alternative but to bat first on a wicket of the sort which, before any long day is done, is bound at some time to give a chance to English bowling. Taking into account the slowness of the outfield, Australia's total for seven wickets can be reckoned as the equivalent of, say, 350 in dry weather. All in all, then, we are not at liberty to congratulate ourselves that the ideal English attack has at last been got together. It can never be anything like complete until it includes a left-handed slow bowler who is master of his length and break.

A big crowd sat round the field when at half-past eleven the

English eleven came forth with mid sunlight softening the white and lovely waterfall of the cricketers' descent down the pavilion steps. As soon as Nichols bowled the game's first ball the scene became quiet as a mouse. This was different indeed from Leeds, where, during the match's most dramatic moments of suspense, our ears were afflicted by noises of some discordant sort—perhaps a newsman rhetorically announcing 'Four down for Yorkshire.'

A QUIET BEGINNING

Nichols and Tate quickly called for sawdust, and soon the green of the field was hideously bespattered like the floor of a butcher's shop. The pitch had a softness that stole power from the attack, though in Tate's first over a ball came from the earth at a speed which made a leg-glance by Ponsford late and impulsive enough to justify the crowd's unanimous 'Oooh!' At the end of the eighth over the Australian score was 11 for none; at this point a voice from the multitude cried out 'Hit 'em!' The impatience was no doubt that of a staunch Lancashire man whose taste for correct cricket had probably been corrupted by the rhetorical recklessness of Watson, Hallows, and other darlings of Old Trafford.

Goddard bowled in Tate's place at 13; his first ball, very short, was directed for three through the leg trap; his third ball was so wide an off-break that though it pitched on the leg stump it eluded Duckworth after turning and went for four byes. Duckworth surveyed the angle of this ball's excessive spin as though with a look of polite reproach. Goddard bowled from over the wicket, and he placed four fieldsmen close to the wicket, beginning at leg and semicircling to, say, forward mid-on, which last-named place was occupied by Chapman, who while Goddard was walking to the bowling place stood in his own beautiful and loose poise, arms folded with right fingers contemplatively stroking his chin—a poise capable of marvellous galvanism at the first hint of swift work to be done. After a while Tate bowled at Nichols's end; and so steadily did he and Goddard pitch a length that in an hour's play Australia scored only 32, and the barrackers were holding very private and tentative rehearsals for tenors, baritones, and basses.

Peebles in his third over sent to Woodfull a ball of delicious length and curve through the air; Woodfull did not play it with his bat, but thrust out his pads, obviously expecting the spin to break away. But the ball travelled straight through, and Woodfull was nearly bowled when his score was 15 and Australia's 33. At twenty minutes

244

to one Peebles, trying for a leg break, was guilty of a terrible long-hop—I am not certain it was not one of Mr. Croome's polyhops. Ponsford hit the ball to square leg, the first authentic boundary of the day. While the wicket was as comfortable as it undoubtedly was hereabout the English attack had reason to be glad that Bradman was watching the game from the balcony near the pavilion clock. Peebles again established the human mortality of Woodfull when Australia were 58 and Woodfull 23. He compelled Woodfull to edge a ball dangerously through the slips just as it was skimming away.

Peebles bowled well, keeping a fuller and more seductive length than he has frequently done this summer. If the pitch had not killed his spin he might easily have taken at least two wickets before lunch. He is a delicious cricketer to watch as he bowls. He is all youthful eagerness as he walks to his bowling place; when he turns round and finds the batsman is not quite ready he seems all impatience, as though the delay has for certain hindered the conception of a perfect googly. He is as lavish with the googly as Grimmett is sparing of it. At lunch Australia were 75 for none; England on the whole could enjoy sustenance with the knowledge that they had escaped by half the punishment any forcing batsman would with ordinary luck have dealt out to bowlers hopelessly handicapped by the wicket.

Woodfull, being a batsman more or less dependent on deflections for his runs, found the sluggish ground quite unable to lend to his strokes any amount of energy. Still he contrived to move slightly quicker than Ponsford, and reached 50 in two hours and ten minutes.

AN ASTONISHING BRADMAN

After lunch both Woodfull and Ponsford opened out their driving technique; twice did Woodfull hit Peebles straight and with a strength which was not hinted at in the narrowness of the preliminary lift-up of his bat. At a quarter to three Australia's score was 106; then Woodfull tried to cut or steer an off-side ball from Tate through the slips. He merely touched it and was caught by Duckworth. And now came forward Bradman. He proceeded to play like a cricketer who never before in his life had seen a spinning ball. Peebles perplexed him sorely. And he appeared to give a chance at the wicket to Duckworth when his score was six. Duckworth fumbled the ball and conveniently did not appeal. To the first ball Bradman got from Peebles he used his pads at the last second, used them to a leg break

245

which pitched on the off stump and went for four byes. The next ball was hit to the on, though the bat's aim clearly was to the off. Bradman had mixed up the leg break with the googly. When he was ten Bradman was missed at first slip from Peebles, and the next ball nearly bowled him as he rather desperately tried to drive. 'God bless thee, Bradman,' one thought; 'how thou art translated!' He fell to a catch at second slip, and as he was attempting to cut or drive square past point a ball that was leaving his bat at the moment of impact we may safely conclude the stroke was speculative and based on no sure notion of the direction of the going-away spin.

The innings was highly significant. I make nothing of the fact that Bradman failed to get runs; it was his turn to fail. What was instructive was his tentative methods against Peebles. The innings justified those of us who throughout the season have argued that the weak spot in Bradman's technique would most likely be found out by slow-medium spin pitching on the wicket and turning away from the bat.

Towards the middle of the afternoon sunshine broke through the clouds, and at last the scene and the day belonged to high summer. But probably the Australians were in no mood to enjoy with any poetical emotions this change in the weather. The wicket began to take spin with some slight greediness. Kippax for a while was as innocent as Bradman in the presence of Peebles's bowling. The first two balls from Peebles were accompanied by appeals for leg before wicket, and Kippax was entirely at the mercy of the umpire on each occasion. He was, for all he knew, a defeated batsman half a dozen times in half a dozen overs.

PONSFORD'S BATTING

The Australian innings now was in the hands of Ponsford. He batted thoughtfully, watched the breaking ball, and, unlike Bradman, did not play against the spin. He scored neat runs on the on side and kept his head down. His use of the passive bat at the right ball qualified him automatically for Lancashire. He seemed set for a hundred when, with Australia's total 184, a lovely breakback from Hammond bowled him. He had been on view for three hours and fifty minutes, and the only fault that could be found with his cricket is that before lunch he might safely have brought into action a more varied and resolute stroke-play than he did.

The ball which bowled Ponsford was significant of much. It is not the custom of Hammond to send along breakbacks on a good wicket. The Old Trafford pitch was at last awakening from the dead, even if it was not definitely kicking. It was to be observed that Hammond had two men at short leg in his field. McCabe found Peebles an insoluble problem, and was out leg before wicket; the use of the pads to a ball nearly a half-volley was proof of a mind darkened with dubiety. When Richardson was bowled by Hammond Australia were 190 for five and the attack very much on top and generally pleased with the world.

GODDARD AND PARKER COMPARED

The crowd were now in the mood to expect a wicket every ball. At tea everybody was estimating the Australian innings at round about 220 all out. A left-handed bowler of sure technique would probably have settled the issue favourably and speedily. Goddard was a disappointment—a sort of second (or third or fifteenth) edition of Parkin. But when Parkin exploited a leg trap the strokes sent into it were made by the reflex actions of batsmen seeking to save themselves from a quick breakback pitched on the off stump (from round the wicket) and spinning to the leg stump. In short, when a batsman got caught out in Parkin's leg-trap he was trying to stop a ball from bowling him. Goddard seldom yesterday seemed likely to bowl a wicket down; and his spin was so tame that no batsman was likely to carry his off-breaks round to the clutching hands of the encircling fieldsmen. There seems to be a notion abroad at the moment that Parker, of Gloucestershire, is not an England bowler—not because he is technically below the Test match standard, but for reasons vaguely psychological. So much is heard nowadays about the 'psychology' or 'temperament' of our England cricketers that I cannot help thinking that they need in the pavilion not only a masseur and dressing-room attendant but also a specialist in the theory and practice of Professor Freud.

At a time when a left-handed bowler would have been considerably inspired by the wicket yesterday—that is, during the hour after the tea interval—Kippax and Fairfax added nearly 49 valuable runs for the sixth Australian wicket. Kippax, once he had settled down, achieved a few fine drives. He was unluckily out, caught off a ball from Nichols which kicked viciously. Nichols also bowled Oldfield at 243; he worked hard and well on a pitch not at all after his heart. He ought not, of course, to have been bowling at all on such a wicket.

The day ended disappointingly for England, because Grimmett

and Fairfax were allowed to hold the eighth wicket fairly easefully until close of play. It was rather sad to see Grimmett playing a perfectly composed defensive stroke against Goddard, whose failure during the afternoon brought home the old saying about the pathos which is born when a beautiful abstract theory is slain by a single concrete fact.

England badly missed a chance after the tea interval of playing themselves on the way to victory; it was provoking to see the tail enders—obviously not happy on a moist pitch —holding up English bowlers. We need not maintain that the wicket was difficult; the point is that the batting after tea was obviously never good enough to cope with any skilfully directed turning ball. As for Bradman's innings, well, as the Bosun in H.M.S. *Pinafore* would say: 'I'm shocked—that's what I am—shocked.' It is alleged that Bradman batted in braces the first time he played in good-class cricket; yesterday his innings not only wore braces, it had its waistcoat on as well.

FOURTH TEST
2nd Day (Old Trafford)

AUSTRALIA
First Innings

W. M. Woodfull, c Duckworth, b Tate	54
W. H. Ponsford, b Hammond	83
D. G. Bradman, c Duleepsinhji, b Peebles	14
A. Kippax, c Chapman, b Nichols	51
S. McCabe, lbw, b Peebles	4
V. Y. Richardson, b Hammond	1
A. Fairfax, lbw, b Goddard	49
W. A. Oldfield, b Nichols	2
C. V. Grimmett, c Sutcliffe, b Peebles	50
P. M. Hornibrook, c Duleepsinhji, b Goddard	3
T. Wall, not out	1
B 23, lb 3, nb 7	33
Total	345

FALL OF WICKETS
AUSTRALIA—First Innings

1	2	3	4	5	6	7	8	9	10
106	138	184	189	190	239	243	330	338	345

BOWLING ANALYSIS

AUSTRALIA—First Innings

	O.	M.	R.	W.		O.	M.	R.	W.
Nichols	21	5	33	2	I. A. R. Peebles	53	9	150	3
Tate	30	11	39	1	Leyland	8	2	17	0
Goddard	32·1	14	49	2	Hammond	21	6	24	2

Nichols bowled three no-balls, Goddard three no-balls, and I. A. R. Peebles one no-ball.

ENGLAND

First Innings

Hobbs, c Oldfield, b Wall	31
Sutcliffe, c Bradman, b Wall	74
Hammond, b Wall	3
K. S. Duleepsinhji, c Hornibrook, b McCabe	54
Leyland, not out	35
A. P. F. Chapman, c Grimmett, b Hornibrook	1
Tate, not out	10
B 3, lb 10	13

Total (for five wickets)   221

To bat: I. A. R. Peebles, Duckworth, Nichols, and Goddard.

FALL OF WICKETS

ENGLAND—First Innings

1	2	3	4	5	6	7	8	9	10
108	115	119	192	199					

Umpires: Chester and Hardstaff.

On paper the balance in the Test match at Old Trafford is at the moment level. But the more one reflects upon the course of the action the more apparent becomes the fact that England have missed opportunities. On Friday they were able to bowl at Australia on a wicket which, though easy to begin with, certainly behaved eccentrically during the afternoon, if it did not grow really difficult. The reliable Australian batsmen were accounted for at a reasonable cost; then, when the ball was turning, an Australian 'tail', admittedly weak at batting, even on a good wicket, was clever enough to hold back the English advance. Good bowling ought to have made an end of Australia's innings for, say, 240 on Friday, after five wickets had fallen for 190. Saturday gave England the privilege of an innings on an easy wicket, fast enough for the exploitation of all the strokes of the game, but not so fast that good batsmen were under compulsion to hurry an instinctive performance of their technique. Moreover, Grimmett was very much out of form, and the rest of the

Australian attack below Test match standards, even if it did maintain the respectable efficiency of the sort of bowling we usually see in an engagement between Leicestershire and Northamptonshire. Yet, despite a brilliant piece of cricket by Sutcliffe when England went in just before lunch, the end of the day saw England struggling still, struggling as they have had to struggle without rest ever since they won by the sweat of the brow at Trent Bridge.

Fairfax and Grimmett deserved high praise for a stand well worth 83 made in circumstances of weather and situation which none but a recognized batsman would choose for the onerous task of scoring his first fifty in a Test match innings. A. C. MacLaren used to say that during every match there comes a moment when a firm grip can be got on the issue by one side or the other. Had England dismissed Australia for 230 or so on Friday, after Bradman, Woodfull, Ponsford, and Kippax were out, and then, on Saturday's easy wicket, had our batsmen taken advantage of a good prelude to the innings by Sutcliffe—but these be vain regrets. Let us hope that opportunity having knocked once at an unanswered door will knock for us again.

The Australians will probably be glad to emerge from this when unbeaten. They must have prepared themselves for trouble game last week they learned that the match was certain to be fought on a wicket of a pace to which their style of batting and bowling is not yet accustomed. England ought always to start favourites at Old Trafford in unsettled weather. The Australians so far have had rather the worst of the wicket, yet here they are holding their own, to say the least. They have played with excellent spirit in an engagement which technically has up to the moment fallen considerably below Test match standards.

MODERATE BOWLING

England will have to work hard to retain the rubber—and it is doubtful whether an adequate attack has yet been gathered together. For the life of me I cannot see that the English bowling in this match has shown much improvement over that of Leeds. Peebles alone has brought to the eleven a bowling technique of fresh ideas and distinction. But how can it be maintained that the English attack in this game has revealed especial powers of penetration in view of Australia's 345, made despite comparative failures by Bradman and Woodfull—and also in view of Grimmett's ability to hold up his wicket in a crucial period for two hours?

When the match was resumed, on a dull morning, Peebles bowled
om the end opposite to the one where on Friday he had done his
est work. Later, after Fairfax and Grimmett had proved themselves
s imperturbable as obstinate for nearly an hour, Peebles attacked
om the Stretford wicket and almost immediately caused the ball
o spin quickly and get Grimmett caught skilfully at short leg by
utcliffe. In the afternoon Grimmett also bowled from the Man-
hester end: not until the last over of the day did he take the end
hich Peebles had consistently demonstrated was the more favour-
ble end for a spin bowler. Hornibrook, I noticed, sent down a
eautiful over to Sutcliffe from the Stretford wicket, only to be
emoved to the other end straightway, where his spin immediately
ost much of its vitality.

The crowd seemed rather disillusioned by the persistent stand of
Grimmett and Fairfax at the fresh of the morning. Not until after
alf-past twelve did the Australian innings finish. Fairfax batted
hree hours and ten minutes for 49; occasionally the crowd quietly
sked him to hit the ball, but on the whole Fairfax's cricket seemed
o tell the people, in Mr Squeers's language, to 'subdue your appe-
ites and you've conquered human nature'.

ENGLAND'S GOOD START

In a doubtful light Hobbs and Sutcliffe played safely through the
alf an hour's cricket in front of lunch, but Hobbs was unpleasantly
it on the body. After the interval we had the finest cricket of the
natch so far. Sutcliffe, at his very happiest, attacked the bowling
esolutely. For the first time in the summer's Test matches he got
id of Grimmett's 'silly' point. Here was a moral gesture as well as
 technical advance. The brilliance of Sutcliffe's play changed the
cene, dispelled the morning's heavy air. From out of the sky came
elicious sunshine, and the light of it flashed on Sutcliffe's bat, on
is flannels, on his handsome face, and on his immaculate hair. He
rove Wall to the off boundary classically; he lay back to Grimmett
nd hit his leg break past cover, then pulled drastically for four to
eg. Another cover-drive off Grimmett, followed by a magnificent
ook off Wall, set the great crowd agog. This was the Sutcliffe who
ears ago first came to Old Trafford and, even during a Lancashire
nd Yorkshire match, made cricket one of the pleasures of life. He
ecaptured the freedom of those salad days; he dealt with Wall as
nce he dealt with Macdonald, hitting him to the on and to leg with
his body erect, his bat sweeping in grand temper across the line of

the short ball. For the first time since the match began we were watching batsmanship which had a personal skill and relish. Why for so long has Sutcliffe held his true strokes in abeyance? His innings on Saturday was the best many of us have ever seen him play in a Test match; he looked the ideal cricketer now, confident and proud of his strength and mastery. The multitude took him to heart; once again Old Trafford called him not Sutcliffe but Herbert.

Sutcliffe reached 50 out of 68 in little more than an hour. Hobbs at the other end was content to play second fiddle in the afternoon's bracing music. He did not time his strokes accurately, and seemed out of sorts. But he brought to the aid of a faltering technique his own experience. Sutcliffe also was painfully hit by a rising ball on the arm. This minor casualty probably was the cause of a slackening in the pace of scoring, just at the moment when the crowd were ready to see the Australian bowling put to waste. Sutcliffe was very clever to get his bat down in time to a veritable shooter from Hornibrook, which spun from the leg to the middle stump. It was after bowling so deadly a ball that Hornibrook was changed over from the Stretford to the Manchester end. Fairfax came on in his place, and Sutcliffe pulled a full toss prodigiously for six.

ENGLISH MISFORTUNES

England's score rounded 100 in as many minutes. Eight runs later Hobbs went after an off side ball from Wall and sent a catch to Oldfield, who had to move a yard to the off to get behind the ball. This was not the only time in the afternoon we were to see England suffer misfortune exactly at a moment when the Australian bowling looked to be well mastered. Hobbs can scarcely have taken off his pads before Sutcliffe lost his wicket too, also through an 'accident' rather than because of an error of batsmanship. He pulled a long hop from Wall deep to the square leg boundary, where Bradman gauged the flight with a quite distressing certainty. Though Bradman tumbled backwards into the crowd there can be no doubting that he took the catch well within bounds. Sutcliffe hit one six and ten fours, and did his best to nail challenging colours to the English mast.

The remainder of the afternoon's play was exasperating to patriots, by reason of the way England pulled themselves out of an uncomfortable position, gained another point of vantage, only to lose ground before close of play. Hammond once more disappointed Old Trafford, where a year or two ago he achieved one of the most radiant innings ever seen on any cricket field. His bat this time was heavy with labour: he played on to a ball from Wall which kept rather low, but never did he appear to have in his hands a blade capable of moving lightly and flexibly. England 119 for three, and the crowd silent where not half an hour since they had made the welkin ring.

DULEEPSINHJI AND LEYLAND

A few minutes of Duleepsinhji's lithe cricket, with Leyland occidentally tangible and solid at the other end, quickly dissipated pessimism. The Australian bowling was given the air of permanent and essential respectability. We could assure ourselves that England had lost three wickets to an attack not really deadly (though Wall bowled well) but rather because Hobbs, Sutcliffe, and Hammond had in a measure been accessories after the act of their own downfall. Duleepsinhji flicked the ball here and there; he cut Hornibrook intimately, the bat touching the ball at the last second as the spin went across to the off. He reached 50 with a leg-glance so fine and thrilling that McCabe, the bowler, threw up his hands to high heaven. Likewise of old would Lockwood call on the gods (in noble numbers) to witness the black magic of Ranjitsinhji's glance to leg, from the middle stump. England 192 for 3, Duleepsinhji and Leyland set, and the time of the delicious July afternoon a quarter to six. The splendid crowd now gave themselves up for the day to summer-time contentment. Then, yet again, at the crucial moment, did the Australians prevent England from getting definitely on top. At 192 Duleepsinhji played a not very decisive stroke to first slip from a ball quick off the pitch and swinging away. Hornibrook held a pretty one-handed catch. Chapman, with Leyland, held the fifth wicket for a quarter of an hour while only seven runs were scored; he was caught at backward point from a low but not very defiant hit. Leyland played an exemplary defensive innings; he was at the wicket nearly 90 minutes before he decided to hit a boundary. Possibly he was wise not to take the shadow of a risk after Duleepsinhji had got out. But after the heartening gesture of Sutcliffe it was with a feeling of promise frustrated that we looked on this cricketer of natural hitting powers being compelled, though thoroughly set, to play for keeps until time for drawing stumps. Tate had to face the ordeal of the closing half-hour; he survived, despite one or two dreadfully dangerous slashes at Wall—reflex actions both!

THE SPECTATORS

A crowd of over 30,000 lent to the afternoon an English bulk of greatness. When the sun shone, the scene was typical of cricket in this land of ours; during the game's silences the crowd, as I saw it from the height of the press box, had an impersonal, almost an institutional, size and immobility. The fancy was made to play with the idea of how, as the years go by, things go on and on, changing yet unchanging. Years ago the summer sunshine at Old Trafford warmed a crowd much the same as Saturday's, while out in the middle it was, in the eyes of time, the same cricketers playing the same game. Spooner and Trumpet and Warner then; Bradman and Sutcliffe now—and tomorrow, well, perhaps it will be any one of the small boys who sat on the grass on Saturday and looked at the match with eyes bright with hero worship.

FOURTH TEST
3rd Day Old Trafford
AUSTRALIA
First Innings

W. M. Woodfull, c Duckworth, b Tate	54
W. H. Ponsford, b Hammond	83
D. G. Bradman, c Duleepsinhji, b Peebles	14
A. Kippax, c Chapman, b Nichols	51
S. McCabe, lbw, b Peebles	4
V. Y. Richardson, b Hammond	1
A. Fairfax, lbw b Goddard	49
W. A. Oldfield, b Nichols	2
C. V. Grimmett, c Sutcliffe, b Peebles	50
P. M. Hornibrook, c Duleepsinhji, b Goddard	3
T. Wall, not out	1
B 23, lb 3, nb 7	33
Total	345

FALL OF WICKETS
AUSTRALIA—First Innings

1	2	3	4	5	6	7	8	9	10
106	138	184	189	190	239	243	330	338	345

BOWLING ANALYSIS
AUSTRALIA—First Innings

	O.	M.	R.	W.		O.	M.	R.	W.
Nichols	21	5	33	2	I. A. R. Peebles	53	9	150	3
Tate	30	11	39	1	Leyland	8	2	17	0
Goddard	32·1	14	49	2	Hammond	21	6	24	2

Nichols bowled three no-balls, Goddard three no-balls, and I. A. R. Peebles one no-ball.

ENGLAND

First Innings

Hobbs, c Oldfield, b Wall	31
Sutcliffe, c Bradman, b Wall	74
Hammond, b Wall	3
K. S. Duleepsinhji, c Hornibrook, b McCabe	54
Leyland, not out	35
A. P. F. Chapman, c Grimmett, b Hornibrook	1
Tate, c Ponsford, b McCabe	15
Nichols, not out	7
I. A. R. Peebles, c Richardson, b McCabe	6
Duckworth, not out	0
B 13, lb 12	25
Total (for eight wickets)	251

To bat: Goddard.

FALL OF WICKETS

ENGLAND—First Innings

1	2	3	4	5	6	7	8	9	10
108	115	119	192	199	222	237	247		

Umpires: Chester and Hardstaff.

A crowd of 14,000 had paid at the gates at Old Trafford yesterday by lunch-time, but there was no play until half-past five, because of rain and a moist, unpleasant earth. The patience of everybody was noble throughout the dreary waiting. Apparently the captains could not agree about the state of the wicket when for the third time they looked at it at four o'clock; naturally enough their strategical points of view were dissimilar. The decision was then, I take it, placed in the control of the umpires, and theirs was the judgment, after a further passage of time, which gave the crowd some little consolation for a prolonged and heroic exercise of one of the cardinal human virtues.

When the game was resumed the pitch played with an astonishing quickness. Leyland was too late for the first ball he received from McCabe and was bowled, after Tate had added one run to England's score of 221 made on Saturday. The light began to fail after Leyland got out. Nichols batted nicely, leaning over with some grace and discretion to the ball on his pads and getting it away for quiet runs. Tate drove McCabe to the off for four; then fell to a catch, cleverly held at mid-on by Ponsford.

In an encircling gloom Peebles shaped creditably against keen bowling which frequently sped from the wicket with a surprisingly angular velocity. Wall had no difficulty with his long run, or with his foothold. Richardson missed Peebles in the slips, and shortly afterwards caught him dexterously. Duckworth came in to great applause, which increased in ardour as he allowed a ball from McCabe to pass him and go for byes. Then the rain came again at a quarter past six and there was light enough still left in the sky for the cricketers to find the shelter of the pavilion. McCabe bowled seven overs for 14 runs and three wickets. The conditions did not favour accurate batsmanship; none the less the batting was clearly that of a 'tail end' which, to say the truth, set in on Saturday at the fall of England's fourth wicket.

FOURTH TEST
4th Day Old Trafford

AUSTRALIA
First Innings

W. M. Woodfull, c Duckworth, b Tate	54
W. H. Ponsford, b Hammond	83
D. G. Bradman, c Duleepsinhji, b Peebles	14
A. Kippax, c Chapman, b Nichols	51
S. McCabe, lbw, b Peebles	4
V. Y. Richardson, b Hammond	1
A. Fairfax, lbw, b Goddard	49
W. A. Oldfield, b Nichols	2
C. V. Grimmett, c Sutcliffe, b Peebles	50
P. M. Hornibrook, c Duleepsinhji, b Goddard	3
T. Wall, not out	1
B 23, lb 3, nb 7	33
Total	345

FALL OF WICKETS
AUSTRALIA—First Innings

1	2	3	4	5	6	7	8	9	10
106	138	184	189	190	239	243	330	338	345

BOWLING ANALYSIS
AUSTRALIA—First Innings

	O.	M.	R.	W.		O.	M.	R.	W.
Nichols	21	5	33	2	I. A. R. Peebles	53	9	150	3
Tate	30	11	39	1	Leyland	8	2	17	0
Goddard	32·1	14	49	2	Hammond	21	6	24	2

Nichols bowled three no-balls, Goddard three no-balls, and I. A. R. Peebles one no-ball.

ENGLAND *v.* AUSTRALIA 1930 TEST SERIES

ENGLAND

First Innings

Hobbs, c Oldfield, b Wall	31
Sutcliffe, c Bradman, b Wall	74
Hammond, b Wall	3
K. S. Duleepsinhji, c Hornibrook, b McCabe	54
Leyland, b McCabe	35
A. P. F. Chapman, c Grimmett, b Hornibrook	1
Tate, c Ponsford, b McCabe	15
Nichols, not out	7
I. A. R. Peebles, c Richardson, b McCabe	6
Duckworth, not out	0
B 13, lb 12	25
Total (for eight wickets)	251

Goddard did not bat.

FALL OF WICKETS

ENGLAND—First Innings

1	2	3	4	5	6	7	8	9	10
106	115	119	192	199	222	237	247		

BOWLING ANALYSIS

ENGLAND—First Innings

	O.	M.	R.	W.		O.	M.	R.	W.
Wall	33	9	70	3	Hornibrook	26	9	41	1
Fairfax	13	5	15	0	McCabe	17	3	41	4
Grimmett	19	2	59	0					

Umpires: Chester and Hardstaff.

Before lunch yesterday it was decided to abandon the Test match at Old Trafford, and a dreadfully wet afternoon confirmed and carried the decision unanimously. We must now hold our souls in patience for the game at the Oval, where one side or the other will die the death, rain or sunshine or the frost of early winter. The Selection Committee in the interim will no doubt consider how the England eleven can be strengthened in batting at no hurt to the bowling. No doubt the name of Ames will crop up again. Something certainly ought to be done to put an end to a 'tail' consisting of Chapman, Tate, Peebles, Goddard, and Duckworth. There was merit in the innings of Nichols on Monday, but with him the question is whether he is likely, on an Oval wicket, to bowl well.

For the purposes of a fight to a finish, the batting of the England eleven, as we saw it at Manchester, would carry nobody's confidence. Only Sutcliffe, Duleepsinhji, and Leyland of the lot looked to be in the Test match class. Hobbs, no doubt, will be much more of himself at the Oval; Hammond cannot be dropped, because he is a useful bowler and an admirable fieldsman. The weak spot in the batting is, of course, Chapman; it is to be doubted, too, whether he is a good captain. We cannot, however, change the leadership at this time of day. It is, indeed, too late to risk any large-scale experiments. despite the sorry fact that the crucial Test match is upon us and we have not yet built up a reliable England eleven. The Australians are at last a team, working together. It is not a great team, true; there is an apparent vulnerability somewhere. That we cannot seek it out exactly is the aggravating thing about this year's Test matches.

The cricket of the England eleven at Manchester was entirely disappointing. On a soft wicket the Australians ought not to have been allowed to score anything like a total of 345. And on Saturday's easy wicket, with Grimmett not in deadly vein, England had a rare opportunity to make runs brilliantly and in bulk. Our recognized batsmen have a habit of getting out at those moments when the game's tide is on the turn; some resolution is lacking somewhere. A match-winner, with great strokes all round the wicket is needed for the Oval. It will be a mistake to suppose that in a fight to a finish the main job for our batsmen to perform will be to stay in. The innings of the most obstinate batsman must sooner or later come to an end; runs will settle the issue at the Oval, not patience. Where there is no time-limit there can be little value in stonewalling as such. I am not certain that it would not be good policy for England to recall Woolley. I fancy that the Australian bowlers were delighted when they knew Woolley had been dropped.

The Manchester match, with all its disappointments, provided us with one cause for keen satisfaction. It revealed the quality of the boy Peebles. He had still a deal to do with his technique but already he can spin the ball; moreover he has enthusiasm and ideas. The England eleven for the next ten years may have to depend heavily on Peebles. We owe much to the great South African cricketer Aubrey Faulkner, because of the skilful and shrewd way he has acted as tutor to the most promising right-handed spin bowler of recent years.

FIFTH TEST
1st Day The Oval

ENGLAND

First Innings

Hobbs, c Kippax, b Wall	47
Sutcliffe, not out	138
Whysall, lbw, b Wall	13
K. S. Duleepsinhji, c Fairfax, b Grimmett	50
Hammond, b McCabe	13
Leyland, b Grimmett	3
R. E. S. Wyatt, not out	39
Lb 12, nb 1	13
	—
Total (for five wickets)	316

To bat: Tate, Larwood, Duckworth, and I. A. R. Peebles.

AUSTRALIA: W. M. Woodfull, W. H. Ponsford, D. G. Bradman, A. F. Kippax, S. McCabe, A. Jackson, W. A. Oldfield, C. V. Grimmett, A. Fairfax, P. M. Hornibrook, and F. Wall.

FALL OF WICKETS

ENGLAND—First Innings

1	2	3	4	5	6	7	8	9	10
48	97	162	190	197					

Umpires: Hardstaff and Parry.

At half-past four on Saturday England looked to be losing the match and the rubber easily, On a beautiful Oval wicket, after more than four hours' play, the score was 197, and five men were out—Hobbs, Whysall, Duleepsinhji, Hammond, and Leyland. England's advantage of winning the toss seemed sadly thrown away; the Selection Committee might well have considered themselves the least fortunate of men. 'We have taken risks with England's bowling,' we can imagine them saying, 'in the hope of giving great skill and staying power to the batting. And now the team's about to crack for 250; and soon, on an Oval wicket, Peebles, Larwood, and Tate will have to tackle Bradman, Woodfull, and the rest—and Larwood is not a Tom Richardson in endurance.' I do not say the Selection Committee did actually commune with themselves in that natural and unphilosophical vein, but they had ample reason to do so—at tea-time on Saturday.

NEW CAPTAIN'S ORDEAL
In this unhappy and trying hour Wyatt faced the ordeal of playing his first innings as captain of England. He had to go through a formidable test of nerve. As he walked to the wicket his imagination possibly saw controversy and sensation like twin ghouls, ready to gloat upon his failure. Arrived at the wicket, Wyatt went through an over from Grimmett which he will no doubt bear in mind to his dying day. He lunged out at the spin once, twice, thrice—and at each lunge, as his bat moved in vacant air, Wyatt's heart must have jumped; 'I am out!—no, I'm not—oh, be praised!—this time—bat to the ball—Lord, now I really *am* out—no?—so help me!' But Wyatt refused to be cast down.

After this terrible over from Grimmett he went in to tea; then he returned with Sutcliffe, who since half-past eleven had stood for England at the wicket's other end like an everlasting pillar. Wyatt now began to play resolute cricket; he got down on his bat, clenched his teeth—you could see him doing it. Possibly he also ground them, like Porthos did in *The Three Musketeers*, only to be told by D'Artagnan, 'Silence, you fool!'—(for they were all hiding in ambush). Wyatt got Wall to leg—half a hit and half a snick. He lifted himself up and cracked quite masterful runs to the off-side. Sutcliffe, strokeless until now, seemed moved to handsome emulation of the young captain's defiant play. And thus did it happen that in the most perilous moment an English innings has known in this season's Test matches Wyatt went fearlessly into a scorching baptism and won though in company with the greatest of all rescuers of lost causes, name of Sutcliffe.

THE GREAT TRANSFORMATION
When Wyatt went in, just before half-past four, the Australians were high on top of the game; at close of play England's position was, on paper at least, satisfactory, though not yet safe. Seldom have I seen a big game so comfortably and quickly transformed; it all happened between five o'clock and half-past six. Just before stumps were drawn the stand by Wyatt and Sutcliffe had put on a hundred priceless runs. Sutcliffe's skill and nerve we, of course, knew and relied upon. With Wyatt it was different. The Selection Committee had picked him to perform a task which in all the other four Test matches proved beyond anybody else's power; Wyatt was there to lend a sound technique to the middle part of the England innings. Without the slightest fuss, Wyatt achieved all expected of him. The

260

crowd exercised its customary healthy instincts and took Wyatt to heart. 'He's got his 'ead on,' said somebody, and he was speaking for thousands.

The day's end gave some consolation for pains and penalties endured earlier on. Australia worked hard to thrust home the gorgeous opportunity which was before them, when half the England eleven were out. But they lacked the really great bowler. The cricket, indeed, was short of greatness throughout the day; it was a case of mediocrity pitted against mediocrity—sometimes it was, to use Mr. Mantalini's language, 'a dem'd case: there never was a dem'der'. I confess that I could not see where the Test match technique or atmosphere always came in during the two hours before lunch, when England scored 71 for one, and between lunch and tea, when England scored an additional 136 for four. It was not merely that the scoring was usually slow; every one of us expected a dour fight and were prepared to revel in it. My disappointment arose not from the competitive aspects of the match, but from the aspects of style and technique.

UGLY CRICKET

It is not cricket when a recognized England player gets the bulk of his runs by holding out his bat, knowing that pace from the pitch will provide enough motive-power to send the ball bouncing away for discreet runs. It is certainly not a Test match in the true and old manner when on a glorious Oval wicket we see half a dozen handsome strokes in three hours. I am not referring to *scoring* strokes— boundaries or anything vain like that. This was a fight to a finish, and, as I say, we in the crowd knew quite well what we had come out for to see. But defensive play, grim as death, can be pretty and distinguished, as Quaife used to show—and Hayward and Albert Ward and Arthur Shrewsbury.

England's cricket was too often ugly on Saturday; until the day's fall, when the Australian attack tired, Duleepsinhji alone batted with relish, and attended to cricket's own love of poise, bloom, and summer-time sweetness. His innings of 50 was made in as many minutes; it came when we were positively aching for a real hit, for the sound of the bat's proper music; it enchanted us for a brief while, then suddenly vanished. Duleepsinhji's cricket came to us like the vision of running water and green, shady leaves which men in a sandy desert see blissfully, deliriously. Sutcliffe so far has been at the wicket just under six hours for 135. At lunch, after 120 minutes, his score was 21. It was a quarter to six before he reached his hundred; in the closing forty-five minutes he made 35, and let us see some of the lovely strokes he had been holding in stony abeyance all day—such was 'the cause, my soul, the cause'.

If cricket were entirely an affair of exhibiting the Christian virtues we should have to canonize Sutcliffe's innings at once. For it was made out of self-denial, patience, fortitude, abstinence, devotion to duty. In all the recurrent adversities to England, he remained the calm, composed Sutcliffe we all know. When a wicket fell at the other end he leaned on his bat and seemed conscious that the sun was shining on his glossy black hair. Nothing dismayed him: he went his ways with his own likeable absorption in his own astonishing qualities. Apparently the idea that he, too, might, like Hobbs and the rest, get out never entered his head. When a fresh batsman joined him, I imagined Sutcliffe was asking himself, 'Now I wonder whether *he'll* manage to stay in?' He batted like a cricketer who that morning had been informed by divine revelation that he was going to make a century for the honour of England. As the afternoon burned away I thought I could see, through the August glow, Sutcliffe wearing a halo.

GRIMMETT'S MASTER

His playing of Grimmett was masterly; he never guessed wrongly about the spin. When it was tossed up, you would see him get it away by means of a straightforward push, the body inclining ever so confidently. But not once, or only once, did he go forward when he ought to have gone back. And every time he decided to hit Grimmett to leg he did so, cleanly and swiftly. As the day went on, I got the impression that Grimmett had given Sutcliffe up as a bad job—till Monday at any rate.

There was probably a suggestion of moisture in the turf at the match's outset. Wall made real pace from the pitch and Hobbs was beaten time and again. We looked for a wicket to fall at his end almost every over for a palpitating quarter of an hour. Then Hobbs settled down. A forcing stroke to the on announced ripeness, his long length of years. The first hour's play produced 22. Hobbs hereabouts let us see a square cut from a short ball by Grimmett; the stroke placed our greatest batsman in a poise the mind will not readily forget. The ball was short and spinning away. Hobbs hit it like a man with a hammer, yet the strength was classically sculpturesque in the ordered contours and rhythms of Hobbs's body and ction. Another royal hit—this time to leg—told us the master was at last entirely himself.

The imagination now saw in his cricket the colours of a full autumn. Every stroke was mellow with experience—until with shocking suddenness the end came. Hobbs hooked a short ball from Wall magnificently for four; from the next ball, which had a fuller length, he tried to repeat the stroke and reach his 50 a few minutes before lunch. The ball probably 'lifted' a little; anyhow Hobbs sent a catch to square leg, where Kippax held it. Thus we had an unfinished symphony of batsmanship; for the end of it was an act quite arbitrary and, as Parson Square would have maintained, it was not in accordance with the eternal fitness of things. (Or was it Parson Thwackum?)

THE DULEEPSINHJI INTERMEZZO

After lunch Wysall was leg before wicket to a fast ball which hit his foot first bounce. And here ensued the intermezzo of Duleepsinhji. Two fours to the on, easeful pulls, set the happy tempo of it. A late cut from Hornibrook for the first time in the long day caused the crowd to see visions. Bloom touched the hour; the cricket was at last in tune with the sun's gracious warmth and light and the blue sky above. Even the unbeautiful, inhospitable Oval began to look a cricket field, as seen in the mirror of Duleepsinhji's batsmanship.

Before he came in, two and a half hours' hard labour had gone to the compiling of 100 runs. But when he did come in fifty runs were made in half an hour. Duleepsinhji passed Sutcliffe's 41 after he had been batting a little over half an hour, and after Sutcliffe had been batting three hours and a half. Out of 65 scored for the third wicket, Duleepsinhji's share was fifty. He then got out trying a straight drive into an uncovered outfield; the spin sent the ball comfortably to mid-off. Critics of the modern school complained that Duleepsinhji should have lost his wicket, trying to hit a four. No such protest would have occurred to anybody of consequence years ago. Duleepsinhji fell through one of the hazards of cricket. Cut out the hazards and you cut out the sport—and that is what is slowly happening to cricket nowadays.

Hammond hit the first ball he received for four; shortly afterwards he drove Grimmett to the off for four. a noble forcing stroke off the back foot. But he, again, was not the old Hammond. His bat seemed lumpish; it bludgeoned the ball into the earth, as though a cricket ball were an evil thing to be stunned and not deliciously sent skimming over the grass. McCabe was bowling at Hammond now, and making pace from the wicket. Hammond played on, stabbing in the way that has recently been spoiling his style. Once more had England been unable to make headway just at a moment when the Australian attack was beginning to waver, as assuredly it was while Duleepsinhji was batting.

Leyland missed his opportunity rather ineptly; he lunged out at Grimmett's spin, and was clean bowled with all three of his wickets exposed. I could almost hear Emmott Robinson's pained protest: 'Maurice, lad, what were t' thinkin' of? Where were thi pads? What dost think the good Lord gave thi legs for, if it weren't to get thi pads in front?'

BRADMAN AND OLDFIELD

My narrative has now arrived at the stage where it begins above— England 197 for 5, with Australia yet again flattered to look a great bowling team. The attack was steady and respectable, with delicious and accurate fielding making it stronger than actually it was in technique. Bradman on the edge of the field moved the crowd to perpetual delight. And Oldfield's wicket-keeping was beyond praise. Once he tried to stump Sutcliffe from a fast 'yorker' which pitched on the leg-side, very close to the return crease. The skill and speed of it all snatched the breath away. Oldfield did his work without the slightest noise or demonstration; he is the most gentlemanly of stumpers.

In review, the day's play can be savoured better than in the actual happening. First the fencing for position before lunch; then the dashing thrust forward by Duleepsinhji; then the setback and the imminent catastrophe. Then, in the lovely afternoon's falling sunshine, the retaliation by Wyatt and Sutcliffe. It was a gruelling day's cricket, swaying now this way, now that. And all the time we knew there was no escape in the end for one side or the other; the mills were grinding out a decision. Where there is no time-limit to a cricket match every ball is significant, fateful—a nail in somebody's coffin.

FIFTH TEST
2nd Day The Oval

ENGLAND
First Innings

Hobbs, c Kippax, b Wall	47
Sutcliffe, c Oldfield, b Fairfax	161
Whysall, lbw, b Walls	13
K. S. Duleepsinhji, c Fairfax, b Grimmett	50
Hammond, b McCabe	13
Leyland, b Grimmett	3
R. E. S. Wyatt, c Oldfield, b Fairfax	64
Tate, st Oldfield, b Grimmett	10
Larwood, lbw, b Grimmett	19
Duckworth, b Fairfax	3
Peebles, not out	3
Lb 17, nb 2	19
Total	405

FALL OF WICKETS
ENGLAND—First Innings

1	2	3	4	5	6	7	8	9	10
68	97	162	190	197	367	379	379	391	405

BOWLING ANALYSIS
ENGLAND—First Innings

	O.	M.	R.	W.		O.	M.	R.	W.
T. Wall	37	6	96	2	S. McCabe	22	4	49	1
A. Fairfax	71	9	52	3	P. M. Hornibrook	15	1	54	0
C. V. Grimmett	66·2	13	135	4					

Wall and Fairfax each bowled a no-ball.

AUSTRALIA
First Innings

W. M. Woodfull, c Duckworth, b Peebles	54
W. H. Ponsford, b Peebles	110
D. G. Bradman, not out	27
A. F. Kippax, not out	11
B 5, lb 5, nb 3	13
Total (for two wickets)	215

FALL OF WICKETS
AUSTRALIA—First Innings

1	2	3	4	5	6	7	8	9	10
159	190								

Umpires: Hardstaff and Parry.

THE OVAL, MONDAY

Today the Australians have made a forcible response to England's total of 405. At one time there seemed little prospect that Australia would lose as many as two wickets for 215: a sudden darkening of the light and a shower of rain, if they did not actually affect the playing conditions, did no doubt steal something from the confidence which strongly marked the cricket of Ponsford and Woodfull while the sun was shining during the afternoon. All sportsmen must wish that bad weather will not spoil the match. The Australians have already deserved a fair deal.

The warm morning began with an over of accurate length balls by Grimmett to Sutcliffe. Each of them was intended to break from leg, but Sutcliffe moved forward with the assurance of a batsman to whom a week-end's interruption of an innings had not really occurred. Then before Wall could send down an over the game was momentarily held up by a policeman standing right in the middle of the sight screen. The players and umpires waved him away, and a hundred voices, forgetting the majesty of the law, told him to move on. But the policeman, though conscious something was wrong, had no notion that it was himself. At last one of his superior officers had to order him out of the batsman's line of vision. It has often occurred to me that for the purposes of duty on a cricket field only those policemen are chosen who, not knowing much about the game, are unlikely to find duty a demoralizing pleasure. We can imagine a posse of them being examined before receiving their orders for the Oval.

'What is a county batsman?'

'A county batsman, sir, is a serious case of loitering in a public place.'

'And what is a bowling screen and why is it painted white?'—'My information upon the subject is as yet incomplete, sir, but I am pursuing inquiries.'

'That will do. Take charge of the Vauxhall end on Monday.'

TRUSTING TO RUN-OUTS?

But let us get on with the game—which is a Test match for the rubber and no laughing matter. Wyatt, like Sutcliffe, settled down immediately. The sound of the bat was sweet and solid, and seldom did either player need to change his first intentions and muscular responses. At half-past eleven Sutcliffe reached 150 out of 344. He had now rendered one end of the wicket a stout barn-door for six nd a half hours. Wyatt hit Grimmett square for four; it was not the troke of a mild-mannered cricketer making his first bow humbly before the austerity of Test cricket. On the contrary, it was the hit of a batsman quite savagely on the look-out for any chance whereby o knock the stuffing out of Australia's hopes.

It is a plain fact that the match had not been in action half an hour this morning before the Australian attack seemed to be so much vain labour under the sun. I began to imagine that Woodfull was trusting to either Wyatt or Sutcliffe running himself out. Once hey nearly did so—and the way Oldfield rushed to the wicket to ake the throw-in suggested that he was beginning to regard his office not at all as a complementary part of the attack. Every over was the eye delighted by a true stroke of the game, yet the batting was now much safer than usually it was on Saturday. In less than n hour 51 runs were scored, and only once in this time did the bowlers and fieldsmen receive a morsel of encouragement. This happened when Wyatt snicked Wall through the slips and Hornibrook missed a swift catch which Oldfield also involuntarily snatched at. Wyatt was 56 and England 356 when the mishap put a break on our galloping optimism.

Just as the August day stood poised at high noon the stand between Sutcliffe and Wyatt was broken. Fairfax caused a ball to flash with unexpected speed from the pitch, and Oldfield caught Sutcliffe most skilfully at the wicket near to the bat. Sutcliffe was roared home to the pavilion with the sun shining on him as though put in the sky especially for the occasion. Not a hair on his head was disturbed—which was very much in keeping with the innings he had played, an innings of nearly seven hours' length, and to the Australians possibly a glimpse into eternity. The stand for the sixth English wicket lasted two hours and a quarter and was worth every run of the 170 made by the reliant batsmanship of Wyatt and Sutcliffe.

ENGLAND'S COLLAPSE

In the light of the disillusioning breakdown of the innings which we were now to witness we could realize that Wyatt and Sutcliffe had staved away certain defeat. Fairfax, who bowled with his proper speed from the ground—his illness at Nottingham temporarily stole vitality from him, a sad loss to Australia—got Wyatt also caught at the wicket by the immaculate Oldfield, whose stumping throughout the English innings had been glorious. Wyatt's vigil endured three mortal hours, and it was an announcement of character as well as of good cricket.

Tate tried hard for a few moments to bat according to modern 'Marathon' methods (as they are called), but you cannot change the habits of a life-time. Tate was stumped, and though Larwood swung his bat hard as he could, England were all out just before one o'clock for a total which a few years ago would have promised victory. Fairfax deserved his wickets; his attack today had much power of penetration. Grimmett, for two hours, was a very pertinacious little man, and the most accurate googly bowler of our age, though, to say the truth, he is sparing of the googly and prefers to spin the ball away from the bat.

PONSFORD'S AGGRESSION

Australia had less than half an hour's batting before lunch. In face of a total of 405 we all expected Woodfull and Ponsford to stonewall until the interval arrived. Consequently we received quite a shock when Ponsford began to attack right and left and hit five boundaries like a man cracking a row of unfriendly heads. Woodfull also got a boundary. Both batsmen behaved with the confident freedom of cricketers on a side that wanted some 40 runs to win and did not wish to have the trouble of coming out into the field again after lunch. At the interval Australia were 36 for none, after 25 minutes of proper and recognizable cricket.

When the game went on, with a vast multitude packed until all individual life in it seemed merged into an impersonal mass, Ponsford continued to play handsomely, and runs were helped along by the presence in the outfield of eager, but rather venerable years. At length Whysall was put in a suitable place at second slip, while Duleepsinhji and Leyland were sent to the boundary's edge. Here was a compliment to Ponsford—any Chelsea Pensioner might well have guarded the outfield at the outset of England's innings on Saturday. Before lunch Duckworth fumbled and dropped the ball when Tate was smothering an appeal for a catch at the wicket against Ponsford.

After lunch, Ponsford was 45 and Australia 57 when Duckworth definitely missed Ponsford from a snick off a ball which came from the pitch viciously. Tate, the bowler, made a gesture of profound mortification at the sight of Duckworth's blunder and Ponsford's escape. Larwood bowled fast, but not dangerously. Ponsford played him with time to spare, whereat Larwood was taken off, after sending down as many overs as Walter Brearley would have needed to get his arm properly into action. Ponsford reached fifty in an hour out of a total of 67. The English attack looked a little blown already, though everybody worked hard, especially the boy Peebles, who would no doubt enjoy the eight-ball over of Australian cricket.

ENGLAND'S ATTACK MASTERED

But Peebles could not spin the ball waspishly on the Oval wicket; moreover, lacking Grimmett's experience, his bowling is without Grimmett's essential insidiousness. It is curious that the Selection Committee, having adopted the notion that googly bowling is disliked by the Australian batsmen, have preferred to give a trial to Peebles, who is an apprentice at the mysterious craft of which Freeman is a master. Ponsford forced Peebles in front of point off the back foot, and the ball was by no means short. It was a stroke that caused the onlooker impulsively to exclaim, 'Oh, splendid, sir, splendid!' The batting put the English innings entirely into a shabby shade. In an hour and a quarter Wyatt was compelled to give work to five different bowlers. When the score was 84 for none at a quarter-past three Hammond and Wyatt were attacking more or less hopefully for England. It is to be hoped that Parker was admiring Hammond's length from a comfortable seat in the pavilion. At this point in the battle's progress Larwood had enjoyed two spells each of four overs. I invite fancifully minded readers to imagine Walter Brearley's commentary on any suggestion that he should ever have taken a rest after bowling four overs.

In ninety minutes Australia reached 100—Ponsford 76, Woodfull 22. It seemed hereabout that England's hope rested in a patriotic providence: heavy clouds were gathering overhead, hiding the sun. The English attack on the flawless pitch looked to be quite harmless by this time. If there were another Test match to be played I can imagine the Selection Committee advertising for 'strong young men wanted, to bowl for England. Must not be afraid of work'. And I can imagine no rush of applicants for the job, except, perhaps, one from a horny-handed yeoman living in Much Hadham, ambitious and tired of cows.

PONSFORD'S FINE INNINGS

Australia's first-wicket stand did not come to an end until the assured rhythm of it had been broken by the tea interval. Ponsford in two hours and a quarter arrived at his hundred. Could any

English batsman, apart from Woolley, score a hundred runs in that time in a Test match when going in against a total of 400? If such another batsman does exist in this country let him appear. We cannot have curtains any longer hiding his merits.

Immediately after tea, in a bad light, Peebles bowled Ponsford, who tried a strangely indiscreet stroke and hit over the ball. Just before tea Peebles had completely beaten and nearly bowled Woodfull, and so the boy deserved his wicket. On the whole, though, Peebles had not given trouble to the batsmen; it seemed to me that his pace was too quick to accommodate his spin, while, of course, a pace rather unnatural to his style went against his flight.

Ponsford's wicket fell at 159. He made 110 in about two hours and three-quarters. It was an innings that always told of an intelligent mind, an opportunist eye, and a thoroughly finished technique. It was cricket according to the true gospel. Ponsford was as watchful for the bad as for the good ball. He cut the off-side ones of convenient length, he drove the overtossed ball, while his on-side strokes from balls on the leg stump were placed to a nicety. He was master of the attack from the moment he saw it—and his one mistake was one of those mischances of war which no man can guard against.

LARWOOD'S DEVICE

Woodfull's share in the first-wicket partnership was wholly accessory to Ponsford. Yet though he stonewalled he did it all very easily. Sutcliffe had caused us to think he was stopping unplayable break-backs. Woodfull's defence not less than Ponsford's attack was calculated to give to England's bowling the aspect of aspiring mediocrity. And mediocre the bowling was indeed. Larwood found himself reduced to the exploitation of two short legs and to balls aimed at the leg stump. It was a run-saving device and a confession of weakness. Larwood bowled only three or four spells of four overs each between one o'clock and the tea interval. The sight of a fast bowler with two slips in his field was 'significant of much,' as a philosopher named Carlyle used to say.

As soon as Ponsford was out the gloomy clouds above burst and a heavy shower drove everybody to shelter—that is, everybody save the thousands of the ordinary paying public, for whom there is no cover at all and few seats at the Oval—one of the ugliest and least hospitable of grounds. The break in the weather threatened to serve Australia a shabby trick, for while the sun shone and the wicket remained as the English batsmen had found it there seemed little reason to ask which side possessed the more resourceful stroke-players. Bad light prevented further cricket until a quarter to six: then the conditions were not in the least summerlike or Australian. The light was not excellent. One appeal had already been successfully lodged against it.

In the changed conditions there was a change of style and colour in the Australian innings. Bradman and Woodfull played wholly defensively—obviously in the hope of better weather tomorrow. Once or twice Peebles caused Bradman to look twice at a ball and withhold a stroke. The bowling of Peebles hereabout seemed to contain one or two problems for the batsmen to speculate upon. A ball from Tate jumped up awkwardly, and Bradman was clever to play it down to the ground. Not until the rain came did Tate make any ball rise abnormally high or did an English bowler command or receive a deal of respect.

WOODFULL'S DISMISSAL

Woodfull and Bradman were quiet but confident for several overs, but after Woodfull had reached 50 he drove Peebles to the off for four and then in the same over was caught at the wicket. Peebles had been promising us another wicket for some time now. It was charming to see him, when he realized Woodfull was really out, go down the pitch and talk to everybody about it. Australia's second wicket fell at 190. It is indeed difficult to believe that had the day kept sunny England's bowlers would have made an advance as considerable as all this. The Australian batsmen are fond of the sun, and after the heartening prelude given to their innings by Ponsford's beautiful play they deserved to go their ways with not even a slight deterioration in the circumstances and sunlight scene which obtained during the England innings. Today's slight rain did not, of course, have marked influence on the pitch, but a sudden transition from ideal to dismal weather was not likely to help the Australians.

At twenty minutes past six Larwood bowled, and the sun came back out of the clouds. And the moment the day looked like summer again the batting became as stylish and confident as it had been earlier on. Bradman at the close of play appeared set for hours ahead unless we have real rain or great bowling. England must look forward to severe work next innings.

271

FIFTH TEST
3rd Day (The Oval)

ENGLAND
First Innings

Hobbs, c Kippax, b Wall	47
Sutcliffe, c Oldfield, b Fairfax	161
Whysall, lbw, b Wall	13
K. S. Duleepsinhji, c Fairfax, b Grimmett	50
Hammond, b McCabe	13
Leyland, b Grimmett	3
R. E. S. Wyatt, c Oldfield, b Fairfax	64
Tate, st Oldfield, b Grimmett	10
Larwood, lbw, b Grimmett	19
Duckworth, b Fairfax	3
Peebles, not out	3
Lb 17, nb 2	19
Total	405

FALL OF WICKETS
ENGLAND—First Innings

1	2	3	4	5	6	7	8	9	10
68	97	162	190	197	367	379	379	391	405

ROWLING ANALYSIS
ENGLAND—First Innings

	O.	M.	R.	W.		O.	M.	R.	W.
T. Wall	37	6	96	2	S. McCabe	22	4	49	1
A. Fairfax	31	9	52	3	P. M. Hornibrook	15	1	54	0
C. V. Grimmett	66·2	18	135	4					

Wall and Fairfax each bowled a no-ball.

AUSTRALIA
First Innings

W. M. Woodfull, c Duckworth, b Peebles	54
W. H. Ponsford, b Peebles	110
D. G. Bradman, not out	130
A. F. Kippax, c Wyatt, b Peebles	28
A. Jackson, not out	43
B 22, 1b, 12 nb 4	38
Total (for three wickets)	403

To bat: S. McCabe, W. A. Oldfield, C. V. Grimmett, A. Fairfax, P. M. Hornibrook, and T. Wall.

FALL OF WICKETS
AUSTRALIA—First Innings

1	2	3	4	5	6	7	8	9	10
159	190	267							

Umpires: Hardstaff and Parry.

The morning began with the chilly presence of autumn some-where, invisible yet, maybe, but surely on the way towards us. Tate and Larwood bowled at Bradman and Kippax on a smooth, hard wicket last night's rain clouds happily did not wholly break. Runs came gently here and there. Bradman, after a clean off-drive for three from Tate's opening over, was content to let his score mount up chiefly as the consequence of strokes designed primarily as defensive measures.

Larwood delivered four overs, then Tate crossed to his end and Peebles bowled at the other. Immediately Peebles caused Bradman to watch every ball closely; one of them got through his first line of defence and hit the pads. Duckworth appealed, and as he did so his right forefinger went up aloft announcing to Umpire Hardstaff what he (Duckworth) thought about it. But Hardstaff had other views. Then Peebles bowled a very ingenious maiden over to Brad-man which everybody applauded. Bradman played through it safely, but each stroke was quite empirical—that is to say, Bradman waited for the ball to pitch before doing anything. He seemed to have worked out no preconceived ideas yet about the way to deal with Peebles. He reached a thoroughly impersonal fifty in ninety minutes.

WYATT'S GOOD CATCH

Meanwhile Kippax had been batting stylishly and well, though not stridently announcing his quality. There seemed little reason to expect another English advance for hours, when at a quarter to twelve Kippax tried to push Peebles's 'googly' to the on. He made the stroke in his own confident way, the ball went into the air, not forcibly but apparently placed to elude Wyatt at short-forward leg. Even as it was going past him Wyatt flung out one hand and made a most welcome and dexterous catch. Kippax's century had looked to be a plant that needed only sunshine to bring it to a full bloom and blossom. Australia's third wicket fell at 267. Peebles had done the hat-trick—save that each successful ball was too widely separated in time and space.

For an hour Peebles bowled eagerly and skilfully; his pace was truer to his style than it was yesterday. He appears this season to be having some difficulty in finding a speed that is quick enough to make his spin difficult to counter and yet not so quick as to prevent it from biting the ground altogether. In June he was bowling too slow. This morning he found the happy medium and was the one factor in the English attack which demanded insight and intelligence in a batsman as well as that technical machinery which on a good wicket can be trusted to move and respond automatically.

With Jackson in, the match had no interest for a while more remarkable than the incredibly insecure wicket-keeping of Duckworth, who was hereabout allowing whole handfuls of byes. Jackson's cricket at his innings' start was as diffident as Mr. Toots. His every stroke seemed to cough apologetically and say, 'It's really of no consequence—please take no notice of me. Watch Bradman; he's much better to look at.'

Jackson's defence had so slender an appearance just now that it was mortifying to see Leyland and Hammond playing him in while Larwood for more than an hour and a half after his four overs at the morning's beginning was wearing his sweater at mid-on. Jackson might have lost his wicket making his first run, but Hobbs, dashing from cover to mid-off, missed the one stump he had to aim at. England could do nothing that was right.

DUCKWORTH'S THIRD BLUNDER

When Bradman was 82 Duckworth missed him off Hammond. Duckworth had now given a second innings to Australia's three highest scorers—to Woodfull at 6, Ponsford at 47, and Bradman at 82. Moreover, he was unable to hold any number of balls clearly. Duckworth's lapses were as inexplicable as they were shocking never before has he kept wicket so fallibly. Bradman went his ways without fuss but with a growing assurance, and at the end of three hours he reached his hundred. He was obviously playing to a plan not to get out. His back-play, very late, allowed him to keep his eye on the ball all the time. Jackson settled down by stages, and at lunch Australia were definitely on top—371 for three.

During the interval torrential rain swept the ground. Here was yet another unchivalrous trick played by luck upon the Australians. All the interruptions by rain in this summer's Test matches have happened in England's favour. At Nottingham, on the first day, when Grimmett was spinning beautifully rain came and left him with a greasy ball to handle: then on the Saturday the Australians collapsed on a damp pitch. At Leeds rain saved England altogether; at Manchester rain ruined the match when the advantage was certainly with the Australians. Last night the change in the weather interfered with the summer sunshine in which Ponsford was always master of the bowling, and now this afternoon rain enabled the English bowlers to get a vitality out of a turf on which before lunch the Australians appeared safely and comfortably set for five or six hundred runs without need for excessive worry.

BRADMAN'S ESCAPES

When the match was continued at three o'clock Larwood attacked with a determination he had not shown at any other time of the day. He made one or two balls rise awkwardly, Bradman edging one not at all handsomely. Also Bradman sent one from Tate without prevision through the slips when his score was 120. Most of us were astonished to see Larwood taken off after sending down only three overs, but Peebles made a better use of the wicket. He completely defeated Bradman, but the ball missed the stumps. A few moments previously Tate had also broken without luck through Bradman's defence. The wicket was lending to the English attack powers which before lunch it had considerably lacked.

Between eleven o'clock and half-past one the Australians scored 156 for one wicket at the rate of a run a minute, yet there were voices in the crowd complaining of the Australians' slow scoring, voices that had acclaimed the English batting on Saturday. Hammond bowled in place of Tate at 398. Twice he caused—or rather the wicket caused—the ball to jump high at an acute angle—once over Jackson's head, the other ball cracking the batsman so painfully on the arm that the game was temporarily suspended. Heavy clouds darkened the scene, and an appeal against the light was granted. Australia deserved to escape from a trap set for them by the patriotic elements.

The batting of Jackson and Bradman while the ball misbehaved or threatened to misbehave was admirable in its coolness. Neither cricketer was ruffled in the slightest. The Australians are England's betters in this match in every way, technically and temperamentally. Seldom has an England eleven been so obviously outclassed as during this present engagement. The scoreboard does not tell half the tale. Bradman's innings became more and more impressive as it went on. It was as quiet as his innings at Leeds was energetic; his back play, despite a bending right knee, always got over the ball and kept it down on the ground. We have now seen Bradman the brilliant and Bradman the shrewd, playing four-day cricket and cricket that takes no heed of the clock. In these different circumstances he has shown command over the appropriate methods; his versatility is astonishing, and he is indeed a great batsman, though I still doubt whether he yet is equal to the challenge of a great spin bowler on a bad wicket.

Jackson was playing charming defensive cricket when the rain came. Not until twenty minutes past six was there any more cricket, and then Bradman and Jackson were received back to the field to the sound of noises intended to be ironical which issued from certain sections of the crowd. The batsmen, of course, did not dream of risking a wicket at this late hour of the afternoon. Thirteen balls were bowled (one carried forward from an over sent down before the interruption) and Bradman scored one run. This brought us to close of play. One wondered whether to admire or to be satirical about the conscientiousness which insisted that in a timeless match not even ten minutes should be allowed to run to waste. Perhaps England optimistically hoped to get Bradman out in thirteen balls.

FIFTH TEST
4th Day (The Oval)

ENGLAND
First Innings

Hobbs, c Kippax, b Wall	47
Sutcliffe, c Oldfield, b Fairfax	161
Whysall, lbw, b Wall	13
K. S. Duleepsinhji, c Fairfax, b Grimmett	50
Hammond, b McCabe	13
Leyland, b Grimmett	3
R. E. S. Wyatt, c Oldfield, b Fairfax	64
Tate, st Oldfield, b Grimmett	10
Larwood, lbw, b Grimmett	19
Duckworth, b Fairfax	3
I. A. R. Peebles, not out	3
Lb 17, nb 2	19
Total	405

FALL OF WICKETS
ENGLAND—First Innings

1	2	3	4	5	6	7	8	9	10
68	97	162	190	197	367	379	379	391	405

BOWLING ANALYSIS
ENGLAND—First Innings

	O.	M.	R.	W.		O.	M.	R.	W.
T. Wall	37	6	96	2	S. McCabe	22	4	49	1
A. Fairfax	31	9	52	3	P. M. Hornibrook	15	1	54	0
C. V. Grimmett	66·2	18	135	4					

Wall and Fairfax each bowled a no-ball.

AUSTRALIA

First Innings,

W. M. Woodfull, c Duckworth b Peebles	54
W. H. Ponsford, b Peebles	110
D. G. Bradman, c Duckworth, b Larwood	232
A. F. Kippax, c Wyatt, b Peebles	28
A. Jackson, c Sutcliffe, b Wyatt	73
S. McCabe, c Duckworth, b Hammond	54
A. Fairfax, not out	53
W. A. Oldfield, c Larwood, b Peebles	34
C. V. Grimmett, lbw, b Peebles	6
T. Wall, lbw, b Peebles	0
P. M. Hornibrook, c Duckworth, b Tate	7
B 22, lb 18, nb 4	44
Total	695

FALL OF WICKETS

AUSTRALIA—First Innings

1	2	3	4	5	6	7	8	9	10
159	190	267	506	570	594	670	684	684	695

BOWLING ANALYSIS

AUSTRALIA—First Innings

	O.	M.	R.	W.		O.	M.	R.	W.
Larwood	48	6	132	1	R. E. S. Wyatt	14	1	58	1
Tate	65·1	12	153	1	Hammond	42	12	70	1
I. A. R. Peebles	71	3	204	6	Leyland	16	7	34	0

Larwood bowled four no-balls.

ENGLAND

Second Innings

Hobbs, b Fairfax	9
Sutcliffe, not out	8
Whysall, not out	6
Lb 1	1
Total (for one wicket)	24

FALL OF WICKETS

ENGLAND—Second Innings

1	2	3	4	5	4	7	8	9	10
17									

Umpires: Hardstaff and Parry

THE OVAL, WEDNESDAY

Significantly enough, Peebles and Hammond were the bowlers when the match entered the fourth day this morning, and after Hammond has sent down two overs Leyland took his place at the Vauxhall end. Parker would have been the better man to exploit the Oval's responsiveness to spin after the heavy showers of yesterday. Peebles and Leyland each was able to turn the ball at varying angles, the widest of which was to be seen and admired from the press box's position on the long-on boundary.

The first ball by Hammond broke and lifted enough to compel Bradman into a half-cock stroke which nearly carried far enough to raise expectations of a caught-and-bowled decision. It was probably this ball which suggested to Wyatt the notion of giving Leyland an early trial. Leyland and Peebles did not pitch the length that draws a batsman out groping for spin; they were both on the short side, allowing Bradman and Jackson time in which to examine the break closely and get legs and bats properly placed. Peebles was rather exasperating because of his persistence with the 'googly', which he exploited ball after ball. The whole point of the 'googly' surely is that it should be a masked ball. To bowl a 'googly' repeatedly is as though a man of felonious intent should go about perpetually disguised, nobody but himself knowing that his whiskers were false.

WYATT AND HIS BOWLERS

After Peebles had bowled half a dozen overs Tate went on instead. This move was difficult to follow. If Wyatt thought the wicket was slightly responsive to spin—which it was, though quite mildly—why should Peebles so quickly have been given a rest? Besides, while Leyland was bowling the new ball could not to his advantage be claimed, and Tate with an old ball is not likely to get any life out of an Oval pitch not definitely fast. Wyatt's changes of bowling throughout the match have been piecemeal, as though made up as he went on; the sense of a plan was not there. If the pitch was of a description likely to suit Leyland this morning Peebles would have been more potential than Tate—especially Tate with an old ball. No captain can decide in six overs whether a bowler is in or out of form unless he is definitely all over the place.

When Tate got a ball through Bradman's defences after making him cock another stroke a little into the air in front of him, far from a fieldsman, the crowd applauded Tate, who made the gestures of a bowler very excited at the prospect of a wicket coming his way.

After achieving this over Tate claimed the new ball, and as Leyland at the other end had gone over the wicket and thus shown a vote of no-confidence in his own spin, the change of tactics was justified up to a point. But I am convinced that there was enough guile in the wicket to help a great spin bowler had one been present. The turf was not, of course, really bad, but a master of break does not depend wholly on a pitch that is sticky.

LEAN TIME FOR THE PROFESSORS

When Australia had reached 450 the innings had lasted some eight hours, and in all that time the professional bowlers of England had been unable to take a single wicket. How untrustworthy the pitch was we could understand from the way Hammond persuaded the ball to jump up several times. Larwood, when he came on at 458, managed to bruise Bradman on the chest, and shortly after this mishap a ball from Hammond rose viciously from a good length and hit Jackson's arm painfully. Yet with all this bruising and battering the score-board read 479 for 3 at half-past twelve.

The batting was admirable in its shrewdness and calm, but it was impossible for us not to deplore the absence from the English team of a bowler with either the spin or pace enough to take advantage of the small but potent amount of evil which was hidden somewhere in the wicket. It was curious to see Hammond's bowling rearing up while Larwood could bump the ball only by bowling so short that nothing but the batsman's physique and personal appearance were in serious danger.

The time of day was past one o'clock before the Bradman–Jackson partnership came to an unexpected and rather fortuitous end, and even now our professional bowling had no hand in the first advance achieved by England for 280 mortal minutes. Jackson mis-hit a ball to extra cover—and the bowler was Wyatt. Jackson's innings was only nominally related to the brilliant young batsman who in Australia has been spoken of as belonging to the aristocracy of the game. He showed rare coolness of mind, and now and again his defensive strokes had the bloom of culture. But it was an outline rather than the substance of batsmanship. He never had the bowling at his command; it was a feminine innings—feminine to the verge of frailty.

DUCKWORTH MAKES AMENDS

After lunch Bradman's innings arrived at an end which must have been predestined by influences of which the English attack were unaware, for he fell to one of the mischances of fortune. He mistimed a cut from a widish ball, and Duckworth did not falter again. For seven hours Bradman had been scoring by means mainly of a back stroke made by a very late stab of the bat in front of the legs. His ability to persist in accurate and thoroughly safe deflections was remarkable; he can even keep an edged stroke through the slips on the ground. He hit only sixteen boundaries in seven hours, and few of them were in front of the wicket. It was a dutiful rather than artistic display; never did he venture beyond the scope of known science. His skill at getting on top of the ball gave us the illusion that he was not really a small but a tall man. The game has not known his like since W. G. Grace, Fry, and 'Ranji' as a prolific scorer, but, of course, 'Ranji' moved the imagination and Bradman never does. He belongs to the economy rather than to the aesthetics of the game.

McCabe for eighty minutes gave us refreshing cricket—and we were all thirsty for it. His strokes were open, free, and dashing with youth's impulse. He hit nine boundaries, then was caught at the wicket by Duckworth, who today was technically more like his true self though vocally still unbelievably subdued. When McCabe got out to Hammond—who bowled consistently—Australia were 594 for six.

WHAT'S IN A NAME?

In this position of the match Fairfax batted half an hour for three. His name is a misnomer, with its associations of ancient knightliness and hauteur. Duckworth actually and brilliantly tried to stump Fairfax, an act of real optimism, especially as Fairfax never left his crease and only once moved his feet, when he nearly trod on his wickets. He was very obstinate for a long time, and then, with Oldfield in, he began to employ his massive shoulders. Oldfield, too, looked for runs, so that in half an hour he and Fairfax scored fifty and were still going along.

England's troubles seemed endless, their path as far from a restful destination as the one trodden by poor Fanny, ill-used by Sergeant Troy—in Hardy's novel,—who kept herself from falling to the ground in a weary journey to the workhouse by pretending that each milestone on the road was the last. Likewise did I imagine that the

English bowlers were not looking as bitterly far ahead as the end of the Australian innings, but were tackling it wicket by wicket, saying to themselves, 'Come on, lads, there goes the fifth—now for the sixth.'

The Oval pitch was easy again by now, and the bowling's only motive power seemed that of hope eternal, though everybody did hard work, and looked it. A magnificent pull by Oldfield suggested that the Australian innings was about to take off its coat and really begin. The seventh wicket made 76 before Oldfield drove a full toss to safe hands.

A LESSON FOR ENGLAND

At tea the Australians had been batting eleven and a half hours—such is modern cricket and modern bowling. What are we to think of it all? In five Test matches on English wickets these Australians have reached totals of 729 for six, nearly 700, and 566. Yet every day in county cricket we are applauding bowling performances while many folk maintain that the game is as good as ever it was. For myself, I am satisfied that Woodfull and his men have rubbed home a fact that some of us have been insisting upon for years—namely, that English bowling is woefully lacking in variety of technique and real ideas. Yet with all its faults who would not prefer an English cricket match to these everlasting grinds imported from Australia? We have not been assisting at one of life's pleasures but the stoniest of duties this afternoon. Only the warm air and sunshine have reminded us it was summer and the time of holiday.

There was quite a stir after tea when Peebles took the wickets of Grimmett and Wall during one and the same over—the first case of a quick fall of two Australian batsmen in the innings. Fairfax arrived at his fifty with the last man in. I cannot say how long he was getting so far, but I can imagine that when he came back to the pavilion somebody remarked on how well he looked! At half-past five Hornibrook was caught at the wicket, Duckworth's appeal this time announcing that he was fully restored to health.

The English bowlers returned to the pavilion with one consoling thought for their private reflection—Australia, after all, had failed by five runs to get 700. Peebles need not be ashamed of his analysis. For a young practitioner of a very difficult craft his figures of six wickets for 204 in 71 overs were highly creditable, and they stood for long and tireless and persistent and plucky work at a job which his more experienced and professional colleagues found far beyond their capacities. Larwood failed sadly—and what a chance was before him on the wicket before lunch today.

A VALEDICTION TO HOBBS

At a quarter to six, in a forlorn cause, Hobbs began to play his last innings for England. Before he took guard the Australians gathered together in midfield and gave him three cheers. The crowd joined in the valediction. It was one of those quick, impulsive scenes which make a man very much in love with cricket and all who play it. We saw the long line of Hobb's years in the moment's emotion from the day his batting dared and achieved on young ambitious feet to this present and full hour of his mastership and fulfilment.

We all were very still while Hobbs and Sutcliffe set about playing themselves through forty-five minutes at a trying day's close. We were scared out of our lives when, with only eight runs scored, a howl of appeal went up from the Australians for a catch at the wicket against Sutcliffe. Whether a chance was actually given did not matter, for, thank goodness, Oldfield dropped the ball. A glorious cover drive by Sutcliffe moved the crowd to proud and delighted noises. Hobbs, too, made the welkin ring with one of his own kingly forcing strokes to the on.

The Oval was on tiptoe of expectancy. Perhaps, after all, England were not beaten yet. But the Kennington clocks had scarcely stopped chiming when faith and the will-to-believe in all of us were harshly and cruelly cast down. Hobbs played on in a fading light to a ball from Fairfax which made a devastating pace from the pitch. No English bowler had been able to give a ball such a wicked increase of speed after pitching. This was the end; bad light stopped the game just after Whysall came in. Today the Oval will witness an English defeat, the loss of the rubber, or some of the most resolute batting seen here for years.

FIFTH TEST
5th Day (The Oval)

ENGLAND
First Innings

Hobbs, c Kippax, b Wall	47
Sutcliffe, c Oldfield, b Fairfax	161
Whysall, lbw, b Wall	13
K. S. Duleepsinhji, c Fairfax, b Grimmett	50
Hammond, b McCabe	13
Leyland, b Grimmett	3
R. E. S. Wyatt, c Oldfield, b Fairfax	64
Tate, st Oldfield, b Grimmett	10
Larwood, lbw, b Grimmett	19
Duckworth, b Fairfax	3
I. A. R. Peebles, not out	3
Lb 17, nb 2	19
Total	405

FALL OF WICKETS
ENGLAND—First Innings

1	2	3	4	5	6	7	8	9	10
68	97	162	190	197	367	379	379	391	405

BOWLING ANALYSIS
ENGLAND—First Innings

	O.	M.	R.	W.		O.	M.	R.	W.
T. Wall	37	6	96	2	S. McCabe	22	4	49	1
A. Fairfax	31	9	52	3	P. M. Hornibrook	15	1	54	0
C. V. Grimmett	66·2	18	135	4					

Wall and Fairfax each bowled a no-ball.

AUSTRALIA
First Innings

W. M. Woodfull, c Duckworth, b Peebles	54
W. H. Ponsford, b Peebles	110
D. G. Bradman, c Duckworth, b Larwood	232
A. F. Kippax, c Wyatt, b Peebles	28
A. Jackson, c Sutcliffe, b Wyatt	73
S. McCabe, c Duckworth, b Hammond	54
A. Fairfax, not out	53
W. A. Oldfield, c Larwood, b Peebles	34
C. V. Grimmett, lbw, b Peebles	6
T. Wall, lbw, b Peebles	0
P. M. Hornibrook, c Duckworth, b Tate	7
B 22, lb 18, nb 4	44
Total	695

283

FALL OF WICKETS
AUSTRALIA—First Innings

1	2	3	4	5	6	7	8	9	10
159	190	267	506	570	594	670	684	684	695

BOWLING ANALYSIS
AUSTRALIA—First Innings

	O.	M.	R.	M.		O.	M.	R.	W.
Larwood	48	6	132	1	R. E. S. Wyatt	14	1	58	1
Tate	65·1	12	153	1	Hammond	42	12	70	1
I.A.R.Peebles	71	8	204	6	Leyland	16	7	34	0

Larwood bowled four no-balls.

ENGLAND
Second Innings

Hobbs, b Fairfax	9
Sutcliffe, c Fairfax, b Hornibrook	54
Whysall, c Hornibrook, b Grimmett	10
K. S. Duleepsinhji, c Kippax, b Hornibrook	46
Hammond, c Fairfax, b Hornibrook	60
Leyland, b Hornibrook	20
R. E. S. Wyatt, b Hornibrook	7
Tate, run out	0
Larwood, c McCabe, b Hornibrook	9
Duckworth, b Hornibrook	15
I. A. R. Peebles, not out	0
B 16, lb 3, nb 2	21
Total	251

FALL OF WICKETS
ENGLAND—Second Innings

1	2	3	4	5	6	7	8	9	10
17	37	118	135	189	207	208	220	248	251

BOWLING ANALYSIS
ENGLAND—Second Innings

	O.	M.	R.	W.		O.	M.	R.	W.
T. Wall	12	2	25	0	P. M. Hornibrook	31·2	9	92	7
A. Fairfax	10	3	21	1	S. McCabe	3	1	2	0
C. V. Grimmett	43	12	90	1					

Fairfax bowled two no-balls.

Umpires: Hardstaff and Parry.

THE OVAL, FRIDAY

At ten minutes to four the Australians won the rubber and England lost this match by an innings and 39 runs. Yesterday's rain laid whatever wan ghost of a chance England ever had of achieving a prolonged struggle. But there could have been only one end to the match, whatever the weather. England went into the engagement with the aspect and behaviour of a side not dreaming of victory.

When the game was resumed a small and silent crowd sat round the field. Woodfull at first seemed unable to make up his mind about the state of the wicket. He opened with Grimmett, then took him off even though the spin bowler troubled Sutcliffe sorely three times in a single over. Wall was given a chance, with Fairfax to see if the ball could be made to rear up menacingly; but though Fairfax hit Sutcliffe on the gloves the altitude he achieved was at the expense of good length. Grimmett then came into action again, and got Whysall caught at first slip from a ball which dropped on the blind length and turned exquisitely away to find the bat's edge. Hornibrook was now asked to contribute left-handed spin to England's difficulties. Woodfull obviously had at last decided that the turf was a slow bowler's ally.

SUTCLIFFE THE FIGHTER

A ball from Hornibrook stood straight up at Sutcliffe. The desperate way Sutcliffe drove at the next ball from Hornibrook, only to mis-hit behind the wicket, did not fill our souls with faith. A great swinging stroke to leg by Sutcliffe was a little reassuring, and, incidentally, it put into a revealing light the lack of an accurate length in Hornibrook's attack. Sutcliffe next pulled Grimmett for four: he had not lost time getting himself into his own fighting vein. And he was not only dogged this time; his bat cracked out a noise of temper and resolution whenever the bowling faltered. Hornibrook for a while proved a disappointing bowler, and Fairfax returned to the pavilion end to bump the ball while Grimmett crossed over.

I mentioned all these moves of Woodfull at risk of dropping into the old tags of cricket reporting ('Richardson relieved Lockwood at the nursery end, and Brockwell bowled vice Lohman'—dear old clichës, much better than the bowling adjectives of these days). I mention them to show that the Australians at the day's outset were very much in the dark about the wicket's state—and, as usual, were embarrassed by conditions which would have rejoiced the heart of Parker or Verity. Fairfax bruised Sutcliffe's body, but not the man's colossal confidence in himself. Duleepsinhji, too, played well, but with a dourness not part of his style or temperament. He did not omit, though, to punch a full toss by Fairfax to the on at a speed which sent flying all the little birds that have throughout the match hopped about on the grass at the long-on boundary.

Duleepsinhji and Sutcliffe batted so skilfully that on the surface of things England looked to have a good chance of making a long fight, but the discerning onlooker saw how the ball was spinning. Some Australian bowler would be sure to pitch now and again the ball of fatal length. Just before lunch Woodfull asked Hornibrook to go on again, and this time his attack was nasty. He sent a ball to Sutcliffe which got up most evilly and struck the top of the bat, and went thence to first slip. It was an unlucky end to an innings of characteristic doggedness and coolness. For two hours and a half Sutcliffe had stood his ground unflinchingly for England and— better still, perhaps—for Yorkshire. . . .

A STICKY WICKET

After lunch the wicket was absolutely on the bowler's side. Hornibrook and Grimmett could put the ball through all manner of tricks: it turned and jumped at acute angles. Yet we are told, by contemporary swerve bowlers, that in wet weather a sticky wicket at the Oval is nowadays an impossibility. Even Mr. Fender, I believe, shares this delusion, caused probably by the fact that no bowler on the Surrey side can spin a ball, weather wet or fine. Today's wicket at the Oval would have finished the match before lunch had there been a Blythe or a Parker in the Australian attack. Hornibrook is not a masterful left-handed slow bowler, but after lunch he was spinning the batsmen into states of mind and body perplexed and tortuous.

Duleepsinhji was out to a ball from Hornibrook that stopped its course after pitching and then sat up like Mickey Mouse; a catch to forward short-leg was the inevitable consequence of this strange compound of spin and varying pace. Duleepsinhji's innings was that of a pedigree cricketer. Hammond, for a few agonizing moments, gave us the appearance of a batsman about to get out every ball. When he was nine he made a slash stroke off Hornibrook and sent a catch to cover, where Grimmett dropped the ball.

THE RIGHT SPIRIT

At a quarter to three England were 154 for four. In three hours today they had scored 130 for three—a brave show on the wicket. But we were to witness cricket braver still. In half an hour Leyland and Hammond scored 53 for the fifth wicket. The ball was hit all over the field. Here was proper cricket, English cricket, inspired by the game's own everlasting spirit of all or nothing, live or die. For my part I would rather play the nation's natural game and lose a hundred rubbers than see our batsmen stonewalling with the score 500 for five. (Not that the Australians have anything to teach English cricket about dull batting.) The partnership of Leyland and Hammond was in the olden style, taking us back to days when nobody was in danger of trial by court martial because he lost his wicket going for a drive. A thousand pities the stand was feebly ended! Leyland played a half-cock stroke with cross-bat, and was bowled by a ball which hit the bottom of the stumps almost on the first bounce.

With Wyatt in, and the end round the corner, Hammond hit the first (and only) six of the match, a grand square-leg hit off a full toss by Grimmett. Wyatt was not so successful as on Saturday, and after he got out England began to carry the ancient dash and animation too far. Tate and Hammond made a risky short run, and then, immediately afterwards, Kippax threw Tate out brilliantly when another short and useless run was being rushed.

Chivalry in a lost cause is a great virtue, but, as the parson said after his prayers for rain had been too liberally granted, 'Lord, let us all be reasonable.' There was no need for England to help the Australians to get wickets today by chancing short runs to hits straight at a fieldsman. The very fact that Hornibrook every other over sent down a difficult ball was sufficient proof of the wicket's untrustworthiness. Hornibrook is by no means a Blythe: he is really a bad bowler whose best ball is superb.

THE REAL HAMMOND AGAIN

The end of the English innings was ennobled by the lion-hearted hitting of Hammond, who was apparently driven by a desperate situation to go back and trust to the strong batsmanship which was his pride and joy a few years ago. He would have served England's purposes well if he had throughout the present season's Test matches put reasonable faith in the gifts given him by nature. Duckworth joined in the merry clouting at the end: one of his hits was much bigger than himself. I must confess, though, that it was with mixed feelings that I witnessed—on a bowler's wicket at that—an eleventh-hour demonstration that the Australian bowling could be driven hard and often. Before the end came Bradman actually missed a catch sent by Hammond to long-off. It is not inconceivable that we shall, when winter arrives think that the fielding and not the batting of Bradman was the more inspired of his contributions to the Test matches.

AN AUSTRALIAN REVOLUTION

It was ten minutes to four when England lost the 'Ashes' and Australia won them. Few of us in May and June expected such an issue for a moment, nor did the Australians expect to beat us. As a fact they at one part of the summer resigned themselves to the worst. Then they realized with Australian opportunism the condition that English cricket was in at the present time. Woodfull and his men jumped to their chance at Lord's after having lost one Test match, and, moreover, after England had batted first and scored over 420. The story of the Australian fight with depression and bad luck to the glorious consummation of their efforts today—it makes a good and heartening story, and I hope to tell it in another article which will sum up the Test matches from as many points of view as I can discover.

England played up well on today's wicket: they showed fight, and that was something. But in the crucial game of the rubber England was without a team. Here was gathered together for the occasion merely eleven cricketers of varying abilities. It is too late now for tears, however: they would be idle and vain. The Australians, of course, deserved to win today, and would have won whatever the state of the wicket because they have since the defeat at Trent Bridge outplayed England at all points, technical and spiritual. And not only have they beaten us fairly and squarely; they have put before us problems which we could not solve even if another Test match had to be played tomorrow. No matter how England shuffled their forces no bowlers could be found capable of getting the Australians out cheaply enough, and no cricketers could be found here capable of mingling in proportion the Australian batsmen's qualities of offence and defence.

It will be churlish and untrue if we say the Australians have won the rubber by un-English cricket. In this last Test match they certainly adapted their batting to the needs of a match without a time-limit, but in the other games they had more than their share of brilliant boundaries.

BRADMAN: AN APPRECIATION, 1930

THE power of genius in cricket is not to be measured by the score-board, and not even by the clock. A Trumper, a Spooner, will reveal art and energy in one or two personal strokes or by some all-pervading yet indefinable poise and flavour. At Leeds Bradman announced his right to mastership in a few swift moments. He made 72 runs during his first hour at the wicket, giving to us every hit of cricket excepting the leg glance. But long before he had got near the end of his innings he was repeating himself; it was as though the sheer finish of technique was a prison for his spirit. He could not make a hazardous flight; he reminded me of the trapeze performer who one night decided to commit suicide by flinging himself headlong to the stage but could not achieve the error because his skill had become infallible, a routined and mechanical habit not at the beck and call of anything so volatile as human will or impulse. When Bradman passed 200 at Leeds I felt that my interest in his play might break out anew at the sight of one miscalculated stroke. But none was to be seen. His cricket went along its manifold ways with a security which denied its own brilliance. Every fine point of batsmanship was to be admired; strokes powerful and swift and accurate and handsome; variety of craft controlled by singleness of mind and purpose. Bradman was as determined to take no risks as he was to hit boundaries from every ball the least loose. And his technique is so extensive and practised that he can get runs at the rate of fifty an hour without once needing to venture romantically into the realms of the speculative or the empirical. The bowler who had to tackle Victor Trumper was able to keep his spirit more or less hopeful by some philosophy such as this: 'Victor is moving at top speed. Well, I'm bound sooner or later to send along a really good ball. Victor will flash at it in his ecstasy—and I'll have him!' The bowler toiling at Bradman cannot support himself by a like optimism. For hours he will see his ordinary balls hit for fours along the grass; then his good one will wheel from his arm, by the law of averages which causes every bowler to achieve one moment of excellence in every hour. But is Bradman ever likely to be so blinded by the radiance of his own visions that he will throw back his head at the good ball, confuse it with the others, and lose his wicket through a royal expense of spirit? Not he; he sees the dangerous ball with eyes as suspicious as those of a Makepeace. Down over his bat goes his head; the blade becomes a broad protective shield—and probably two pads will lend a strong second line of defence. It is not a paradox to imagine some bowler saying to Bradman, with strict justice, after Bradman has punished five fours in one over and cannily stopped the sixth ball: 'For the Lord's sake, Don, do give a fellow a chance and have a hit at her!'

The genius of this remarkable boy consists in the complete summary he gives us of the technique of batsmanship. In every art or vocation there appears from time to time an incredible exponent who in himself sums up all the skill and experience that have gone before him. It is not true that Bradman has inaugurated a new era in batsmanship: he is substantially orthodox in technique. Nearly all his strokes at Leeds could very well have been used as illustrations to C. B. Fry's thoroughly scientific and pragmatic book on batsmanship. But Bradman shows us excellences which in the past we have had to seek in different players; nobody else has achieved Bradman's synthesis. It is, of course, a synthesis which owes much to the fact that Bradman stays at the wicket longer than most of the brilliant stroke players of old ever dreamed of staying. Perhaps he is marked off from the greatest of his predecessors not so much by technique as by temperament. It is hard to believe in the possibility of a more masterful stroke player than Trumper was, or Hobbs in his heyday. But when Trumper and Hobbs were great batsmen it was customary for cricketers to try to get out when their scores went beyond, say, 150. How many times has Hobbs thrown his wicket away after reaching his century? Bradman brings to an extensive technique the modern outlook on cricket; a hundred runs is nothing to him; he conceives his innings in terms which go far beyond Trumper's or Macartney's most avaricious dreams. He has demonstrated that a batsman can hit forty-two boundaries in a day without once giving the outfielders hope of a catch; he has kindled grand bonfires of batsmanship for us. But never once has he burned his own fingers while lighting them.

When I think of an innings by Macartney I do not think entirely of cricket. My impressions of Macartney's batting are mixed up with impressions of Figaro, Rossini's Figaro, a gay trafficker with fortune but a man of the world; hard as iron though nimble as wit; an opportunist wearing a romantic feather in his cap. And when I think of an innings by Trumper I see in imagination the unfurling of a banner. Not by Bradman is the fancy made to roam; he is, for me, wholly a batsman living, moving, and having his being in cricket. His batsmanship delights one's knowledge of the game; his every stroke is a dazzling and precious stone in the game's crown. But I do not find his cricket making me think of other and less tangible things; the stuff of his batsmanship is skill, not sensibility. In all the affairs of the human imagination there must be an enigma somewhere, some magical touch that nobody can understand and explain. You could never account for Macartney, Ranjitsinhji, Spooner, Trumper, in terms of even a marvellous technique. Bradman, as I see and react to him, is technique in excelsis. I could write a text-book on him with comprehensive and thoroughly enlightening diagrams. Could anybody have written a text-book saying anything that mattered about the batting of Johnny Tyldesley!

The really astonishing fact about Bradman is that a boy should play as he does—with the sophistication of an old hand and brain. Who has ever before heard of a young man, gifted with quick feet and eyes, with mercurial spirits and all the rapid and powerful strokes of cricket—who has ever heard of a young man so gifted and yet one who never indulged an extravagant hit high into the air? Until a year or two ago Bradman had seen little or no first-class cricket. Yet here is he today, bringing to youth's natural relish for lusty play with a cricket bat a technical polish and discretion worthy of a Tom Hayward. A mis-hit by Bradman—when he is dashing along at 50 runs an hour—surprises us even as a mis-hit by Hayward did when he was in his most academic vein. How came this Bradman to expel from him all the greenness and impetuosity of youth while retaining the strength and alacrity of youth? How did he come to acquire, without experience, all the ripeness of the orthodox—the range and adaptability of other men's accumulated years of practice in the best schools of batsmanship? The cricket of Trumper at the age of 21 could not be accounted for, but we were content to accept it in terms of spontaneous genius. Besides, there was always the rapture and insecurity of the young man in Trumper. But while we can account for Bradman's batting by reason of its science and orthodoxy we are unable quite to accept it—it is too old for Bradman's years and slight experience! The genius who thrills us is always unique but seldom abnormal. If Bradman develops his skill still further—and at his age he ought to have whole worlds to conquer yet—he will in the end find himself regarded not so much a master batsman, but as phenomenon of cricket.

As I say, the remarkable fact about Bradman's batsmanship is its steady observance of the unities. At Leeds he was credited with the invention of a new kind of hook. But there was no scope at Leeds for any sort of hook, ancient or modern. The ball never rose stump high on the first day; how can any batsman hook a ball that does not rise at a sharp angle from the ground? I have never yet seen Bradman perform the hook stroke, but I have seen him pull often enough. The pull, indeed, is one of his most efficient hits; it is timed to perfection, and the sound of it is as sweet as a nut. But it is not correct to think Bradman does not drive in front of the wicket.

At Leeds more than half of his forty-six fours were drives in front of the wicket. His drive and cut, indeed, were much more frequently to be seen than his pull and leg hit. The secret of his stroke-power lies in his ability to move quickly backwards or forwards, making the length short or overpitched. The area of the wicket wherein a ball can be pitched that is a good length to Bradman is considerably narrower than that which is defended by all our county batsmen, Woolley excepted. He judges the direction of the attack rapidly; never is he to be seen lunging forward, stretched speculatively out; never does he fall into that 'two-minded' state which compels a batsman to make 'A-shaped bridges down the wicket feeling awry in the air for the ball,' to quote C. B. Fry. Bradman clinches Fry's celebrated Fallacy of Reach: 'The Fallacy of Reach is fatal to true cricket. None but a giant by advancing the left foot and pushing out down the wicket can reach within feet of the pitch of a good length slow ball or within yards of the pitch of a good length fast ball. Why, the very thing the bowler wants one to do, what he works to make one do, is to feel forward at the pitch of his bowling.' Bradman plays back or else goes the whole way of the forcing stroke on punitive decisive feet. When he is as a last resort compelled to play forward, he actually goes back on his wicket to do so, and his legs are behind the bat, and his eyes are on the ball. So strong is his back play, and so quick his eyes and feet, that it is fatal to bowl a short length at him. Yet, so far, that is the mistake the English bowlers have made against Bradman. Frankly they have not 'stood up' to his punishment. Flattered by everyday batsmanship (right foot rooted behind the crease) English bowling has wilted at the sight of a bat that is busy and resolute; hence an attempt to take refuge in short bowling, a safe enough dodge in front of a cricketer who cannot cut. Bradman has thrived on bowling which he has been at liberty to see all the way, to see pitch yards in front of him. If he has a weak point Robins, by accident or design, found it out occasionally at Trent Bridge. Every time (which was not often!) that Robins sent a well-flighted ball to Bradman, pitched on the middle stump and spinning away, Bradman was without an exception observed then to be thinking hard, entirely on the defensive. It is not, of course, for the pavilion critic to presume to know the way that Bradman can be got out cheaply. But it is surely not presumptuous for anybody to suggest that the short-pitched ball is about the last of all to send to a batsman with Bradman's voracious appetite for fours and his range of hits.

He has all the qualities of batsmanship: footwork, wrists, economy of power, the great strokes of the game, each thoroughly under control. What, then, is the matter with him that we hesitate to call him a master of style, an artist who delights us, and not only a craftsman we are bound to admire without reserve! Is it that he is too mechanically faultless for sport's sake? A number of Bradmans would quickly put an end to the glorious uncertainty of cricket. A number of Macartneys would inspire the game to hazardous heights more exhilarating than ever. . . . But this is a strain of criticism that is comically churlish. Here have we been for years praying for a return of batsmanship to its old versatility and aggression; we have been desperate for the quick scorer who could hit fours without causing the game to lapse into the indiscriminate clouting of the village green. In short, we have been crying out for batsmanship that would combine technique and energy in proportion. And now that a Bradman has come to us, capable of 300 runs in a single day of a Test match, some of us are calling him a Lindrum of cricket! It is a hard world to please. Perhaps Bradman, by making a 'duck' in the Manchester Test match, will oblige those of his critics who believe with Lord Bacon that there should always be some strangeness, something unexpected, mingled with art and beauty.